Building the Sustainable Web

How to Create Web Products That Respect People and the Planet

Chris Chinchilla
Ines Akrap

Foreword by Chris Adams
Director of Technology and Policy, Green Web Foundation

Apress®

Building the Sustainable Web: How to Create Web Products That Respect People and the Planet

Chris Chinchilla
Berlin, Germany

Ines Akrap
Munich, Germany

ISBN-13 (pbk): 979-8-8688-2520-0
ISBN-13 (electronic): 979-8-8688-2521-7
https://doi.org/10.1007/979-8-8688-2521-7

Managing Director, Apress Media LLC: Welmoed Spahr
Acquisitions Editor: James Robinson-Prior
Development Editor: James Markham
Editorial Assistant: Gryffin Winkler

Cover designed by eStudioCalamar

Distributed to the book trade worldwide by Springer Science+Business Media New York, 1 New York Plaza, New York, NY 10004. Phone 1-800-SPRINGER, fax (201) 348-4505, e-mail orders-ny@springer-sbm.com, or visit www.springeronline.com. Apress Media, LLC is a Delaware LLC and the sole member (owner) is Springer Science + Business Media Finance Inc (SSBM Finance Inc). SSBM Finance Inc is a **Delaware** corporation.

For information on translations, please e-mail booktranslations@springernature.com; for reprint, paperback, or audio rights, please e-mail bookpermissions@springernature.com.

Apress titles may be purchased in bulk for academic, corporate, or promotional use. eBook versions and licenses are also available for most titles. For more information, reference our Print and eBook Bulk Sales web page at http://www.apress.com/bulk-sales.

Any source code or other supplementary material referenced by the author in this book is available to readers on GitHub. For more detailed information, please visit https://www.apress.com/gp/services/source-code.

If disposing of this product, please recycle the paper

Thanks to my wife for losing all the weekends
while I was working on this.

—Chris Chinchilla

To my daughters. May the digital world
you step into be lighter and kinder.

—Ines Akrap

Table of Contents

About the Authors

Chris Chinchilla is a tech writer, developer, podcaster, journalist, and video maker with a long history of creating and editing content for the tech industry. In a past life, Chris worked for sustainability organizations and is a passionate advocate of sustainable technology and currently works with non-profit organizations to create more sustainable and eco-friendly tech solutions.

Ines Akrap is a front-end engineer and educator with over a decade of experience building high-performance, accessible, and sustainable websites. With a background in computer science and telecommunications, she brings an engineering mindset to modern web development. Ines contributes to the W3C Sustainable Web Guidelines and speaks internationally about responsible, user-centered design and the future of a more efficient web.

About the Technical Reviewer

Anita Schüttler is a computer scientist and expert in digital sustainability, Green Software, and the Circular Economy. As Head of IT Sustainability of an IT company and Co-Chair of the German Green Software Association, she works on advancing digital sustainability in her company as well as the wider IT industry.

Acknowledgments

Thanks to the CNCF Environmental Sustainability TAG, especially Niki Manoledaki, Antonio Di Turi, and Ross Fairbanks and Chris Adams for putting up with my questions.

Thanks to Ines for working with me.

—Chris Chinchilla

This book would not exist without the many people who shaped my thinking and supported me throughout this journey. I have been fortunate to learn from and be inspired by more people than I can possibly name here, especially within the web performance and web sustainability communities, whose shared knowledge, respectful debates, and drive to make the web better are reflected throughout this book.

I want to thank Chris for bringing me into this project. I learned so much and had so much fun working together.

To Fabian Krumbholz, for introducing me to web performance and laying the foundation for how I think about building for the web today.

To Claire Thornewill, my partner in crime from the early days of exploring web sustainability, back when we believed we could read every resource that existed on the topic. Thank you for the shared passion, curiosity, and the many discussions about how to make the web a better place.

To everyone in the W3C Sustainable Web Interest Group, thank you for the amazing work you contribute to the guidelines and for the thoughtful discussions in our Thursday meetings. A special thanks to Tzviya, Alex, Tim, and Mike. I learned so much from you, and our weekly calls kept me connected and inspired, especially during my parental leave.

Huge thanks to Anita for your thoughtful technical review and for the many helpful hints along the way. You introduced me to new tools, asked the right critical questions, and helped sharpen the parts that needed more precision. I'm grateful for your time, attention to detail, and all your support.

To James and the publishing team, thank you for your patience and understanding that life keeps lifing. Your flexibility made it possible for this book to be written alongside major life changes.

To my family and friends, for listening to me talk about this topic way more than they would probably like to.

And finally, to my husband Samir. Thank you for being my favorite rubber duck, slightly annoying devil's advocate, and my biggest cheerleader. For being the most amazing dad to our girls and holding the fort while I worked on this project. Without you, this would have been a chapter and a half at most.

—Ines Akrap

Foreword

I work in an organization called the Green Web Foundation, oriented around the idea of a fossil-free Internet, so when Chris Chinchilla approached me to write a foreword for *Building the Sustainable Web*, it was very easy to say yes.

If you work in the tech industry, even in 2026 the chances are fairly high that education about the environmental impact of the services you build and operate is something you have to take responsibility for, rather than being something built into any formal education you went through yourself.

So if you've ever found it a tad overwhelming once you decide to go down this path, you're in good company—there's so much to learn, at so many parts of the stack! In addition, a lot of the time it's not clear where to focus your attention first, and spend your limited social capital at work if you're arguing for a more sustainable solution for your team to use.

With this in mind, I'm really grateful that Ines and Chris have put the time into writing *Building the Sustainable Web* and sharing their own experiences. They've built the tools themselves, they've used the software that's out there, and they've been in the meetings, making the case to colleagues for greener choices and seeing how standards get thrashed out for measuring the environmental impacts of digital. Being able to learn from the lessons they share is invaluable.

They give a really helpful overview of what you need to know about supply chain associated with building digital services, and dive into the details where as a practitioner you have the ability to make measurable changes.

When I was reading the advance copy, they also managed to make me laugh out loud at least once with a well-chosen meme, and the personable tone of the book makes what can be a dry and detailed subject so much more alive and accessible.

I hope you enjoy this book as much as I did.

—Chris Adams

Chris Adams is the Director of Policy and Technology at the Green Web Foundation, and the co-chair of the policy working group in the Green Software Foundation, as well a director of climateAction.tech, a community of more than 10,000 technologists working to build climate action into their practices at work.

Introduction

Every digital product is the result of countless decisions. How it is built. Where it is hosted. What it contains. How it is maintained. Most of those decisions are made quickly, under pressure, with the next deadline in mind.

This book is about the wider impact every one of those decisions can have. It explains what sustainability means in the context of digital products and how it belongs in every one of those decisions, not as an afterthought, not as a separate workstream, but as part of what it means to build well. It covers the full stack, from infrastructure and back-end services to front-end development, design, content, and marketing, and what the rise of AI means for all of it.

Depending on your role, some chapters will feel immediately relevant and others less so. Feel free to skip, mix and match, and get the most out of the parts that speak to your work.

Chapter 1 looks at the size of the problem, why you should care, and how you can motivate colleagues and clients to also care about solving the problem.

Before diving into the practical, Chapter 2 looks at the measurements the rest of the book will use, why it uses them, who created them, and their limitations.

Chapter 3 covers product decisions. While programmers and designers can play their part, if those in charge of product decisions and direction are on board with sustainability-minded design from the outset, then later stages are much easier.

Chapter 4 starts at the application stack's lowest point and covers choosing hosting providers, architectural decisions, orchestration, and more.

Chapter 5 covers the backend services that run on top of that infrastructure. Although invisible to users, these are often the services and applications that have the largest impact on sustainability, bills, and performance. It looks at the impact language and application architecture choices have and other potential impacts of these decisions.

Chapter 6 covers the design implementation of an application and how to optimize the choices you make for sustainability.

Chapter 7 looks at optimizing the front ends of applications and services, the ways that users interact with you, and what you've built.

With an application or service built, Chapter 8 covers populating it with content and marketing it worldwide. After all, a responsible application only remains that way if you continue to treat it that way.

Chapter 9 looks beyond predominantly web-based applications and services to the sustainability of other applications and considerations such as AI, streaming versus downloading, and more.

Finally, Chapter 10 looks at what's next in this fast-moving space and, once again, tries to convince you why you should apply all that you've learned in this book.

CHAPTER 1

The Carbon Footprint of Application Development

Chris Chinchilla[1]

[1]Berlin, Germany; https://chrischinchilla.com/

Pickup your phone. I'm sure it's near you. Open an app and scroll through the never-ending list of text, images, and video.

Open some items on the list and read or watch them.

Play a game for a few minutes.

Send some messages to friends, and make sure you include some emojis or GIFs!

Is there a desktop or laptop computer near you? Open it or turn it on. Launch an application. Check your emails. Work on designs. Write code. Run tests.

Did you interact with any other services today? Did you book a movie, get something delivered, or deal with someone in retail or customer service who was likely tapping away on their device to help you?

Digital devices are everywhere in the modern world. They are often connected to each other in small or large private or public networks, ferrying bits and bytes back and forth almost constantly. Behind every interface you see is a plethora of backend services, shuttling an equal, if not greater, amount of data between each other and the thousands of other people using them daily.

Using some of these services and tools costs us money, and we are generally aware that we also cost the supplier money. However, there are hidden costs we are less aware of. One of those is the cost to our environment—the environmental impact of our digitally connected world.

C. Chinchilla and I. Akrap, *Building the Sustainable Web*, https://doi.org/10.1007/979-8-8688-2521-7_1

How Big Is the Problem?

At the moment, exact measurements are hard to come by, but various reports estimate the carbon impact of "the Internet" to be 3.7% of global greenhouse gas emissions. This is the same as the airline industry, an industry we tend to think of far more when considering environmental impact. Many of these values were reported in 2019 before the massive uptick in online work and consumption caused by the COVID-19 pandemic, and the same report predicted emissions would double by 2025. However, as you will read in this book, there are now many efforts in place to help monitor and reduce this impact, so maybe this prediction won't come to pass.

3.7% equals around 1.6 billion tons of CO_2 emissions every year. This is such a large value it's hard to visualize or contextualize. Looking at some smaller examples can help.

According to Mike Berners-Lee, in his 2010 book *How Bad Are Bananas* (extrapolate the numbers from there), a typical business user creates 135kg (298 lbs) of CO_2 emissions from sending emails every year. This is equivalent to driving 320km (200 miles) in an average car. Bear in mind these values ignore personal emails, spam, and more.

Another big impact is video consumption. The International Energy Agency reports that one hour of streaming video equals about 36 g of CO_2 emissions. Say the average person watches 8 hours a week. Then this equals about 1.2km (3/4 miles) driven in an average car. This doesn't seem so high, but this is just one person, and again, much of the reporting data is from before 2020, so while it includes watching video on streaming sites, it doesn't include the impact of the countless video meetings we now find ourselves in.

In many of these cases, I can hear the collective shuffling of many of you grabbing your nearest digital device to send an email worth 4g of CO_2 to state that surely the impact of passive and active video consumption is less than getting in a car and driving to the cinema or flying to a meeting. Well, yes, maybe.

As always, and as you will see many times in this book, "it depends." A lot of people don't drive or fly to these engagements. But perhaps the easiest point to make in this case is that often deciding to visit the cinema or meet in person is an intentional decision, so it is less lightly considered. However, because attending an online meeting or scrolling absent-mindedly through YouTube or TikTok is so easy, it's less intentional and more wasteful.

Setting this conjecture aside, it's time to introduce yet more.

What Is "the Internet"?

Looking wider than some of the specific examples above, what does "the Internet" even mean?

Not every device connects to what we call the public Internet. Do these calculations include all the mobile devices, customer service tablets, and other specialized devices? Does it include the impact on your computer or phone when you browse and use those ad-laden apps and websites? What about the countless gadgets and gizmos that don't connect to any network but still chug away, drawing power or using batteries? Would it even be possible to factor these disconnected devices into any calculations? And what about the cost of manufacturing and shipping these devices?

If you start to consider that unless you wander in the wilderness, you'll likely see digital devices everywhere around you. You encounter dozens, if not hundreds, per day. So, while our best metrics claim 3.7%, I argue that the hidden numbers make this value far higher.

And why does this matter, why should you care, and what can you do about it?

No matter how small, almost all of these devices run code written and designed by someone. They use infrastructure designed and built by someone, even if that infrastructure is just a solo and lonely disconnected device.

If you're reading this book, I assume you care about the environment and the future of a healthy, sustainable, and enjoyable planet. I also assume that if you're reading this book, you have some form of interaction with code, what it runs on, or the design and experience of code. While you could argue that in the grand scheme of things, there are bigger impacts on the planet than our work, this is the sector we work in, and all of us doing our part will help. On the positive side, our sector is full of metrics, flexibility, and constant iteration, so it is perfect for change and optimization.

Currently, our main way to monitor this impact is through energy consumption mapped to a carbon impact calculation. It's not an ideal method, but it is our best right now. Depending on what you're measuring and where in the stack it is, these energy consumption values can come from provider billing records or directly from monitoring hardware or virtual hardware such as containers.

This book will cover a lot of these metrics, changes, and optimizations across the whole stack of application development to delivery and marketing.

We are still in the early days of energy consumption monitoring, and almost every vendor, provider, infrastructure, and programming language choice represents things subtly differently. A handful of projects and tools are looking to standardize these inputs into metrics that are at least actionable. The book will cover each of these tools in the relevant chapter and how to integrate them into your workflow.

But before we dive into those large topics, let's dwell a little longer on some of the other related impacts of software and hardware on certain sectors and groups.

How to Motivate Others

While you, the reader, may be motivated to improve the software and hardware you work with to lower its environmental impact, those you work with and have to justify your efforts to may not be. Fortunately, there are other positive impacts of reducing the energy consumption of software that may help you.

The first is cost, which is probably a motivation that will motivate many others. Reducing the energy consumption of services and applications generally costs less to run. In these times of financial cutbacks and the questioning of throwing more money at "cheap resources," reducing and streamlining them saves impact on the environment and the wallet.

Secondly, more efficient apps give users a better experience and probably save them energy and money, too. We are all familiar with complaining about applications that eat up too much battery. Imagine! By making more energy-efficient applications, you save money, help the planet, and bring a smile to your users' faces! What's stopping you?

From Data Centers to End Users

While this chapter earlier argued that some of the energy consumption of "the Internet" isn't so visible in terms of metrics, by far the largest energy consumer, while well reported, is perhaps the least visible to end users. The data centers and interconnected infrastructure that we now rather loosely (among other terms) call "the cloud" are increasingly everywhere. As developers, designers, and product owners, we have become used to throwing yet more services and compute resources at a problem.

- Is the application running too slow? Throw more cloud instances at it.
- Need more storage? Bolt-on more, storage is cheap after all.

- Monitoring? There's a service for that.
- Need to cope with demand? Add a load balancer or two.
- Monetization? Add advertising and tracking pixels. Oh, and, of course, something to measure its effectiveness.
- Everyone needs artificial intelligence and machine learning now, so train some models, add a chat interface, or, failing that, use someone else's.

And so on.

At the very end of all of this are end users. When we scroll endlessly through walls of text or images, or watch movies, play games, or take VoIP calls, we rarely think about the massive amount of software and infrastructure behind the scenes processing all of this. At University, one of the concepts that stuck with me was that of "abstraction," making something incredibly complex look far simpler than it was. Many modern apps submerge the huge iceberg of complexity they use under a small fingertip swipe.

Behind the scenes are myriad servers flashing lights in countless racks, fed by hundreds of colored cables, hosted worldwide in thousands of data centers. Between all of these run larger cables, and between continents run a surprisingly small amount of larger and longer submerged optic fiber cables that provide the high-speed backbone of our connectivity. As a small aside, my Grandfather helped lay the precursors to these in the form of gigantic reams of copper wires. He once told me that "optic fibers" are the future, and here I am 30 years later, telling you how submerged beneath our feet in the modern world are nearly a million kilometers of them.

Depending on the application's architecture and its infrastructure, that single tap could send a trail of digital signals circling around the world and back again.

Frankly, all of the technology that makes this work generally seamless is incredible, but, yes, you guessed it, it uses a tremendous amount of energy.

Strangely, one of the easiest and largest groups to gather data on but generally under-reported is end users. Almost all modern desktop operating systems and browsers (which are already operating systems to many users) have a monitoring application that can measure and show impact, almost always in the form of energy consumption.

Yet, because there are billions of end users, often using more than one device, with no motivation or mechanism to report these impacts centrally, it's almost entirely unreported, aside from extrapolating usage percentages from electricity usage, which is possible but inaccurate.

But let's try.

Let's take a couple of globally popular websites: BBC News, Facebook, and Wikipedia.

Measuring their energy impact in the **Firefox profiler** on my MacBook M1 Pro, I see the following impacts of each site:

- **BBC news**: 2.2mWh/1.1mg CO_2e
- **Facebook**: 5.5mWh/2.7mg CO_2e
- **Wikipedia**: 0.512mWh/0.25mg CO_2e

For this exercise, I picked **the most popular page from the BBC on June 26, 2024** to test for the BBC and **a random Wikipedia page** that seemed to represent an "average" page to me. For each of these pages, I started the profiler, scrolled from the top to the bottom, and selected the entire profile range to get the total readings.

For Facebook, I used my home feed, logged in, cleared caches, and scrolled down for 10 seconds.

Of course, these are all approximations. We also don't exactly know how many pages each unique user viewed, and generally, as the same user browses multiple pages, caches and other optimizations kick in to make the pages lighter.

When loading each page, I disabled any content and ad blockers (more on that in Chapters 7, 8, and 9), accepted all cookies, and opened the page in a private window to get the, well, the "worst" experience.

Now, here are the rough monthly page views for each of these sites:

- **BBC news**: 1.2 billion (**Reported in April 2021**)
- **Facebook**: 2.989 billion monthly active users in this case as "page views" with Facebook aren't so clear (**Reported in April 2023**)
- **Wikipedia**: 25 billion (**Reported in May 2024**)

Let's say the traffic is a 50/50 split between mobile and desktop. This is probably not accurate at all, and at least for the BBC and Facebook, they also have apps, but it's harder to get those numbers and harder to separate out the traffic per destination and user. Of course, if you are measuring the impact of your own services and applications, then you have these numbers and can be more precise. But it's fine for this "back of the envelope" calculation for illustrative purposes.

- **BBC news:** 1,320kg CO_2e per month

    - Equivalent to 3,361miles driven by an average gasoline-powered passenger vehicle

- **Facebook**: 8,220kg CO_2e
    - Equivalent to 20,933 miles driven by an average gasoline-powered passenger vehicle
- **Wikipedia**: 6,400kg CO_2e
    - Equivalent to 16,298 miles driven by an average gasoline-powered passenger vehicle

I converted the CO_2 emissions above to kilograms, multiplied that by the number of users, and then used the **EPA Greenhouse Gas Equivalencies** Calculator

Ironically, despite having the lowest emissions per page, Wikipedia's sheer usage scale makes it much higher in the results.

In isolation, these numbers don't seem that bad. But bear in mind that these are rough, only per month, and just three websites. Granted, they are three of the most popular websites, but **billions** of websites exist.

The most significant fact to remember is that this is just the impact on users. It doesn't include the impact of running these services, which is likely much larger per user, per view, and per month.

At this scale, you can start to see the justification behind making small improvements. Saving 1mg per view has a bigger impact overall.

Regulations and Standards

Currently, most of this book's content encourages you to make changes because it's the right thing to do. However, there's a high likelihood that regulations may force some industries and developers to report their carbon impact in the not-so-distant future, especially in more highly regulated regions such as the European Union. Much like the current reporting on larger consumer goods in some regions, this won't necessarily mean the regulation will mandate doing anything about that impact. But that time might come, and in the meantime, much like the white goods labeling, consumers and users will use the reporting to make their own consumption decisions. Energy impact might become a competitive advantage even on digital goods and services.

When potential customers decide between various options to meet their needs, they weigh up different factors. These can include features, price, terms, and the team. However, when all of these are roughly equal or balanced, they can also look deeper into a company's profile and how it aligns with their ethical perspective. If a product uses more sustainable development techniques and practices and, most crucially, can prove it, a customer might choose it over another product, even if the costs are different.

At the time of publishing, **the European Commission had already adopted a rating scheme for data centers**. If plans remain on track, the Centers must report their ratings to a yearly database. I can't tell if this database is public or if there will be any private or public repercussions for "bad" data. However, it's a start, and with European data centers accounting for 3% and rising EU electricity demand, it's a growing issue that reflects global numbers.

Other policies in development, with a specific focus or mention of digital services, include the following:

- **France's Digital Environmental Footprint Reduction Legislation**
- **California's Corporate Data Accountability Act**
- **The UK's greening government ICT and digital services strategy**
- **The EU's corporate sustainability due diligence directive**
- **The EU's Energy Efficiency Directive**
- **Germany's Energy Efficiency Act**
- **India's Business Responsibility and Sustainability Report**
- **The USA's proposal for climate-related disclosure**

However, the past few years were years of massive potential political change, so it remains to be seen how many of these proposals remain and are enforced at the time of publication.

I wonder if there will ever come a time when all services and/or sites will have to report sustainability metrics more widely. If all websites had to carry white-goods style labels for their direct and indirect consumption, how would that look? How far down the stack would a provider have to go? The current labels don't include the impact of production or disposal. So, would an impact label for a website or service also include the data Center impact? What if the service uses multiple hosts and architectures? Will the rating change depending on where the user accesses it from? Will it factor in the impact on the user and the implementation impact?

With the best will in the world, it's a lot more complex than putting an energy rating on a fridge!

However, things seem to be moving toward some form of reporting or regulation, so even if it's not clear right now what that could be, it makes sense to start preparing and informing yourself about it. Get ahead of the completion date for when it's mandatory, which is why I hope you're reading.

Summary

This chapter covered the broad view of the environmental impact of digital technology and why it matters for anyone involved in software development, design, or product ownership.

It looked at the rough impact of our industry and how it compares to other industries, but also how defining quite what "the Internet," "ICT," or our industry even includes, is a challenge.

It covered different ways to motivate those in your team or company who may not be as motivated by reducing environmental impact, be that financial, regulatory, or otherwise.

The next chapter digs into some of the frameworks and models to measure carbon impact of software, and from then on, this book aims to be a practical guide across the full application development stack. The book breaks down each role and responsibility into chapters for each. In your project, team, or company, these roles may all be undertaken by the same person. Or maybe you're interested in finding topics to take to other team members and encourage them to try and apply in their work. This could be a book that one person reads from cover to cover, or maybe you pass from team member to team member.

CHAPTER 2

Estimating the Impact

Ines Akrap[1]
[1]Munich, Germany; `inesakrap.com`

About six years ago, I bought a hybrid smartwatch. Wearable tech was taking off, but I already knew I didn't want another screen in my life. This one looks like a regular, old-school watch. It tells the time and date, it doesn't interrupt me, and it quietly tracks a few simple things: my sleep, my daily steps, my heart rate, and the workouts I remember to turn on. Over the years, the watch became more useful than I expected. I could see how my activity dropped every winter, how stress affected my sleep patterns, and how small daily habits made a measurable difference. Friends who use wearables say the same. The numbers aren't perfect, but they make trends visible, and that visibility is what makes the data valuable. You stop guessing. You start understanding. Tracking a handful of personal metrics is straightforward. Tracking the environmental impact of digital products is not. But the principle is identical: until you measure something, you're only guessing. And guessing your way toward sustainability won't take us far.

In Chapter 1, we looked at the scale of the problem and why digital services have a meaningful environmental impact. In this chapter, we start unpacking why measuring that impact is so difficult, what we can realistically estimate today, and how those estimates help us make better decisions.

Even rough data can help us:

- Identify where the biggest impacts come from.
- Set improvement goals and track real progress.
- Communicate your efforts with more honesty and clarity.

Digitization brings huge benefits, but it is not impact-free. Designing and building digital products responsibly starts with understanding their impact, and measurement, however incomplete, helps us do that.

C. Chinchilla and I. Akrap, *Building the Sustainable Web*, https://doi.org/10.1007/979-8-8688-2521-7_2

Sustainable vs. Green

Before we go deeper into measuring impact, we need to address two words that often get used interchangeably: green and sustainable. They are related, but not the same, and the difference matters for everything that follows.

When people describe something as green, they usually mean it reduces environmental harm. In digital work, this often means cutting energy use, lowering carbon emissions, or running on renewable electricity. Green is important, but it focuses on a single dimension.

Sustainable is broader. It includes the environment, but also people and long-term economic health. A sustainable web product uses resources responsibly, respects attention and privacy, supports accessibility, and remains maintainable for years rather than months. It avoids decisions that create hidden costs for users, teams, or the planet later.

This wider perspective is reflected in the United Nations' Sustainable Development Goals, shown in Figure 2-1. The SDGs span climate action, responsible consumption, decent work, inclusion, and more. Not every goal applies directly to the web, but they serve as a useful reminder that sustainability is multidimensional.

Figure 2-1. *The UN's Sustainable Development Goals*

In this book, we explore the sustainability of digital products. We look at emissions and infrastructure, but we also look at clarity, accessibility, user experience, and the long-term health of what we build. A sustainable digital product is not only lighter for the planet. It is clearer for users, easier to maintain, and more respectful in how it uses attention and data.

Measuring Sustainability

Now that we have a broader definition of sustainability, the next question is what we can actually measure. This is where things get complicated. Sustainability spans environmental, social, and economic dimensions, and each of these areas comes with its own indicators, methodologies, and blind spots. Even large organizations with dedicated sustainability teams struggle to capture these metrics consistently.

Before we narrow our focus to the digital world, it helps to understand the common categories used across industries and why they are so challenging to apply in practice.

Environmental Metrics

Environmental impact is typically the most visible part of sustainability. It is assessed through indicators such as carbon footprint, water usage, energy consumption, waste management, and biodiversity impact. Tools like Life Cycle Assessment (LCA) aim to quantify these impacts from raw materials to end of life. They are incredibly useful, but they depend on detailed data that is rarely complete or standardized.

Social Metrics

Social sustainability focuses on aspects like labor practices, community engagement, human rights, and employee well-being. Metrics include fair wages, workplace safety, diversity and inclusion, and community development initiatives. Social Return on Investment (SROI) and other social auditing frameworks help quantify these aspects.

Economic Metrics

Economic sustainability focuses on long-term viability. It evaluates financial performance, economic impact, and governance practices. Metrics include profitability, economic value generated, tax contributions, and sustainable investment strategies. Tools like the Global Reporting Initiative (GRI) and the Sustainability Accounting Standards Board (SASB) provide standards for reporting on economic sustainability.

Integrated Approaches

Because no single set of metrics captures the full picture; most organizations rely on a combination of frameworks such as GRI, SASB, or LCA. These help create a more balanced view across environmental, social, and economic dimensions. Still, even with these tools, sustainability measurement remains difficult. Data is inconsistent, the boundaries are unclear, and priorities evolve as technology and expectations change.

This high-level view already shows why sustainability is hard to measure in a clear and consistent way. Digital products make things even more complex. A single interaction involves hardware, global networks, backend services, and whatever is happening on a user's device. Before we dive into the methods for estimating these impacts, it helps to step back and understand what the Internet looks like underneath the "cloud" most people imagine.

The Internet We Don't See

An average Internet user may access 10 to 20 websites per day. That number is much higher for me, as it is most likely for anyone whose job depends on the Internet and accesses It from different devices.

Our typical interaction with the Internet is simple. We open an app or a browser, ask for something, and get something back (hopefully) a moment later (Figure 2-2).

Figure 2-2. *Connecting to the Internet*

We understand the devices we hold. Smartphones, tablets, and laptops feel real and tangible. Many of us spent hours researching which one to buy, comparing models, reading reviews, and scrolling through online shops. We get excited when a new device arrives and annoyed when it slows down, breaks, or disappears. These devices have become an everyday part of our lives.

Most homes also have a Wi-Fi router, usually blinking somewhere in a corner. My grandmother still refers to it as the "resilver," a holdover from when she first got a satellite TV receiver. It is the one that usually gets the blame when a video freezes, or the dinosaur game appears again.

For many people, this is where the physical world ends, and the "cloud" begins. If we search for images of "the Internet," we will mostly end up with glowing dots and abstract floating lines, as shown in Figure 2-3.

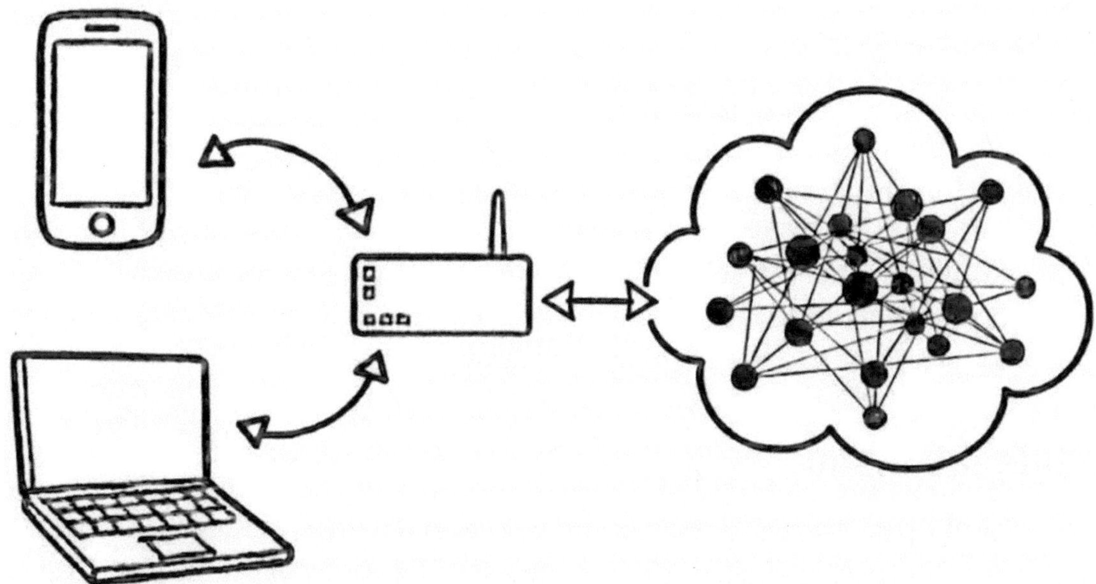

Figure 2-3. *The Internet Abstraction*

But the cloud is not really that magical.

It is hardware.

Servers, routers, switches, antennas, and cables make up the infrastructure that moves our data around the world, as illustrated in Figure 2-4.

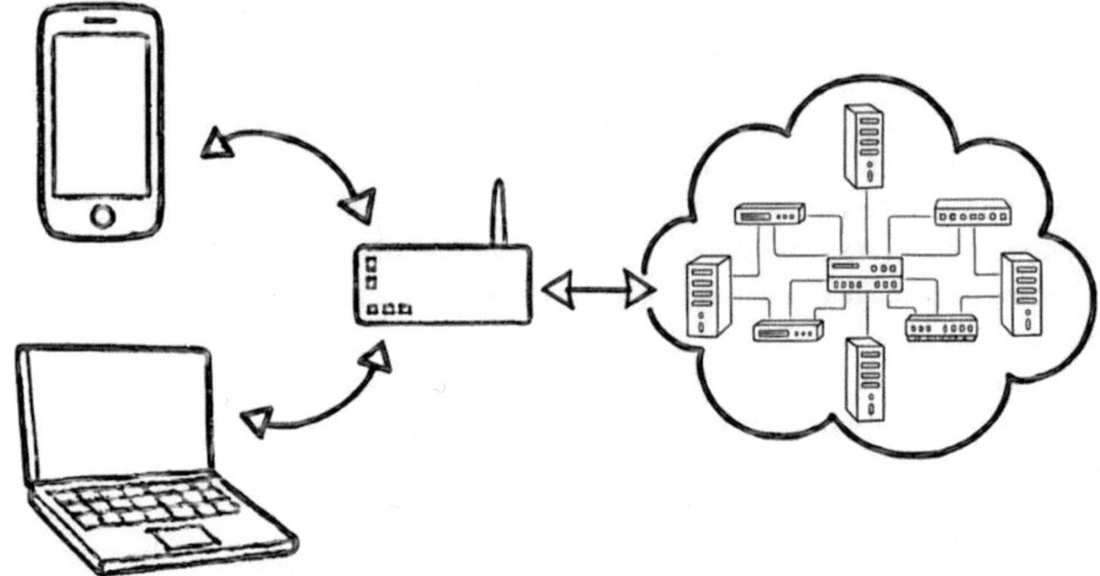

Figure 2-4. *The Internet is hardware*

It never stops to amaze me how this intricate network works and how it works this fast, as well as how many physical devices are actually a part of it. Everything that makes the Internet work is physical. Every device in this network requires resources to be produced, electricity, and often water to run and cool, and eventually becomes waste when it is replaced with something newer and faster.

Inside the Cloud

If we follow the path of a request beyond our devices and routers, the next stop is the data center. This is what people mean when they say, "the cloud." It isn't abstract. It isn't floating anywhere. It is a collection of buildings full of machines.

A typical data center houses long rows of servers, along with the networking equipment, storage systems, and cooling systems needed to keep them running safely (Figure 2-5). Some facilities host thousands of servers. The largest operate at a scale that is difficult to even imagine.

***Figure 2-5.** Inside a data center*

From the outside, a data center usually looks like a plain warehouse. On the inside, it is one of the most energy-intensive types of buildings in the world.

Chapter 4 explores these facilities in more detail. For now, the key idea is that digital services run on physical machines that consume energy and resources. To complete the picture, we also need to look at the machines closest to us. The smartphones in our pockets are built from just as many components and materials as the servers they connect to.

Anatomy of a Smartphone

When we zoom in on the devices closest to us, the picture becomes just as physical as the inside of a data center. Figure 2-6 shows a disassembled smartphone. Inside a small device are components that work together to run apps, connect to networks, store data, and display information. The processor handles instructions, memory (RAM) keeps data ready for quick use, and storage holds apps, photos, and files. The battery powers the device, while the screen, cameras, microphones, speakers, and various sensors make it usable. Antennas and radios enable cellular, Wi-Fi, Bluetooth, and NFC communication.

Figure 2-6. *Disassembled smartphone*

That is still quite abstract though. What are these components? The processor, memory, and storage are primarily made from silicon-based semiconductors. The battery is typically lithium-ion, using materials such as lithium, cobalt, and nickel to store energy. The display is made of specialized glass and indium tin oxide for touch functionality. The casing and frame often use materials such as aluminum, glass, and plastics, while other components, including cameras and speakers, incorporate rare-earth elements and metals such as copper and gold. Many different materials, most of us don't even know what they look like in their raw form. The only thing we are very familiar with is the end product itself.

Seeing the physical reality behind the "cloud" is only the first step. The harder part is figuring out what to measure so we can turn that understanding into action. That's where we go next.

What to Measure

Once you start looking at the physical layers behind digital products, another question appears almost immediately: what should we actually measure? Sustainability encompasses people, the planet, and prosperity, so the list of possible metrics grows rapidly. To keep things manageable, this book focuses on digital products and services that are accessed over the Internet. Even a simple site involves many moving parts. Think of a website you use often, or one you worked on recently.

Let's start with the user.

They arrive on different devices, with different screen sizes, processing power, battery levels, and network conditions. They stay for various reasons and for different lengths of time. All of this shapes their experience and the resources they consume.

Then look at delivery.

A site may load from cache, a nearby server, or a data center on another continent. Hosting choices, content delivery networks, reliability, and distance all influence cost, performance, and resource use.

And then the people behind it.

Teams design, build, test, and maintain digital products. They use devices, software, infrastructure, and time. They work remotely or onsite. They make trade-offs that affect accessibility, clarity, performance, cost, and long-term maintainability.

Most organizations already track many of these factors, but usually for financial or UX reasons. They measure what affects conversions, performance budgets, infrastructure costs, and team velocity.

But how about the planet?

And here, the measurement landscape becomes almost empty. What do we track? How does a digital service affect the environment? Isn't moving from physical to digital supposed to reduce impact?

Reality is harder to ignore. Extreme temperatures, fires, floods, and weather instability are shaping life around us. According to the United Nations, carbon emissions from fossil fuels remain the largest driver of climate change, responsible for more than 75% of all greenhouse gas emissions and nearly 90% of carbon dioxide emissions.

Wait, what do fossil fuels have to do with digital services?

Carbon Emissions

Before we go deeper into fossil fuels and digital services, we need a quick note on what we mean by "carbon." In this book, carbon is used as shorthand for CO_2e, which stands for carbon dioxide equivalent. CO_2e is the standard way to express the combined warming effect of all major greenhouse gases in one comparable number.

Carbon dioxide (CO_2) is the most common greenhouse gas, but it is not the only one. Methane, nitrous oxides, and fluorinated gases can trap far more heat than CO_2. CO_2e converts their impact into a single unit, so we can talk about climate impact without juggling different gases and their warming strengths.

When you see "carbon" or "emissions" in the rest of this book, read it as CO_2e. This keeps the language simple while still accurately reflecting the science.

Emission Scopes

To understand where emissions come from, organizations use a framework called emission scopes:

- **Scope 1** covers direct emissions from sources a company owns or controls. This includes fuel burned in company vehicles and emissions from boilers and generators in company buildings.
- **Scope 2** covers indirect emissions from purchased energy, such as electricity, heating, cooling, or steam. It represents the carbon footprint of the energy a company buys to power its operations.
- **Scope 3** covers all other indirect emissions across a company's value chain. This includes employee commuting, business travel, waste, supply chains, and the emissions created when customers use the company's products or services. For most organizations, Scope 3 is by far the largest category.

Digital products sit almost entirely in Scope 3, because their impact comes from electricity use, networks, cloud hosting, and hardware manufacturing outside a company's direct ownership.

How Do Digital Services Emit Carbon?

What do fossil fuels have to do with digital services? Short answer: **Electricity**.

Even with ongoing growth in renewable energy, much of the world still relies on fossil fuels for electricity. Each time someone loads a page, streams a video, or opens an app, the systems behind it consume electricity. The emissions from that activity depend on how the local grid produces power.

The emissions from digital products are diffused across multiple layers of infrastructure. These layers include

- **User devices**: The end user devices, such as computers, smartphones, and tablets, consume energy while people interact with digital services.
- **Network infrastructure**: Data moves through routers, switches, cell towers, and cables. All these draw electricity continuously, not only when traffic flows.
- **Data centers**: These facilities house the servers that store and process data. They are energy-intensive buildings with substantial cooling requirements to keep equipment within safe operating ranges.
- **Cloud platforms**: Cloud services run on physical servers inside data centers, but they add an extra layer of virtualization and orchestration. This makes the system more flexible and scalable, but also more complex when it comes to understanding where emissions occur.

The energy used across these layers makes up what are usually called operational emissions. These are the emissions from electricity consumption during use: devices turned on, networks moving data, and servers running applications.

Grid Carbon Intensity

To understand electricity-related emissions, we need one key idea: **grid carbon intensity**. It describes how dirty or clean electricity is in a specific place. More formally, it measures the amount of CO_2e emitted to generate one kilowatt-hour of electricity. A grid that relies heavily on coal or gas has a high carbon intensity. A grid with more wind, solar, hydro, or nuclear has a lower one. This means the same activity, whether a page load, a video stream, or a file upload, can produce very different emissions depending on where the electricity comes from.

Tools such as Electricity Maps (shown in Figure 2-7), WattTime, and the Carbon Aware Computing API (Based on Frauenhofer Energy Charts) and Ember's Global Electricity Data platform provide real-time data on grid carbon intensity, showing how electricity is generated at any given moment.

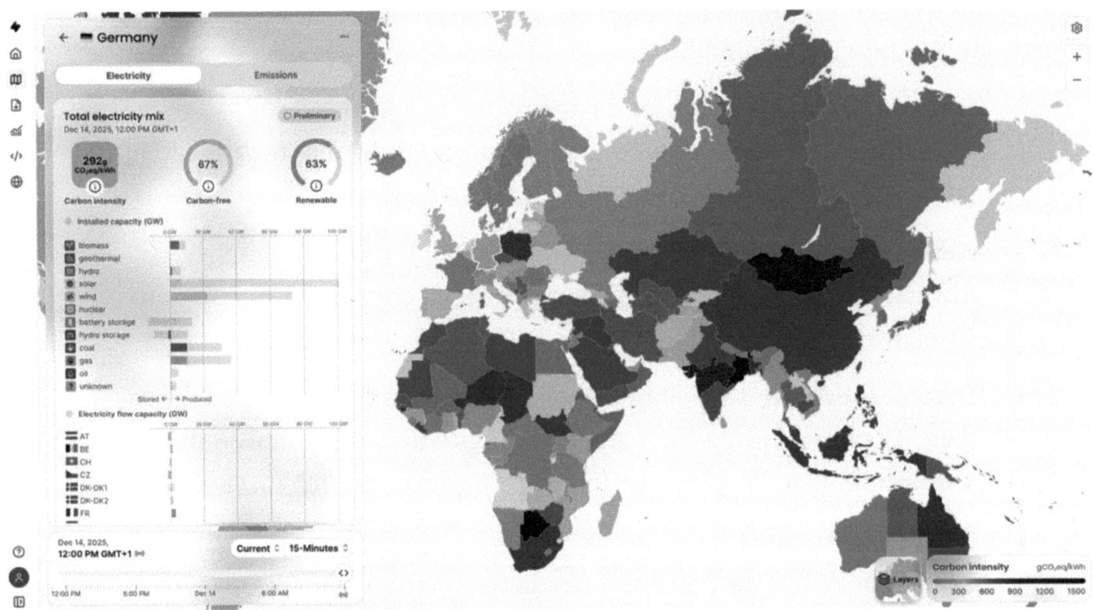

__Figure 2-7.__ Electricity maps app view

Embodied Carbon

Electricity emissions tell only one part of the story. A large share of the total footprint of digital technology comes from making the hardware in the first place. Extracting metals, refining materials, manufacturing chips, assembling components, shipping devices across the world, and eventually dealing with disposal or recycling all generate emissions long before a phone, laptop, or server is ever turned on.

This part of the footprint is known as **embodied carbon**. And for many devices, it dominates the total.

Independent life cycle assessments from research organizations across Europe consistently show the same pattern. Smartphones, for example, generate most of their lifetime emissions during manufacturing, not during use. Depending on the model and study, **around 70–90%** of a smartphone's total footprint comes from material extraction, component production, and assembly. For laptops, tablets, and desktop machines, the share varies, but production is still a major contributor.

Carbon from using and making devices explains a lot, but it still leaves gaps. Digital systems rely on resources and processes that create other environmental and social impacts that carbon numbers alone won't show.

It Is Not Just Carbon

Running servers and cooling data centers require large volumes of fresh water. Mining and refining the metals used in chips, batteries, and screens come with ecological damage and, in many regions, serious labor concerns. Waste from short device life cycles adds pressure on recycling systems that are already far from effective.

These impacts don't behave like electricity use. They don't scale neatly with page loads or traffic volume, and they aren't visible in emissions charts. But they are part of the same system and part of the sustainability story we need to understand.

And just as this picture is already complex, another force is accelerating many of these pressures.

And Then There Is AI

Could this be the longest you have been reading something about technology without seeing those two little ever-present letters?

Training large AI models consumes significant energy and drives demand for new hardware. Since the current AI boom began, more data centers have been built, more equipment has been produced, and several companies have moved further away from their climate targets rather than closer to them. The environmental cost of AI is growing quickly.

That is why Chapter 9 takes a closer look at the environmental side of AI. The field is moving fast, so specific numbers will change, but the underlying patterns stay the same. Our goal is to help you understand those patterns so you can make sense of the impact even as the technology evolves.

The Tale of the Team That Came Close, or Did It?

Now that we have covered the foundations, here is a story about a team that came surprisingly close to building a tool that could estimate the carbon emissions of an entire website.

There was once a group of web performance enthusiasts, people mostly working in front-end web development, who realized that optimizing how those bytes get transferred over the wire before they display something amazing on our screen is actually a very fun activity. I'm not sure if persuasion or luck got this group to get management approval and money to dedicate their work to their passion.

They knew that doing this at scale meant automation. So they embarked upon a quest to build their own Real User Monitoring (RUM) tool.

There are two complementary methods for measuring the performance of the website: synthetic or lab testing and Real User Monitoring (RUM). **Lab tests,** which many of you have probably done before, are in-depth analyses of the site to determine potential issues using tools such as Google Lighthouse, Webpagetest.org, Yellowlab.tools, etc. These tools simulate different connection speeds and different device screen sizes, load the site in those conditions, and report all the issues they found and some of the reasons why the site is potentially not performing well. They allow us to see **WHAT** the problem really is.

The second method is slightly newer and less used in this area. Real User Monitoring (RUM) tools work very similarly to any site analytics tools for measuring conversions, visits, etc. A small script is added to the site that collects data during the session and, in the end, sends them to the database, from which they are extracted and displayed in a nice dashboard that allows us to perform data analysis. The only difference between "Analytics" and "RUM" tools is in the data that they collect. With RUM tools being web performance-focused, they only collect data such as page load speed, amount of assets, Core Web Vitals, etc. As its name says, RUM tool measures website performance from real users and allows us insight into that dataset. This method enables us to see **IF we even have a problem and WHERE it is.**

While developing their RUM tool, the team found an open-source JavaScript library called CO2.js. It claimed to estimate CO_2e emissions of websites and apps. It caught their attention immediately. They were already using Sustainable Web Design principles in their consulting work, so adding emissions estimates to performance data felt like a natural next step.

Most website carbon calculators follow a simple three-step model:

- Measure the page weight of the website.
- Convert page weight to energy consumption.
- Convert energy consumption to CO_2 equivalent emissions.

All you need is data and a formula and the team quickly discovered that CO2.js implemented two emissions estimation models (formulas): 1byte and the Sustainable Web Design (SWD). After a few debates, they settled on trying out the Sustainable Web Design Model.

Sustainable Web Design Model

The SWD Model, illustrated in Figure 2-8, is an open-source collaboration between Wholegrain Digital, Mightybytes, Footsprint, EcoPing, and the Green Web Foundation. It has evolved across several versions, aiming to refine emissions estimation as research improves.[1]

The key word here is estimation. Because digital emissions come from many sources, precise measurement is currently impossible. Models offer the best available approximation.

The SWD model creates an energy profile of a website by using data transferred over the wire as a proxy. Three sub-systems segment their results into

- **Data centers**: Energy that is required to house and serve data.
- **Networks**: Energy used by networks to transfer data.
- **User devices**: Energy used by end users interacting with a product or service.

Using combined information from a few different research, these segments account for a portion of the total system energy used:

[1] The percentages described reflect version 3 of the SWD model, which was available to and used by the team in our story. At the time of publishing, the model is at version 4, which refines the methodology further, including updated data sources and a more nuanced approach to embodied emissions across all three system segments. You can learn more about the current version on the Green Web Foundation website.

- **Data centers:** 22%
- **Networks:** 24%
- **User devices:** 54%

Each system segment is further divided into two categories that we have already discussed: operational and embodied emissions. This allows for the extraction or filtering of data by these categories.

To get the final emissions estimation number, the model multiplies the calculated energy number with grid carbon intensity, **which makes data transfer and carbon intensity two key inputs for this model.**

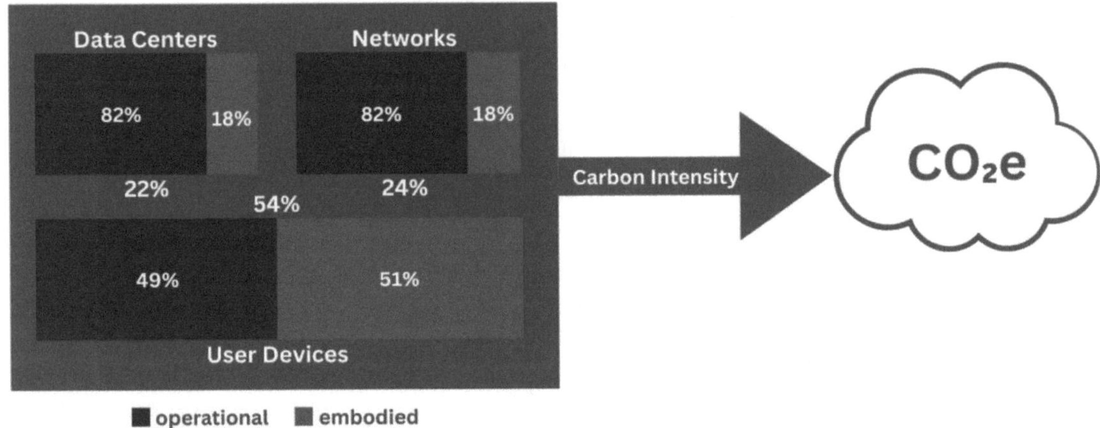

Figure 2-8. *The Sustainable Web Design model*

The model allows adjustments, such as renewable-powered hosting (Chapter 4) or accounting for cached content and returning visitors (Chapter 7). It aligns with the GHG Protocol Corporate Standard. It can be used to estimate emissions from websites, apps, downloads, streaming, and API responses.

Real-Time Full-Site Estimations

The idea felt almost magical: real-time emissions estimates for every page visit across a whole website.

There was a catch. To make the calculation accurate, the RUM script had to collect precise page-weight data from each session. That extra data added more bytes to every request. Processing and storing it created even more load. The team found itself facing a very tricky question: **Can the impact of having the information be annulled by the amount of data required to obtain it?**

There was no perfect answer. They compromised by collecting page-weight data from a sample of sessions and extrapolating the rest. Precision was lost, but the system became usable.

Once integrated, the dashboard came to life. Real-time emissions graphs. Filters by page type, country, and screen size. Trends over time. A single number that could, in theory, appear in a company's sustainability reporting. It felt like a glimpse into the future.

To Estimate or Not to Estimate

Why was this so exciting? Because measurement changes everything. If you can measure emissions, you can identify problems, compare results, and track improvements. The SWD model had mostly been used in lab tools that analyze a single URL. But testing one page is misleading. Homepages are often the most optimized pages on a site. Other pages can be far heavier.

RUM tools check for every session across the whole site and allow us to see exact user behavior. Lab tests usually don't simulate page interaction, such as clicking and scrolling, which can drastically affect page weight (I have seen up to 18MB !!! of difference), making lab test results very imprecise compared to RUM, which collects real users' inputs. As a cherry on top, having a dashboard with graphs plotting changes over time, allowing for alerts and budgets, and filtering to check where the issues arise was the "please don't wake me up" moment.

Even though real user data allowed this model to be fed with as precise data as possible, it was still fed to a model, and by their very nature, models are imprecise. They can be useful, but they are always wrong. So, having this number was an absolute dream, but it came with a lot of responsibility and controversy. In addition to the question of the balance between positive and negative impacts that data collection and processing can create, ongoing debates center on how flawed the model really is and the extent of its negative impact.

The biggest problem is that data transfer is not a good proxy for electricity and carbon emissions. That is something everyone agrees on. Why? Well, not every byte of data is equal. Once bytes are transferred over the network, they still need to be processed by the browser, and some require significantly more processing and memory than others. When data transfer serves as a proxy, storing files locally can result in estimated emissions being reported as 0, which may be far from the truth. If we also consider that screens on laptops and phones are among the biggest energy consumers (looking at a page for longer can require much more energy than the initial load) and that networks are constantly 'on' regardless of whether data is passing through them, it becomes clear why this debate persists.

Even though everyone agrees this is not right, opinions differ on whether it can be useful. It boils down to a fundamental question of **why we want to use this estimation**: to report emissions, work on optimizations, raise awareness, or show we are the "greenest."

Greenwashing

Claims about "green websites" or "low-carbon digital services" have become more common, often without strong evidence. As you've seen, the reality is complex. Any emissions estimate comes with caveats, assumptions, uncertainties, and boundaries that are easy to gloss over.

The simpler the number, the easier it becomes to use it in marketing without nuance.

New regulations in the European Union and shifts in US guidelines aim to reduce unsubstantiated sustainability claims. In some cases, misleading statements can result in penalties. We explore this in more detail in Chapter 3.

Conclusion

If this chapter feels like a lot, that is because it is. Once you start asking what the impact of a website actually is, the picture expands fast. Electricity grids, manufacturing, mining, water, working conditions, and now AI hardware races. None of this shows up in an analytics dashboard. It is easy to miss.

We now know at least three things.

First, digital is physical. There is no cloud without buildings, machines, cables, and materials. Every interaction sits on top of that.

Second, we cannot talk about impact honestly without estimates. We rely on models, grid data, and life cycle assessments. They are imperfect and always will be, but they are the only way to get closer to reality.

Third, numbers are not neutral. The same estimate can guide better decisions or end up as a marketing claim with no context behind it.

The story of the RUM tool and CO2.js reflects this tension. It shows what is possible with current methods and where the limits are. It is exciting to see a CO_2e number for a page view. It is also uncomfortable once you see how many assumptions sit behind that single number.

So the real question is not whether we can measure everything perfectly. We cannot. The more useful question is what level of estimation is good enough to inform better decisions without pretending we have certainty where we do not.

The next chapter moves from the big picture back into the work you do every day. We look at digital products and services themselves, who shapes them, and where impact is created inside a product lifecycle. Even with imperfect data, these are places where decisions matter.

Summary

This chapter explores why measuring the impact of digital products is difficult and why we need to try it anyway. Sustainability spans environmental, social, and economic dimensions, and each part of a digital service touches physical systems we rarely think about.

We went beneath the abstraction of the cloud and saw the hardware behind every interaction: devices, networks, and data centers, all drawing electricity whose emissions depend on the local grid. We also saw that a large share of the footprint happens before anything is powered on, through manufacturing and materials.

Carbon is only one part of the picture. Water use, mining impacts, and labor concerns all sit in the same system. The rapid growth of AI adds new pressures through increased energy demand and hardware turnover.

Finally, we looked at an example of current estimation methods. Models like the Sustainable Web Design model help reveal patterns, but they come with uncertainty and require care to avoid misuse or greenwashing.

The key idea is simple. Digital products have a real impact. Measuring them is imperfect, but it remains the most reliable way to understand where those impacts come from and where change is possible.

References

Internet Use and Environmental Impact

- **Google Search/Sites Visited Statistics (SEMrush)**: https://www.semrush.com/blog/google-search-statistics/
- **United Nations – Causes and Effects of Climate Change**: https://www.un.org/en/climatechange/science/causes-effects-climate-change
- **Visual Capitalist – How Top Economies Generated Electricity in 2024**: https://www.visualcapitalist.com/charted-how-top-economies-generated-electricity-in-2024/

Energy Grids and Carbon Intensity

- **How Energy Grids Work – Green Web Foundation**: https://www.thegreenwebfoundation.org/news/how-energy-grids-work/
- **Electricity Maps – Real-time Grid Carbon Intensity**: https://www.electricitymaps.com
- **WattTime – Automated Carbon-aware Emissions Signal and API**: https://www.watttime.org
- **Carbon-Aware Computing API (Fraunhofer Energy Charts)**: https://www.carbon-aware-computing.com
- **Ember – Global Electricity Data Platform**: https://ember-climate.org/data

Hardware Manufacturing and E-waste

- **Fraunhofer IZM – Life Cycle Assessment of Consumer Electronics**: https://www.izm.fraunhofer.de
- **Fairphone – Life Cycle Assessment Reports**: https://www.fairphone.com/en/sustainability/impact-reports/

- **Product Environmental Footprint Category Rules (PEFCR), European Commission Joint Research Centre**: https://susproc.jrc.ec.europa.eu/product-bureau/product-groups
- **United Nations University - Global E-waste Monitor**: https://globalewaste.org
- **Reducing Embodied Carbon (European Commission)**: https://ec.europa.eu/environment/news/reducing-embodied-carbon-key-achieving-sustainable-construction-2021-12-14_en

Data Centers and Infrastructure

- **IEA - Data Centres and Data Transmission Networks**: https://www.iea.org/reports/data-centres-and-data-transmission-networks
- **Uptime Institute - Data Center Energy Efficiency Reports**: https://uptimeinstitute.com
- **Masanet et al., "Recalibrating global data center energy-use estimates" (Science, 2020)**: https://www.science.org/doi/10.1126/science.aba3758
- **Andrae & Edler - Global Electricity Usage of Communication Technology (MDPI)**: https://www.mdpi.com/2078-1547/12/3/14
- **Ericsson Mobility Report**: https://www.ericsson.com/en/reports-and-papers/mobility-report
- **GreenIT.fr - Impacts Environnementaux du Numérique dans le Monde 2025**: https://greenit.eco/nos-etudes-et-essais/impacts-environnementaux-du-numerique-dans-le-monde-2025/

Measurement and Models

- **Sustainable Web Design Model**: https://sustainablewebdesign.org/estimating-digital-emissions/
- **DebugBear – Why Website Carbon Emissions Are Hard to Measure**: https://www.debugbear.com/blog/website-carbon-emissions
- **Fershad Irani – Why Web Performance Tools Should Report Website Carbon Emissions**: https://calendar.perfplanet.com/2023/why-web-perf-tools-should-be-reporting-website-carbon-emissions/
- **Digital Greenwashing – Mightybytes Guide**: https://www.mightybytes.com/blog/digital-greenwashing-guide/

CHAPTER 3

Rethinking Product Decisions

Ines Akrap[1]

[1]Munich, Germany; `inesakrap.com`

Take a moment to look around; how many digital devices do you see? Phone, laptop, tablet, perhaps an e-reader. Beyond what we actively use, many spaces now include connected TVs, smart speakers, and other "smart" devices that stay online quietly in the background. Digital technology has become a constant presence in our daily lives, often in ways we barely notice anymore.

This constant connectivity is reflected in how much time we actually spend online. According to recent global data, Internet users aged 16 to 64 spend an average of six hours and forty minutes per day using the Internet across devices. That adds up to roughly 101 days a year. Almost one-third of our lives is spent online. Let that sink in for a moment. Figure 3-1 shows how this time has grown over the past decade, and how usage has steadily shifted from desktop computers to mobile devices worldwide.

C. Chinchilla and I. Akrap, *Building the Sustainable Web*, https://doi.org/10.1007/979-8-8688-2521-7_3

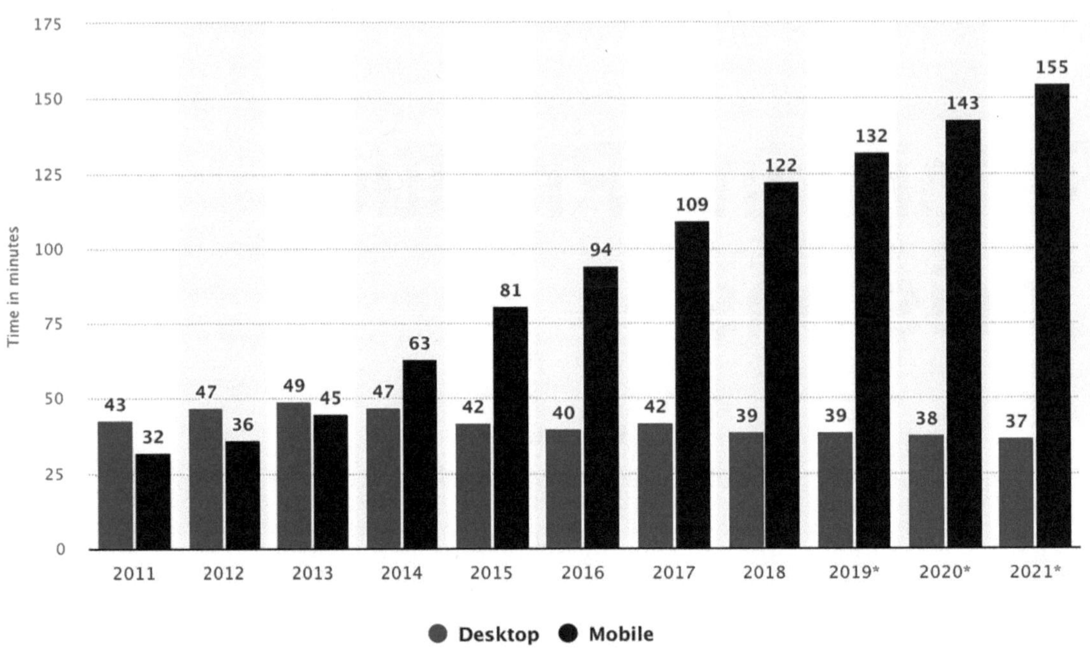

Figure 3-1. *Daily time spent with the Internet per capita worldwide from 2011 to 2021, by device (Statista 2024)*

I used myself as a test subject for this topic, and the result, which showed that I was above average, did not surprise me at all. I work remotely using my computer, and as someone who needs to physically write, sketch, and visualize things all the time, my tablet is non-stop in front of me, ready to receive new notes. The moment I clock out, I pick up my smartphone to catch up with family, friends, and the news, and indulge in my daily dose of social media. I use the Internet to read, learn, exercise, shop, research, relax, order food, pay bills, and almost everything else. I still go to the grocery store in person, but it is also becoming an extreme activity whenever my kids accompany me, so I am increasingly considering using those "click and collect" services.

The Internet and digital services have reshaped how we live, work, and solve problems. We can do things today that once felt impossible. But the systems that make all this possible also create impacts we rarely notice, and by overlooking those costs for so long, we've allowed the conveniences of our digital world to cause harm in places we don't see.

Digitalization isn't the problem. It can create enormous value for people and, in many cases, even support sustainability goals. The issue is that many of its hidden costs go unexamined. Once we understand those costs, we can design in ways that avoid them. In Chapter 2, we unpacked what the "cloud" actually is and saw the first signs of the real infrastructure behind digital products and services. Before we dig deeper, we need one shared definition: what exactly do we mean by a digital product? According to the Sustainable Digital Infrastructure Alliance (SDIA)

> *A digital product or service is what a company or a consumer might buy. It is always made up of software or a combination of software and hardware and, therefore, deals with data, which represents its inputs (by the users), which it transforms into outputs.*

Basically, these are any goods that exist in a digital format: eBooks, courses, memberships, programs... all the apps and content we interact with daily, mostly online. The sheer volume of digital products being created today is hard to grasp. Because they bring convenience to everyday life and don't require the same up-front investment as physical products, they can appear faster than we can process them. At times, it feels like the only thing that might slow this growth is legislation.

To keep this book focused, the digital products we discuss are websites and web applications. Let's define those as well.

According to the Cambridge Dictionary, a website is a set of pages of information on the Internet about a particular subject published by a single person or organization. On the other hand, a web application is a computer program designed for a specific purpose that can be used on the internet rather than downloading it.

This chapter looks at the foundations of website and web application ideation. We'll get to the hands-on techniques and technical guidance in later chapters, but first, we need the groundwork. Before any design or development choices are made, the most important thing to build is the right mindset.

World Wide Waste

If the why of "why-do-we-even-need-to-make-Internet-more-Sustainable" is still not fully there, let me share a quote by Robert Swan with you:

> *"The greatest threat to our planet is the belief that someone else will save it."*

Exactly. We're at a point where every effort counts, big or small. If you're familiar with compounding, you already know how tiny actions can accumulate into something powerful over time. It works in both directions. One by one, small pieces of trash create massive landfills. One by one, tiny atoms of CO_2 released over decades add up to global warming that we're now struggling to contain. The same applies to digital decisions. A choice that feels insignificant today, once multiplied across millions of users over many years, can create huge consequences. The Internet is compounding in the wrong direction, but we can change its trajectory.

I guarantee you've had an idea for an app at least once in your life. Maybe you noticed a feature missing in something you use every day, or maybe you were joking with friends and someone said, "We should make that app." It's hard to keep count of how many ideas like that we've all had over the years, and even harder to picture how crowded the Internet would be if every one of them actually came to life.

Let's go one step further. How many of these ideas originated on the Internet but never gained traction? Or had an initial hype where everyone predicted it would be "the next big thing" for a week, and then that same everyone returned to the comfort of their well-known and loved services. How many services have you created accounts for over the years, just to do a quick run-through and decide that you don't really like it, and never log in again? It sounded like a good idea, but its implementation was not exactly how we imagined it. And of course, the inevitable thought appears: *maybe it's time for my version.*

Recently, I came across a service that looked interesting, so I started exploring. I liked what I saw and created an account, only to discover that I had a two-week free trial that would roll into a monthly subscription. Oh, wait. Billing. I had to pay for this. That wasn't what I expected, and as someone who only pays for services I truly need and use, I wasn't ready to make that commitment. I closed the tab and moved on. Over the next couple of weeks, I received a handful of check-in emails reminding me that my trial was ending. And then something unexpected happened, something I had never seen before. I received an email offering me two options: continue by becoming a paying customer, or simply do nothing, which would lead to my account and all associated data being deleted. As someone who has worked in digital sustainability for years, I was genuinely surprised. The service proactively removed all trial accounts that did not convert. It's a simple but powerful example of good maintenance, breaking negative compounding, and respecting data privacy. Left untouched, those inactive accounts would have quietly piled up into terabytes of unused data, contributing to storage growth and the eventual need for more data centers. Instead, they were wiped. The only data this service keeps is the data it actually uses from active customers.

The main question here isn't whether we need web applications and services but whether we need **this many**. Are all of them genuinely useful, or are most simply creating digital waste? In Gerry McGovern's book *World Wide Waste* (a fantastic read, highly recommended), he argues for reducing digital waste by focusing on the "Three

R's": recycling useful information, radically reducing digital creation, and removing pollution-causing data. **Spoiler alert: a big part of reducing the Internet's carbon footprint is just cleaning up and getting rid of the things we don't need.**

Start with Why

There are several key questions to answer before creating a sustainable application, but the first one is crucial: **Why should we develop this website or application in the first place?**

Some of the most common answers are going to be

- To solve a specific problem
- Because there is a gap in the market
- To improve an already existing application
- To make money
- To learn how this technology works
- To share my thoughts or knowledge with others
- To help a particular community

All of these are valid reasons. But every coin has two sides, and the question we rarely ask is: **"Why shouldn't we create this website or application?"** That question forces us to look beyond benefits and confront the potential risks, harms, and unintended consequences our product might create.

Creating new websites and web applications usually boils down to benefiting a specific person, group, or community:

- **Person**: I want to learn, I want to earn.
- **Group**: Our company needs its communication tool, or our team has a particular way of managing its time and tasks.
- **Community**: How about an app where everyone with the same problem can connect and share their thoughts and tips?

What often happens is that the focus stays on the benefits for that small circle of people. What usually doesn't enter the discussion are the potential negative effects—on the target group, on the people around them, and on the wider ecosystem that supports all of this. And that wider context matters. **The climate crisis has already put basic human needs at risk: access to food, water, clean air, and shelter. If that isn't enough to make us ask "Why not?" before creating something new, I'm not sure what is.**

There are many examples of digital services that have created substantial negative impacts over the years. Let's start with the most obvious one: social media.

The Sustainability Impact of Social Media

Social media was invented to facilitate communication and connection among people, enabling them to share information, ideas, and experiences more easily across distances. The early motivations behind social media were rooted in the desire to create virtual spaces where people could interact in real time, form networks, and build communities, regardless of geographical barriers. Sounds incredible: new technology, solving problems of distance communication, filling the market gap... However, having social media omnipresent in our lives turned out not to be so great. I seriously doubt that any of us, as consumers, ever thought about what negative impact clicking that "Sign-up" button could have on us and our lives. No one thought that people sharing only small, curated glimpses into their "perfect" lives would be responsible for so many cases of anxiety and depression. No one thought that the ability to be connected with anyone anywhere, anytime could have negative consequences on people's sleep and, therefore, health. No one thought that tools used to ease communication would actually negatively affect real-world in-person communication and, with that, often harm even the closest relationships.

Next time you visit a bar or restaurant, take a moment to notice how many people are typing or scrolling on their phones instead of being present and engaging with those around them. Bonus exercise: Notice how many of those are children.

Should we be worrying about this as users? I would like to know if the product team has conducted thorough research on human psychology to understand how these services may have a negative impact on people. Did everything just move too fast for this not to even be a question until it was too late? Was the research done and discarded because profit prediction was just too good? Or was it maybe decided that "we are not responsible for how people use it"? This opens up many discussions about the ethics of product design, but we won't go deeper into that here. It could easily be an entire book on its own.

And with all that, did anyone ever stop to ask how much energy these systems would use, or what carbon emissions they might produce? I doubt it. As they evolved, focusing on profit over anything else and monetizing our attention, social media applications reached a point where their success meant harm to us and our planet.

Recently, I came across an estimate suggesting that TikTok's annual carbon footprint may be in the same range as that of a small country. The exact figures vary depending on the methodology, but the point is clear: **a single digital service can reach a scale where its environmental impact rivals that of an entire nation.** That should concern all of us.

Brad Smith, Microsoft Vice Chair and President, once said: **"Every day when we go to work, we will decide whether tech is used for good or ill... technology has no conscience, but people do, and we must exercise our conscience."** The first step toward making conscious choices that benefit people and the planet is to educate ourselves as much as possible, so we can identify potential negative outcomes and advocate for the positive ones.

All Stakeholders

As the next step in the process of creating a website or web application, right after we answered why and hopefully why not, is to define the stakeholders. Around the 16th century, the word "stake" was used for "something put up as a wager" or "something placed at hazard," and by the 18th century, it evolved slightly to "a personal interest" or "something to gain or lose." Therefore, stakeholders are those who have something to gain or lose. So, you may be sensing my next question here: Have we always included **everyone** who has something to gain or lose when defining our stakeholders?

In September 2023, Apple released an ad titled "Mother Nature Needs a Status Report." The ad itself sparked criticism, especially for portraying Apple as more environmentally responsible than many believe it is. But it also did something very important: it introduced a non-human persona (humanized, in this case) as a stakeholder in a highly visible way. With millions of views, it pushed the idea of non-human stakeholders into the public conversation in a way few examples had before.

A brand that has been using this idea more quietly, but far more authentically, is Patagonia. On September 14, 2022, the company announced: "Earth is now our only shareholder." The message was simple: environmental responsibility is not a campaign, it is a governing principle.

Patagonia and Apple operate in very different worlds, but both examples point to the same idea: the environment can be treated as a real stakeholder. Once you start thinking that way, the conversation around product decisions changes. And you don't need to overhaul an entire company to adopt this mindset. Any team, on any project, can begin widening the circle of who is affected.

Your Environment-Centered Stakeholders

Earth, or "Mother Earth," is a persona many people can imagine, but you don't have to use the same one. Depending on what you're building, it can be more helpful to be very specific. Your non-human stakeholder might be a forest, a river, an endangered species, farmland near a new data center, or a local community's water supply. Defining a concrete persona makes it much easier to ask meaningful questions about impact. We encourage you to do this exercise with your team. Digital products can affect places and systems that rarely appear in traditional project discussions.

The Indirect Human Stakeholders

Once you start looking beyond the immediate user, it becomes clear that many stakeholders are affected indirectly. These are people who may never interact with your product but still feel its consequences. A parent whose child is overwhelmed by social media. A community living next to a water stressed data center. A teacher supporting students who are exhausted from late night scrolling.

They don't appear in user research or analytics dashboards, yet they are part of the system your product touches. Including them in early discussions broadens the perspective of the team and helps you spot avoidable harm before it happens.

What Makes a Website and Web Application Sustainable

In Chapter 2, we discussed some of the challenges associated with measuring the impact of digital products across various sustainability dimensions. We also introduced some basic concepts related to these dimensions: environmental, social, and economic—people, planet, and prosperity. The next question we would like to answer here is what makes digital products sustainable. And to make it more specific: what makes websites and web applications sustainable?

Prosperity

We are all familiar with what makes a website and web application prosperous. This part has been well-researched and is one that most businesses, and therefore, product teams, care about. Some digital products are made with the primary goal of generating income (in many different ways); some do that as a side effect. Very few do not have that goal in mind whatsoever. It is easy to find resources with tips and tricks on this topic. Let's also make one thing clear: designing the site to make a profit is not a bad thing, far from it. **However, a website that makes a profit should not harm people and the planet as a consequence.**

People

Creating products and services is much about understanding people's needs and delivering what meets them. We discussed this at the beginning of the chapter. However, we also scratched the surface of the topic of products and services being designed without considering the harm they can bring to the very people for whom they are intended.

One crucial topic that arises when discussing design for people is accessibility. I learned about this topic and realized its importance in the first weeks of my first front-end developer job. I was going through a company enablement program, and one of the sessions introduced me and my colleagues to this important topic. I can't stress enough how grateful I am for that, as learning about the topic and its importance made me incorporate it into my default mode of creation, which is how accessibility should be approached. **Built in, not bolt on.** I also can't express how excited I was when I found out that having an accessible website would become a law, because it was extremely challenging to push this as a requirement during the product development process before that. So why accessibility, and what does it have to do with sustainability anyway?

There is a common misconception that accessibility is only about designing for people with permanent disabilities such as blindness or deafness. This misconception has led to the topic and its associated issues being ignored and pushed to the back of the agenda for years. However, accessible design is actually defined as "designing for everyone." It's about not excluding people because of a permanent disability, a temporary limitation, or a situational constraint.

Let's do a quick example. One of the requirements for a website to be accessible is to provide captions for videos. It's not an easy one, well, at least it wasn't before we had AI available. This feature would often be discarded as unnecessary because our users can simply listen to the video, and what is the worth of doing this for the few with hearing disabilities? However, how often have you been in a situation where you are about to watch a video, for example, on public transport, and you don't have your headphones handy? How many times have you been using your device with one hand and were not able to perform an action because the button was "too far"? I can keep going with these types of examples for a while, but I believe this is already enough to see how these are not edge cases but everyday situations for many. Designing our services to be accessible to anyone, everywhere, and in any situation they may be in, can easily lead to more sales.

Let me share one more example, my favorite one from the non-digital world: the elevator. A fully able-bodied person can use stairs to reach the upper floors of a building, making elevators an accessibility feature for those who cannot. But who are those? Only people with permanent disabilities, or parents with strollers, new tenants moving in heavy furniture, an average-fit person with hands full of groceries, and, well, anyone just feeling lazy that day. It is essential for a few, and useful for nearly all.

Another core aspect of designing for people is **choice**. Giving users control so they are neither excluded nor harmed. We look at this in detail in later chapters, but it belongs here as part of the mindset.

With all of us being different from one another, it's logical that our web-browsing preferences differ too. Dark mode is an easy example. I prefer working in dark mode, so when websites finally started offering that switch, it felt like a small but very real improvement. One simple option instantly made reading more comfortable for me. And dark mode is just one case. Many features we treat as standard don't work equally well for everyone. Decorative images can slow pages down or waste mobile data for people who just want to read. Animations might look fun to some, but others find them distracting, and for some they can even trigger serious medical symptoms. None of these elements are inherently good or bad. They just affect people differently.

That's why offering choice matters. Giving people the ability to turn off extras, simplify the interface, or control the visual experience makes the product usable for far more people. This isn't about adding endless settings. It's about recognizing that the "default" does not serve everyone equally and allowing people to decide what works for them.

Building the best product for our users is already a challenging task. Expanding that thinking to design for everyone can feel overwhelming at first, but it becomes far more manageable when the whole team adopts this mindset. A shared approach makes inclusive, flexible design a natural part of the work rather than an extra layer added later.

Before we begin turning ideas into an actual product, there is one more element to add to this mindset.

Planet

To achieve a sustainable digital product, we need to design it for everyone, make it profitable, and ensure it is balanced with the surrounding ecosystem. This means making sure it does not harm the planet and, in turn, everyone who depend on it.

In Chapters 1 and 2, we looked at how digital services affect the environment. Most of the impact comes from the CO_2e emitted when fossil fuels are burned to generate the electricity needed to manufacture and power our devices. We also touched on the fresh water required to cool data centers and the mining needed to extract materials for hardware. With that in mind, how can we design websites and web apps that are actually "green"?

Chapter 2 also established that manufacturing a device carries a heavy environmental cost long before anyone turns it on. Earlier research put this at roughly three-quarters of a device's total footprint. Newer studies show that the exact split shifts over time as devices stay in use longer and services become more energy intensive, but the underlying message remains the same. **Making new devices is resource-heavy, energy-intensive, and environmentally expensive**.

A few years ago, a friend shared with me an interesting anecdote that provides a perfect starting point for this discussion: her father had to buy a new smartphone because the parking app he was using was no longer supported by his old device. The "old" device was approximately two years old. That means that a digital product (a mobile phone app) offering a digital service (parking payment) has made the device obsolete. Not being able to use the app they need made a person throw away a perfectly good device, as well as spend money on a new one. And we all know that the app did not make itself that way.

> ***It is always software that forces hardware to be thrown away.***
>
> ***—Max Schulze, Founder of the Sustainable Digital Infrastructure Alliance (SDIA)***

This is the part we don't talk about enough. Software decisions have a direct physical impact. Every time an app becomes heavier, or drops support for older devices, or demands more CPU and RAM just to display simple content, it shortens the lifespan of perfectly functional hardware. And when hardware dies early, the environmental cost of manufacturing new devices is triggered again and again.

We all know that feeling when we buy a brand-new device, unbox it, remove all the stickers, and see the welcome screen for the first time. As I age, the setup process becomes more of a hassle than an excitement. Still, I appreciate the moment when I realize I can perform my everyday tasks faster and more efficiently than before. The issue is that the speed and efficiency honeymoon phase typically lasts for a year or so, and then we often go back to feeling that our device is slow and begin thinking about an upgrade. That is, of course, if we are wealthy enough to afford regular swaps.

What I find interesting is how quickly we start calling a device "slow" when, not long before, it was considered "blazing fast." Has anything changed about the device itself? Not really. Applications become increasingly demanding, consuming more CPU and battery power, and sometimes becoming entirely unavailable if the device is considered outdated. And it doesn't have to be this way.

This isn't only about phones. Many of us feel this pressure in our work devices, too. Throughout my career, I received a new work laptop every two to three years. Right now, I sometimes feel frustrated with my one-year-old, extremely high-end device because it occasionally slows down or gets stuck. A one-year-old device that is mainly used for browsing, cloud-based applications, and a few video calls a day. On paper, it is the best laptop I've ever had. In practice, modern software is pushing it harder than it should.

The root of this forced renewal is often the growing weight of modern websites and web apps. As a service grows heavier, with a larger DOM, more JavaScript, assets, and trackers, it demands more CPU cycles and RAM from the device just to display a single page. That overhead has a real environmental cost, especially when multiplied across millions of users.

And this leads directly into another important topic: **the device inequality gap**. Not everyone is browsing on a brand-new high-end device. The average global user has a mid-range or older phone, and for many people, upgrading frequently is simply not an option. When services assume fast devices and fast connections, they exclude people who cannot or should not have to upgrade, and they accelerate global e-waste by pushing devices into early retirement.

With e-waste now one of the fastest-growing waste streams in the world, compatibility becomes a crucial part of a sustainability mindset. When a product works well on older or lower-spec devices, it reduces unnecessary hardware turnover. It ensures more people can access the service without frustration, wasted time, or repeated failed attempts that also generate avoidable emissions.

Bringing It All Together

Sustainable digital products balance three things at once: people, prosperity, and the planet. These are not competing goals. When they are considered together, they strengthen each other.

Designing for **people** means building products that include rather than exclude. Accessibility, choice, and flexibility make products usable for more people, in more contexts, with less friction. They reduce frustration and increase trust and loyalty. Designing for **prosperity** means creating value in a way that is both resilient and does not exploit people or resources. A profitable product that relies on dark patterns, exclusion, or constant hardware upgrades is not sustainable. A product that serves people well tends to perform better financially over the long run. Designing for the **planet** means recognizing that software decisions have physical consequences. When services become heavier or more demanding than they need to be, they shorten device lifespans and accelerate e-waste. When they are efficient, compatible, and respectful of resources, people can keep their devices longer and use them with less energy.

Sustainability becomes much easier to work with when teams share a common understanding of what "good" looks like. The W3C Web Sustainability Guidelines, led editorially by Alex Dawson, are one attempt to describe that shared direction. They aren't something you need to follow line by line, and they won't solve every challenge for you. What they offer is a practical way to bring sustainability into everyday product decisions, so teams treat it the same way they treat performance, security, accessibility, or usability. Sustainable products aren't about perfection. They grow from consistent decisions that respect people, support the organization, and reduce unnecessary strain on the planet.

So what happens when the product is already live, full of past choices you didn't make? That's where many teams start. Sustainability isn't a reset button. You can introduce it gradually, even in products that have been around for years.

What If We Already Have a Product

In an ideal world, we would incorporate all aspects of sustainable design into a website or web app from the very first ideation workshop. But most of us don't work in that world. We work on existing products that have years of decisions behind them, and we can't always apply what we've learned right away. The good news is that building a mindset for designing and developing sustainable sites can start at any point in a product's life cycle.

> ***The best thing about making software sustainable is that we can make a difference and reduce emissions with just one single deployment.***
>
> ***—Anita Schüttler, Head of Sustainability (neuland)***

Many strategies of sustainable design and development can be easily applied to even the oldest code bases, and improvements can be made with a single deployment. The first steps would be to initiate discussions about this topic within the product team and allocate some time for education. Once all team members are familiar with what website sustainability means for their role, it shouldn't be too hard to find opportunities for quick wins.

Clean Up Old or Start from Scratch

Nothing like that clean, fresh, blank project that gives us flexibility, creativity, and the opportunity to start from scratch. If you have been working on a legacy project for years, getting a fresh start is usually even more satisfying. We get to re-design everything that was initially designed years ago and has been giving us headaches. However, is starting from scratch always the best approach? It depends.

When site rebuild decisions are being made, most of the time, the main topic ends up being the budget. It, of course, costs to do a project from scratch, from purchasing new technology to paying people who will handle ideation, design, implementation, testing, content creation, etc. These discussions can last months or even years, with new project costs being justified in terms of potential benefits. Yet one major cost is almost always missing from the conversation: the sustainability cost.

Imagine that after reading this book, you become eager to build a sustainable website. You sit down, open a new document, and start drafting a proposal. You want to apply every principle right away, and starting from scratch seems like the simplest path. But is it really the best one? Before opening a blank page, the first step should be to open the current website or application and evaluate what is already there. Maybe your existing product is already closer to sustainable practice than you think. Maybe it isn't, but improvements could still be reached more easily, quickly, and with far less impact than a full rebuild. And yes, sometimes a rebuild is the right answer. But it is important to remember that rebuilding costs more than money.

Designers sketching new flows need their laptops, which means energy. Developers rewriting code use energy and generate new storage needs in data centers. Teams meet on calls, exchange files, write documentation, and sometimes travel. All of this has an environmental footprint, even before a single user loads the new site.

There is also the operational side that we rarely acknowledge. A rebuild not only consumes resources when people are actively working. CI pipelines run on every commit. Automated tests run on every branch. Dev and test environments stay online long after working hours. These systems consume electricity and cloud resources continuously. The impact starts to accumulate long before the new version launches.

I've seen many rebuilds driven by a switch in underlying technology, which can be a valid reason. But the question should always be: why are we switching? Is the new technology genuinely better for users and the team, or is it simply newer and more exciting? It is important to remember that new does not always mean better or faster. **If the new site performs worse on older hardware, is it truly an improvement?** Many modern frameworks and tools add weight, not efficiency.

Rebuilding to simplify, remove unnecessary complexity, and return to well-designed basics is often where "it depends" leans toward "yes." Over time, as product teams change and features pile up, maintenance becomes harder, and the product becomes increasingly bloated. Regular refactoring should prevent this, but in the real world, it often doesn't happen.

High-quality products are easy to maintain, extend, and refactor when needed. That is what already makes them sustainable. But building such a product requires time, resources, and a shared mindset across the team—and those are usually the first things to slip under pressure.

It Takes a Team

This is one of the crucial messages in this chapter. When talking about any product development, we all know how many roles are involved, and every single one of them has a responsibility in making the end product great.

Throughout my career, I have often seen topics such as accessibility and performance pushed mainly by developers. Great engineers take quality seriously, and with tools such as "blame" and "annotate" showing exactly who wrote what, no one wants their name next to something they're not proud of. But even the best intentions collide with real-world constraints. Large enterprise projects come with limited budgets, tight timelines, shifting priorities, and many stakeholders. Trade-offs have to be made, and this is exactly when team alignment becomes critical.

Creating websites and web apps that are good for users and good for the environment, not just profitable, is impossible unless the entire team is on board. Everyone needs at least a basic understanding of what sustainable design and development mean for their role. Otherwise, a single decision can unintentionally undo everyone else's effort.

This is also where trend-driven mandates tend to surface. Decisions like "we need AI in the product" often arrive top-down, driven by market pressure or competitive signaling rather than a clearly defined user need. When that happens, design and development teams may end up implementing features simply because they are expected, not because they solve a real problem. Sustainable teams need the space to question these decisions: what value does this bring, what does it cost in complexity and energy, and what happens if we choose not to ship it at all? And if such features are introduced, user control matters. They should be optional, clearly communicated, and easy to turn off.

This is where adoption strategies matter. Teams that successfully integrate sustainability usually start small: a short knowledge-sharing session, a single backlog item to improve something obvious, a shared document outlining what "good" looks like, or adding one sustainability metric to an existing dashboard. These tiny steps make the topic visible without overwhelming anyone. Over time, they help the team build shared language, shared expectations, and shared responsibility.

And once the team is aligned, metrics become useful. They are not the goal, but they help everyone see progress and understand where adjustments are needed. When sustainability becomes a team habit rather than a side project, the quality of decisions changes. That is when the work starts to have a real impact.

And Metrics

What is your product? What is its main goal? Who does it serve? And how do you want your product to make the world a better place?

These are just some of the questions we can ask ourselves to establish the context before attempting to define any metrics. Each product is unique and should be treated as such, rather than being compared to a product that is very different from it. For example, the page weight of a blog page should definitely be smaller than that of a product category page.

Many development teams define their key performance indicators (KPIs) to evaluate the success of their projects or products. They usually provide a good focus for the team, indicating what matters and helping with crucial decision-making. It is essential to distinguish between KPIs and metrics. All KPIs are metrics, but not all metrics are KPIs. KPIs are strategic and measure performance based on specific business objectives and goals. Metrics measure the success of everyday business activities that support the KPIs.

Some of the usual metrics for website or web application projects can be

- **Unique visitors:** Counts individual users who access your site within a specific period, indicating audience reach
- **Traffic by source:** Differentiates visitors based on how they found your site, such as organic search, direct, referral, or social media, helping you evaluate the effectiveness of your channels
- **Sessions:** Measures the total number of visits, including repeat visitors, serving as a volume indicator for engagement over time
- **Pageviews:** Tracks the total number of pages viewed, helpful in identifying popular content and user interests
- **Average session duration/average time on page:** Indicates the average time users spend on your site or specific pages, highlighting engagement levels and content relevance
- **Page load time:** Assesses how quickly your website loads for users, which directly influences user satisfaction and SEO ranking
- **Bounce rate:** The percentage of users who leave your site after viewing only one page; a high rate may signal issues with relevance or usability

- **Conversion rate:** Percentage of visitors who complete a desired action (e.g., signing up, making a purchase), showing how effectively your design and content drive business results
- **Error rate and server response time:** Monitor technical performance and site reliability, as these are crucial for user experience and operational stability
- **Exit rate:** Indicates the percentage of users who leave a particular page, helping to identify drop-off points in user journeys
- **Return on Investment (ROI):** Assesses the effectiveness of your website or web application in delivering measurable business value

From these, we can set KPIs to be some of the following examples:

- Decrease the average page load time below 2 seconds by year-end
- Increase website conversion rate to 5% in Q3
- Grow unique website visitors by 30% over 6 months
- Increase online sales revenue by 20% in the next year
- Make our website conform to the Web Content Accessibility Guidelines (WCAG) at level AA before June 27, 2025

It is easy to see how these can help everyone in the team stay on track, keep focus, and deliver what matters most. In my experience, most KPIs fall into two categories: prosperity and sometimes people. Almost none consider planetary boundaries. That is something we can change.

Defining sustainability-focused KPIs during product ideation and design is one of the most effective ways to ensure the entire team treats sustainability as a real requirement rather than an afterthought. As discussed in Chapter 2, it is challenging to measure the full environmental footprint of a digital product. But the tools and frameworks available today make it possible to estimate meaningful parts of it.

Metrics such as page weight, number of requests, energy consumption, water usage, and carbon intensity can be combined to create sustainability KPIs that guide decisions throughout the product's life cycle. They don't need to be perfect to be useful. What matters is that sustainability is measured intentionally and discussed alongside other goals.

I Am Not Convinced

Back in 2019, I presented a talk on the importance of web performance and accessibility in website design and development at a meetup targeted at UX designers. After about 30 minutes of me talking about many aspects of how these two topics are essential to address to have a happy user, we came to the Q&A section, where a person (let's just note, very corporate looking) raised their hand and asked me: "But why would I do this?" At that point, I was still not a mother of a small child asking why around 43,791 times a day, so I was a bit taken aback to get a question I had just spent 30 minutes answering. I reiterated some of the key points from my presentation, but the person didn't seem convinced. A few more whys came my way from the same person. I have to admit that I was already getting slightly frustrated that the message was not coming through (and it was a relief seeing that I was not the only one in the room). As I became desperate, I blurted out, "Well, accessibility is on its way to being regulated by law, so not complying with the standard could bring your company legal issues." After that, the person said, "Oh, ok," and sat down.

I felt slightly defeated having to use this argument; however, that interaction, being very early on in my advocacy for a "better web," may also have given me a bit of a reality check and clarity on how the "building for people" message will not always resonate with everyone. Some need a different kind of motivation.

Today, accessibility is regulated. The European Accessibility Act became fully enforceable since the end of June 2025, making accessible digital services a legal requirement across the EU. We are now on the other side of the journey I was describing back in 2019. What used to be "optional" guidance is now law. And that shift is exactly what many in the web sustainability community are working toward as well.

Laws and Regulations

It would be awesome if we could say that sustainability is next in line, following the path accessibility took toward regulation. But reality is far messier. Regulations are emerging, but slowly and inconsistently. Some proposals are strong, others are weakened during negotiation, and many are voluntary for now. What is clear, though, is that environmental impact is no longer an optional conversation. Policymakers, organizations, and standards bodies are all paying more attention, and digital teams will increasingly be expected to understand and justify the footprint of what they build.

Here are some of the regulations that currently shape, or soon will shape, expectations around digital products and services:

- **EU Accessibility Act (EAA)**: The EU now requires many digital products and services to meet accessibility standards. It is one of the clearest examples of a long-standing best practice becoming a legal obligation, and it shows how topics that were once "nice to have" can become mandatory.
- **The EU's Digital Product Passport (DPP) and the Ecodesign for Sustainable Products Regulation (ESPR)**: The rollout of Digital Product Passports is happening gradually, expanding to more product groups over time. The aim is greater transparency across product life cycles, including materials, origin, environmental impacts, repairability, and disposal. While some environmental requirements have been softened in legislative negotiations, the overall trajectory is toward more accountable and traceable products, including the physical infrastructure that supports digital services.
- **EU Energy Efficiency Directive (EED)**: Requires monitoring and reporting of energy and water performance for large data centers, increasing transparency around the infrastructure supporting digital services.
- **The Corporate Sustainability Reporting Directive (CSRD) and ESRS:** Large organizations must report on their Scope 1, 2, and 3 emissions. For digital teams, this includes the footprint of digital operations, products, and suppliers.
- **EU Artificial Intelligence (AI) Act**: The environmental footprint of AI is increasingly being discussed in regulatory circles. As AI systems grow more energy- and material-intensive, policymakers are examining how they should be measured, reported, and potentially regulated, particularly regarding data center demand.
- **EU Green Claims Directive**: This proposal aimed to require environmental claims to be clear, evidence-based, and verifiable. The legislative process was suspended in June 2025 following political

disagreement. Anti-greenwashing rules are still advancing through the Empowering Consumers for the Green Transition Directive, which applies from September 2026. Digital services that make environmental claims will still need to back them up.

- **France's RGESN (Référentiel Général d'Écoconception des Services Numériques):** France is the first country to publish an official national standard for the ecodesign of digital services. It provides detailed criteria for building lower-impact websites and applications and is gradually becoming mandatory for public sector services. Many see it as a preview of how digital sustainability regulation may evolve elsewhere.

Most of these rules focus on transparency rather than prescribing specific technical practices. This leaves a gap between legal requirements and day-to-day design and development choices. Community standards help fill that missing layer. The W3C Web Sustainability Guidelines offer teams a shared reference for good practice. They're voluntary for now, but they give a clear direction and may influence future regulation, much like WCAG did for accessibility.

And regulation is only one force pushing organizations in this direction. The real momentum often comes from the market itself.

Market Demands

More and more consumers are shifting toward and even demanding "sustainable products." In my everyday life, I've noticed a significant shift in the cosmetics industry. Recycled and biodegradable packaging, refill options, fewer harmful chemicals, and transparency about animal cruelty and labor practices were almost impossible to find a few years ago. Today, when I come to the store to restock my bathroom cabinet, I finally have a choice. A choice to go for a more sustainable option.

It is essential to offer the same choices to customers of digital products and services. Many people would like to adopt more sustainable practices, but this becomes almost impossible when there are no alternatives and no market signals that such options exist.

Digital is following that same pattern, just more slowly. Sustainability considerations are now appearing in software procurement, especially when organizations select components of their digital stack. I've noticed more teams asking about environmental impact during these evaluations, something that was not common in the past. These questions are still high-level today, but they signal a clear shift. Once customers can compare digital products on sustainability, expectations will rise quickly.

Employees Demand

Many people want to make a difference, and that motivation spans all generations. Yes, younger professionals often arrive with strong expectations around sustainability, but they are not alone. I've met many mid-career and senior experts who are rethinking what kind of impact they want their work to have, sometimes prompted by their children's questions, sometimes by a desire for meaningful change after many years in the industry.

For employers, this should matter. Sustainability culture is becoming a real factor in attracting and retaining talent. Losing experienced people is expensive, and failing to meet the expectations of new ones is equally risky. A company that takes sustainability seriously simply becomes a more appealing place to work, regardless of generation.

Cost

Sustainability often pays off in the long term, not just in abstract ways. In addition to the point from the previous section, where fulfilled employees tend to stay longer and reduce hiring costs, many operational improvements driven by sustainability also lead to very real savings. A lot of sustainable practice is simply efficiency: improving systems, removing what is not needed, and cleaning up waste. That almost always lowers costs.

To add a quick personal experience here, in one large e-commerce project I worked on several years ago, we were looking into ways to improve website delivery speed. We quickly realized that we might have found a gold mine when we discovered that none of the requests were cached (see Chapter 7 for more details). By flipping a switch to enable this functionality, we reduced the customer's bills by about 80%. Eighty. The website delivery speed also increased significantly, resulting in a better user experience and higher conversion rates.

Sustainable decisions often look like this. You remove waste, the system becomes faster, and the business becomes more efficient. It is good for the planet, and it saves money. That combination is hard to argue with.

Conclusion

Designing sustainable websites and web applications can already sound overwhelming. And it is. Hannah Smith, Director of Operations for the Green Web Foundation, created a fantastic visual (Figure 3-2) that shows the gap between what people think sustainable Internet means and what it actually involves. Some of these topics we covered in this chapter. Others will show up in the chapters ahead.

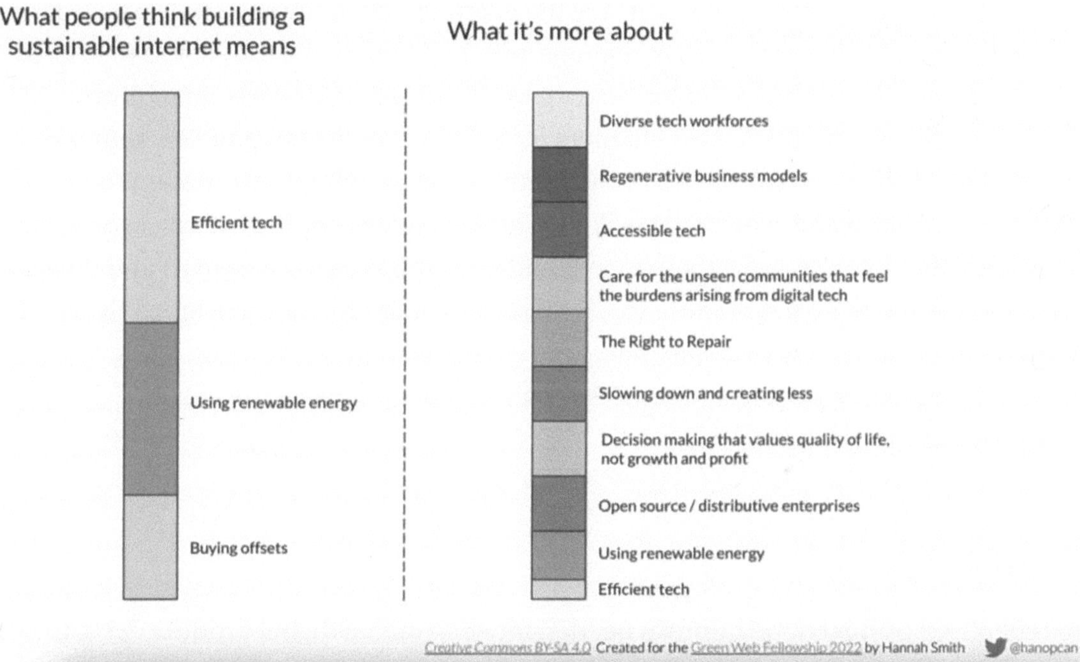

***Figure 3-2.** Building Sustainable Internet by Hannah Smith*

One of my secrets to battling overwhelm comes from author Anne Lamott, who, in her book *Bird by Bird*, shares advice that her father gave her brother when they were kids, and I believe this advice can be well applied in our case of overwhelm:

> *Thirty years ago, my older brother, who was ten years old at the time, was trying to get a report on birds written that he'd had three months to write. It was due the next day. We were out at our family cabin in Bolinas, and he was at the kitchen table close to tears, surrounded by binder paper and pencils and unopened books on birds, immobilized by the hugeness of the task ahead. Then my father sat down beside him, put his arm around my brother's shoulder, and said, "Bird by bird, buddy. Just take it bird by bird."*

Page by page, line by line, byte by byte. You can translate this advice into whatever works best for you and your team. Keep it in "bird by bird" form if you like. Turn the birds into your stakeholders. Count how many of them don't lose their habitats because your product doesn't require yet another data center to be built in theirs.

If your role sits anywhere near product management, strategy, or decision-making, it's important to recognize the influence you already have. I hope this chapter has given you enough grounding to see where sustainability fits into digital product work and enough inspiration to start applying it. Try the exercises, even the unusual ones. Define your non-human stakeholders. Give them names. Look into what they stand to lose. It may feel strange at first, but it builds the empathy that sustainable design requires.

And then keep going. The next chapters move from mindset to practice, showing how product, design, development, infrastructure, and architectural decisions all influence environmental impact. We will look at the choices behind interfaces, the code that powers them, the systems they run on, and even the growing role of AI and how its demands reshape our digital landscape. Bit by bit, the path forward becomes clearer. The goal is not perfection. It is to create digital products that help your organization prosper while also supporting people and reducing unnecessary strain on the planet.

That journey starts here.

Summary

This chapter introduced the mindset needed for sustainable digital product design. We looked at why digital services have real physical consequences and why every new feature, framework, or product should be questioned through both "why" and "why not." We explored how past product decisions contribute to digital waste, device obsolescence, and environmental impact, and why thinking in terms of all stakeholders, direct, indirect, and non-human, leads to better outcomes.

We also broke sustainability into its three core dimensions:

- People (access, inclusion, choice)
- Planet (resource use, energy, device longevity) and
- Prosperity (value that doesn't depend on waste)

Finally, we examined how existing products can be improved, why team alignment matters, and how metrics, regulations, market forces, employee expectations, and cost all contribute to a growing demand for sustainability in digital services.

The mindset is the foundation. The next chapters show how to put it into practice through architecture, design, development, infrastructure, and even AI. One decision at a time, you can steer a product toward a future where digital experiences support people and prosperity without compromising the planet.

References

Definitions

- Website, Cambridge Dictionary: `https://dictionary.cambridge.org/dictionary/english/website`
- Web Application, Cambridge Dictionary: `https://dictionary.cambridge.org/dictionary/english/web-app`

Digital Behavior and Environmental Impact

- **Daily time spent with the internet per capita worldwide from 2011 to 2021, by device**, Statista:

  `https://www.statista.com/statistics/319732/daily-time-spent-online-device/`

- **Digital 2024: Global Overview Report**, DataReportal (We Are Social & Meltwater):

  `https://www.datareportal.com/reports/digital-2024-global-overview-report`

- Daily screen time over a lifetime, Fortune:

  `https://fortune.com/well/article/screen-time-over-lifespan`

- TikTok carbon footprint estimate, The Guardian:

  `https://www.theguardian.com/technology/2024/dec/12/tiktok-carbon-footprint`

- **Global E-waste Monitor 2024**, United Nations University:

  `https://www.itu.int/en/ITU-D/Environment/Pages/Publications/The-Global-E-waste-Monitor-2024.aspx`

- What people think building a sustainable Internet involves vs. what it might actually be, Hannah Smith, Green Web Foundation:

  `https://www.thegreenwebfoundation.org/news/what-people-think-building-a-sustainable-internet-involves-vs-what-it-might-actually-be`

Sustainability, Design, and Organizational Behavior

- Apple, *Mother Nature Needs a Status Report* (advertisement):

  `https://www.youtube.com/watch?v=QNv9PRDIhes`

- Patagonia, *Earth is now our only shareholder*:

  `https://www.patagoniaworks.com/press/2022/9/14/patagonias-next-chapter-earth-is-now-our-only-shareholder`

- **Sustainable Digital Infrastructure Alliance (SDIA)**:

  `https://sdialliance.org/`

- Web Sustainability Guidelines (W3C):

  `https://www.w3.org/TR/web-sustainability-guidelines/`

- Sustainability and employment, People Management:

  `https://www.peoplemanagement.co.uk/article/1893574/employer-commitment-sustainable-development-motivate-employees-perform-best`

Legislation and Regulation

- EU Accessibility Act (EAA):

  `https://eur-lex.europa.eu/eli/dir/2019/882/oj`

- Ecodesign for Sustainable Products Regulation (ESPR) and Digital Product Passport:

  `https://eur-lex.europa.eu/eli/reg/2024/1781/oj`

- EU Energy Efficiency Directive (EED) 2023:

  `https://eur-lex.europa.eu/eli/dir/2023/1791/oj`

- Corporate Sustainability Reporting Directive (CSRD):

  `https://eur-lex.europa.eu/eli/dir/2022/2464/oj`

- European Sustainability Reporting Standards (ESRS):

  `https://eur-lex.europa.eu/legal-content/EN/TXT/?uri=CELEX:32023R2771`

- EU Artificial Intelligence Act:

  `https://eur-lex.europa.eu/eli/reg/2024/1689/oj`

- Green Claims Directive proposal:

  `https://eur-lex.europa.eu/legal-content/EN/TXT/?uri=CELEX:52023PC0166`

- France's RGESN (Référentiel Général d'Écoconception des Services Numériques):

  `https://ecoresponsable.numerique.gouv.fr/publications/referentiel-general-ecoconception/`

Books

- Lamott, Anne. *Bird by Bird: Some Instructions on Writing and Life.* Anchor Books, 1995.
- McGovern, Gerry. *World Wide Waste.* Silver Beach, 2020.

CHAPTER 4

Infrastructure

Chris Chinchilla[1]
[1]Berlin, Germany; https://chrischinchilla.com/

What does infrastructure mean?

This chapter takes it to mean two distinct but related concepts, and depending on your computing background and history, you may only consider one of them to be correct.

First, it means all the hardware and physical infrastructure that goes into creating one or more servers. This could include everything in a data center of any size, from the building and its walls, cooling, power supply, and racks to the cables, screws, and light fixtures. All of these times have an environmental impact: when commissioned, decommissioned, and when in use.

Second, it refers to all the server operating systems, low-level software, and various infrastructure as code (IaC) tools and platforms common in modern application development, testing, monitoring, and delivery. The lines between these and what Chapter 5 covers regarding backend code are blurred, but this chapter aims to include anything fundamental to getting an application and services running. Some common examples are software such as OpenStack and Kubernetes, OpenTofu and Terraform, and continuous integration and delivery tools and providers.

Both are large topics with many subtleties and details that one book chapter cannot cover fully. I am also far more experienced with the software side of infrastructure and less so with the hardware side, which is the more significant part of the problem in terms of emissions.

Throughout the research for this chapter, I read many reports and spoke with many people who are far more experienced with building and running data centers and the workloads that run in them than I am. As you might imagine, it's a highly specialized business with various opinions and practices on sustainable design and operation. So, treat this chapter as a hopefully comprehensive collection of starting points for further investigation.

C. Chinchilla and I. Akrap, *Building the Sustainable Web*, https://doi.org/10.1007/979-8-8688-2521-7_4

This chapter begins with the size of the problem. As Chapter 5 outlines, much of the impact of "the Internet" and information communication technology (ICT) is measured through data centers. These numbers are easier to find, but as you will see, they do not always represent the full picture.

The Size of the Infrastructure Problem

In the year or two before the time of writing (2024–25), all of the largest three cloud hosts (Often called "Hyperscalers" by the industry) were aiming to reduce their cloud footprint and energy costs. Whether motivated by cost savings, regulation, public interest, or genuine altruism, most Hyperscalers put effort into reducing energy and implementing policies, practices, and technologies to help lower their environmental impact. That all changed with the combination of the advent of the new wave of generative artificial intelligence (Gen AI) and the downturn in revenue from other sources from 2023 onward. While Chapter 9 covers that in more detail, broadly, we know that technology companies are racing into scaling AI at an unprecedented level, not only reversing some of their environmental commitments but going backward and increasing emissions in some cases as profit and new products take precedence over all other priorities.

Setting aside the environmental impact, data centers need to draw power from somewhere, and their high energy usage is starting to cause concern for the jurisdictions in which they are based.

Many companies base their European data centers in Ireland, a small country. According to the Irish Times and the International Energy Association's (IEA) 2024 report, data centers already use around 20% of the electricity generated in the country, which is predicted to be over 30% by 2026, more than all urban households. While Ireland is a popular location for data centers, it's not the only one, and the IEA report also predicts that demand is likely to rise even in less common locations such as Denmark. In Denmark's case, the current energy consumption is lower (2% in 2022), and the 2026 rise is more dramatic, to 15–20%. I had never expected London to be a major location for building data centers, but apparently, it also can't cope with the power demands and has a large backlog.

The same Irish Times article states that Google Ireland, who wanted to build the data center, didn't make enough effort to use renewable energy or integrate with the national grid or local area in a longer-term sustainable way. It's an interesting example of how no matter what the financial or job-creation (and generally, data centers don't employ many people, in this case, only 50 new jobs) promise, an energy system can't conjure new power plants or grid infrastructure overnight. Sometimes, hosting and technology companies create their own power infrastructure. In another recent demonstration of a company rolling back sustainability commitments, Microsoft wants to reopen the Pennsylvania Three Mile Island nuclear power plant, shuttered since a partial meltdown in 1979, to power what many see as AI energy demands. Microsoft recently hired from the energy industry to fill a role called the "Director of Nuclear and Energy Innovations." That a role with that name even exists shows how crucial a reliable power supply is to hyperscale cloud hosts. Amazon Web Services (AWS) is buying a nuclear power plant in Northeastern Pennsylvania from an energy company. Interestingly, AWS already claims to be the largest buyer of renewable energy, so hyperscale hosting companies buying independent power sources isn't anything new, but like many factors in technology, the increased scale is. All across the tech sector, investments in nuclear-related startups are rising and Amazon, Google, and Meta have all pledged to triple their investments in nuclear by 2050.

Nuclear power receives mixed opinions and responses in the sustainability movement, and it's not a discussion I want to enter into here. Instead, I want to focus on computing companies buying and running power plants and typically keeping their presence much quieter when compared to the fanfare they make when acquiring or investing in renewable energy. Granted, buying and retrofitting an existing plant has less impact than building a new one, but it feels like the wrong incentive and another step toward the corporate dystopias present in fiction for decades.

While many hyperscalers talk about their renewable energy usage (and they do invest heavily in it), the constantly running nature of data centers means they can't rely solely on the relatively intermittent nature of renewable energy without large capacity battery or non-renewable power sources. While the United States is seeing an increase in renewable investment and usage, renewables and nuclear are still 10–20% of total supply and the east coast houses a lot of US-based data centers (that famous AWS us-east-1 region), where supply is mostly natural gas.

Before generative AI took the world by storm, a trend we're yet to see will last. The guiltiest party for data center energy consumption was crypto mining. In a double whammy for the environmental impact of data centers, mainstream interest is also up for cryptocurrencies, and their energy demand still features highly. According to Wired, desperate for something to replace dwindling oil revenue, one Texas town invited the World's biggest Bitcoin mine to open there. Much like the case in Dublin, the current grid can't cope with the demand and would need to double its capacity in the next few years to cope. It's unlikely that a country like the United States, already with an ailing energy infrastructure, could build this capacity even if it wanted to. Recent content from MIT Technology Review stated that with the thirst for data center power from US companies and the current administration set to rise, the cost of electricity for consumers is also likely to rise to pay for the infrastructure needed.

Aside from the impact on the power grid, data centers also generate a lot of noise, and while they are generally not that close to houses, this noise disturbs local wildlife, which has its own impact on the environment. Finally, data centers can pull a tremendous amount of water from the local supply, which, while spoken about less than the energy impact, can cause more dramatic problems for local communities.

According to their sustainability reports from the past two years, Microsoft's water consumption has increased from 4,196,461 cubic meters in 2020 (the reference measurement year) to 7,843,744 cubic meters in 2023. One can only wonder what it will be in 2024. It's unclear how many of the numbers in the sustainability report relate to cloud operations, but I would guess a significant part of them.

To make a comparison. The US Environmental Protection Agency (EPA) put the water consumption of an average family of four in the USA at 400 gallons per day in 2017. That's about 1.5 cubic meters per day. According to the Fraunhofer Institute, these numbers are significantly lower in Europe. It's roughly 130 liters per person per day in Germany, which is 34 gallons. So 34 multiplied by four is 136 gallons or 0.5 cubic meters per day.

The rest of the chapter sticks with the US numbers. Microsoft's 2024 water consumption equals roughly 5.25 million American households, effectively just over 20 million people.

While humans could just about cope without electricity, as we did for 1000s of years, fresh (desalinated) water is a complete necessity and an increasingly scarce resource that is less spoken about outside the developing world. There is plenty of saline water (sea water, for example), but desalination is an expensive and energy-intensive process.

It's harder to extract the impact of individual components of data centers or even software and hardware. To get an idea of the energy impact of a data center in isolation or the impact of a data center doing "nothing," you could start with how much the average data center runs "idle." It's equally hard to define what "idle" means but to have some value, I define it as a server with no application running aside from the operating system or any of the essential tools and services outlined in Chapter 5 to get your application running.

Compounding the problem, it's hard to get exact numbers for the percentage of time servers run idle. A Kepler project blog post (a popular tool for monitoring Kubernetes, which will be covered later in this chapter) references the SPECpower benchmark, which puts active idle power consumption at 20% to 60% of the power consumed at maximum utilization. So, let's take an average of 30%. Think about it. To make a quick estimation, that's 7 hours a day, nearly a full workday, where a server is just sitting, waiting to do something. That's 2628 hours a year per server. As part of the 3.7% of global emissions mentioned in Chapter 1, this means that 1.1% of global carbon emissions are caused by servers basically doing nothing, waiting for someone to ask to post a cool new photo.

According to the Kepler blog, the actual energy consumption ranges from 100 Watts to 1300 Watts, equivalent to the power consumption of a classic light bulb. Again, taking a conservative estimate and using an average of 600 Watts, that's just over 4 kWh per server day running idle.

To be clear, these are active servers doing nothing. As the SPECpower report puts it, they are "active-idle." While shutting down active-idle servers is an option, it's not always practical or the most effective option. There are many server use cases, especially in dedicated servers, on-premise servers, model training, or semi-regular log and reporting jobs where traffic and usage levels are reliable and where it is possible to turn servers off when not in use, but for many workloads or larger co-located servers, this is harder to manage, and they are often still left running and idle.

However, sleeping idle servers and processes is an option. The wake time for most modern hardware and payloads that run on hardware, such as virtual machines and container runtimes, is fast enough not to be an issue in most use cases these days. Sleeping needn't only apply to servers but also to network devices.

Generally speaking, over-provisioning is the bigger issue with servers, networking, and other cloud infrastructure. Users have too many resources dedicated to a task, "just in case." From server hardware all the way down to virtual machines, containers, memory, storage, and CPU, with modern computing, we tend to plan for "what could happen." This is expensive and wasteful.

According to a report from the University of Berkeley way back in 2007, networks, much like servers, are also provisioned for worst-case and busiest-hour loads. The report states that many networks are utilized at less than 30% capacity and experience long periods of idle time. Relatively speaking, network devices often consume substantially more energy when idle than idle servers. The report implies that most of the energy consumed in networks is wasted. Network hardware and software is a big topic. Even a sub-topic such as running it more efficiently could run to its own small book, as it is another one of those "unseen costs" of cloud computing, and when you start considering the data pipes coming in and out of data centers and snaking all around the world, it has its own, almost separate environmental impact, so it's worth noting. If you want to dig further, look at the resources of the "Greening of Streaming" organization.

Report after report outlines the issue of over-provisioning and waste, which also impacts businesses financially. StormForge reported in 2021 that 48% of respondents knew they were wasting money, and 75% said reducing that was a priority. More interestingly, the top reasons were complexity, over-provisioning, and just to "be safe." Thirty percent said they reached the settings they use (largely with Kubernetes for this report) by trial and error or by leaving them on default.

In 2023, Flexera reported that, while waste had improved, its respondents estimated they were wasting about 23% of their cloud spend. However, Flexera is a vendor focusing on reducing cloud waste, so their report respondents are likely somewhat more engaged with the issue.

In a conversation I had with Arwel Owen, a consultant specializing in SAP applications and deployments, he said that many, especially those new to the paradigms of cloud computing, still think like they are using fixed physical machines. They plan capacity for the next five years as if their applications' resources are unmoving, inflexible, and can't be changed. Instead, they should embrace the rapid flexibility and dynamism of cloud computing and plan for the next five months or less. However, hyperscalers often give large discounts to companies that reserve fixed instances for longer time spans, so the cost/carbon trade-off isn't compelling. As someone who has mostly operated in the open source world, aside from knowing they are "big business," I have very little visibility into the proprietary SaaS systems of companies such as SAP. Arwel gave me a quote, which I feel he has given a few times thanks to its impact (if you forgive the pun).

> "90% of the world's largest companies run SAP, and 85% of carbon emissions come from (the business of) SAP customers."

I took a quick look into SAP's sustainability reporting, and without undertaking extensive research to extract the values of the world's largest companies, I wondered what its emissions data was. Bear in mind that customers run SAP software with a mix of cloud and on-premise installations, so exact numbers are even harder to extrapolate. It's challenging to find details, but they do at least acknowledge their potential impact and their efforts, and according to SAP's 2023 report, they are carbon neutral. The details of what this means aren't clear.

Either way, you can see why "right-sizing," a method of ensuring you use server resources appropriate to usage, is so important.

Cost of Manufacture and Embodied Carbon

About ten years ago, I was involved in a very different sustainability project in Melbourne. And I remember someone saying to me (and I have no numbers to back this up) that an unsaid secret of much of the sustainability movement at the time was that when it discussed moving to more renewable energy and homes, was that the environmental and resource cost of building everything needed from solar panels and wind turbines to wall insulation was too great for the planet to supply. In short, we didn't have enough resources to make the green transition, and generally, everyone hoped that technology manufacturing would become more efficient in the future. I can't remember when I heard this statement, but I assume that technical transformation came somewhat true. There is a similar problem with sustainable computing. If your strategy is to "replace everything with new hardware." While it's fairly easy to monitor the carbon impact of most of what's running on hardware, the carbon cost of the hardware (called embodied carbon) itself is easy to forget.

Most technology hardware becomes more energy efficient with each new generation. That's not to say it uses less power (or water) but is more efficient. Returning and paraphrasing a line I heard and saw many times while writing this book.

> "Greater efficiency means people will do more, and there is no net saving."

This is known as the "Jevons paradox" or the "rebound effect."

And while running newer hardware such as CPUs may be more efficient, manufacturing them and disposing of older models isn't necessarily more efficient. According to reports from S&P Global in 2024, Taiwan Semiconductor Manufacturing Company (TSMC), one of the world's most advanced chip manufacturers, could account for nearly 25% of Taiwan's electricity consumption by 2030. Though it currently only accounts for around 8%, its consumption has doubled from around 110GW in 2016 to 250GW since it started manufacturing 3-nanometer chips. This time frame mostly coincides with the wider technology industry's increased reliance on TSMC. While not as high, Intel and Hynix's electricity consumption is around 90GW and 125GW, respectively.

According to the OECD, water consumption is often overlooked and poorly reported across the board of data centers and chip manufacturers. A report from S&P Global states that chipmakers globally consume the same amount of water as Hong Kong. And each new generation of chips needs more water. Fabrication plants use ultra-pure water (freshwater with high purity) to rinse silicon wafers between each process. The more advanced the chip, the more process steps are needed and, thus, the more water is consumed.

And again, while most industrial processes are becoming more efficient over time and plants can and do use recycled water, it's an increasingly scarce resource. Taiwan has experienced multiple droughts, and half its water supply is precarious, falling during typhoon season, mostly around summer. Chip manufacturing companies are increasingly using electricity and water-intensive processes. While all companies cite sustainability policies, it's uncertain how many will stand against revenue and profit targets. And all of this is just the chips used in servers. There's also casing, power supplies, and much more. Later, this chapter presents some tools that can estimate the embodied carbon of your servers. However, average values for the embodied carbon of the average data center and server are hard to find and involve life cycle assessment processes that are beyond my knowledge and the scope of this book. However, depending on the process and the components, for AI purposes alone, according to the OECD report, they could be anything between 15% and 30% of the environmental impact of a server throughout its lifespan.

Emission Scopes

As you read about carbon emissions and data centers, you often see a reference to reported "scopes," which match the definition laid out by the Greenhouse Gas protocol standards. There are three, which for data centers are loosely broken down to

1. **Scope 1**: Direct emissions from processes such as gas escaping from cooling systems, often called "fugitive emissions" or diesel for uninterruptible power supplies (UPS).

2. **Scope 2**: Indirect emissions from electricity, heat, or steam consumption. Most of what this book deals with falls into this scope. Interestingly, it's referred to as "indirect," especially as more data centers generate their own power directly.

3. **Scope 3**: Other indirect emissions, often from manufacturing and end-of-life processes. This includes "upstream" emissions related to the producing the services and products and company sells, such as those from suppliers to the party reporting scopes, purchased goods, travel, waste, and more. It also includes "downstream" emissions related to the consumption of the products and services the reporting party sells, such as transportation, usage, end of life, and more.

The last section covered scope three emissions, which are large, and depending on the industry can be in the 90% plus range of a reporters' emissions.

This Microsoft Cloud for Sustainability API calculation methodology is a good start for more details on these scopes related to data centers.

Also Datavizta hosts a lifespan impact calculator and a cloud instance impact calculator for a quick overview of server impacts and scopes.

Circular Servers

I am sure many of you reading this section don't make servers, and I don't want to end this section with such defeatist gloom. Even if you don't build servers, you can always make better decisions with the vendors you use. Cloud service providers above a certain size tend to build their servers and hardware, and this also means that, if they choose, they can focus on longevity and recyclability.

France's OVH (which hosts around 4% of public websites globally) claims to be the only global cloud provider that manufactures and (more crucially) dismantles them at the end of life. This means they reuse many components or, at worst, dispose of and recycle them responsibly. They then use some of these components in older, lower-end servers, which are perfectly good for many common use cases, such as low-traffic websites.

On a smaller scale, and only available as a private cloud, kraud.cloud buys a CPU and then builds the rest of each server themselves. Arvid E. Picciani, the company's founder, told me they even consider aspects such as power supply to reduce the potential waste of conversion between AC and DC current.

What Goes into the Emissions of a Data Center?

So far, this chapter has examined the size and details of the problem but not what's behind it. This section looks at each aspect of modern data center infrastructure and how much it contributes to its energy impact.

Heating and Cooling

After the actual servers, the biggest energy consumer inside a data center is often cooling. Servers emit a lot of heat, which, if not counteracted, will damage the servers. Ideally, and in most recently built data centers, the level of cooling usage is more reactive, meaning that it scales to meet demand. There are data centers where cooling is smarter, utilizing colder weather outside, local natural water sources, or rerouting the heat into secondary uses. For example, Deep Green partners with hosting providers to use the heat generated to warm water and use that warm water for other uses, often heating water for pools or central heating. Heeta is another example, supported by British Gas, a natural gas provider in the UK. Interestingly, for heating reuse to work, the servers need to run warmer, requiring less cooling. The data center also needs to be located near enough an area that requires heating.

Some data centers use more efficient server rack layouts to allow for better heat dissipation, while others place racks with little regard for the heat they output and its effect on the servers nearby. Some data centers use average off-the-shelf cooling with little regard for efficiency to match cooling demand, while others use better systems with more optimized layouts. New energy-efficient cooling options are also emerging, such as Phononic, that instead use solid state cooling rather than rely on liquids, gases, or motors. Either way, even in the case of data centers that use more efficient systems, cooling servers doing very little or doing unnecessary work is still wasteful. A further complication is that more energy efficient cooling systems tend to use more water and water efficient cooling systems tend to use more energy. As always, it's a balancing act.

According to the Federal Energy Management Program (FEMP), a data center that takes a less efficient approach to server cooling may only use less than 40% of its energy consumption on actually running servers. In contrast, a more efficient data center uses closer to 60% on running servers. The fact that an efficient data center can still consume up to 50% of its energy needs on cooling shows how hot things run and how much impact reducing the workloads running on servers could have on overall consumption.

Network: Internal and Global

It's easy to focus on a data center. Most of us have seen pictures of these large, anonymous buildings in the middle of nowhere. We can imagine our application churning away on some server nestled among rack after rack of blinking lights and spinning fans. But we think less about how requests get to and between those data centers and our users. In reality, massive cables crisscross the world, dozens under oceans and likely billions over land. As mentioned in Chapter 1, my Grandfather used to work on ships laying giant copper cables under the sea, the precursor to the optic fibers we now use. Way back when I was too young to know what he meant, he told me that "optic fibers are the future." He was right to a scale he could have probably never imagined.

Transmitting data back and forth across the cables also has a carbon impact. Again, this is due to the hardware that sends and switches this data and the embodied costs of creating, installing, and maintaining that hardware.

Although the lines between the two industries are blurring, you can also add the carbon impact of communications networks not directly related to server and ICT traffic, such as land and mobile phones, to these numbers.

A recent IEA report showed the impact of the two industries, and they are remarkably similar.

	Data centers	Telecommunications
2015	200 TWh	220 TWh
2022	240–340 TWh	260–360 TWh
Change	+ 20–70%	+ 18–64%

This summary is thanks to a talk by Romain Jacob, who pointed out that communication hardware isn't as smart as servers running software. They are as under-utilized and over-provisioned as many servers, their energy consumption has little to do with traffic load, and they are technically always "on," often even if there's no cable plugged in.

Much of this provisioning makes sense. Providers don't want any chance of significant downtime or lost traffic, but it's often handled in a less-than-smart approach. Regarding what you can do about it, sadly, there is not much you can do apart from reducing how much data you send back and forth between applications and services (see Chapter 5 for discussions on microservices vs. monorepos and architectural design). Romain presented findings from a tool called "Hypnos," which can turn off ports and links in a networking switch. However, they found that "turned off" wasn't the same as "powered off," and the tests saved less than 1% energy consumption, often because the pluggable transceivers in routers that cables are often plugged into generally still draw power when plugged in, even if their port is switched "off."

On the positive side, networking hardware manufacturers are starting to notice and take action, and workarounds are possible with port configuration.

Lighting

According to the same FEMP report, while lighting is generally one of the smallest consumers in a data center (around 1–2%), it should be motion-triggered and almost always is, as often data centers reduce the amount of human presence around server racks for security, stability, and cleanliness reasons anyway. Using low-energy LED lighting reduces heat and energy consumption in the data center.

The Impact of Choice

Unless you read this and operate data centers, there's not much you can do to manage their efficiency apart from letting your wallet decide and choose vendors that provide details and options around the ancillary hardware they use around servers.

For a list of hosting providers generally more optimized for sustainability or who at least offer more sustainable options, take a look at the Green Web Foundation's Green hosting directory.

app.greenweb.org/directory

There is a lot of "greenwashing," or the act of issuing misleading information about green credentials in this space. So, the green hosting directory includes verified and linked evidence for a service's inclusion.

It's easy to criticize the three largest hyperscale hosts, mostly because they are so widespread that they dominate any statistic. However, on the positive side, all three have tools that help you assess and adjust deployments based on their carbon impact. A further caveat is that these tools do not all report equally, so you need, to a degree of comparative research, to really compare.

Amazon Web Services (AWS) offers a handful of resources, including a carbon footprint tool, organizational policies for sustainable deployments, lower-emissions Graviton servers, and spot servers, which run workloads in unused server capacity.

Microsoft Azure has the Emissions Impact Dashboard to show the overall impact of services, the carbon optimization tool to provide more actionable insights, a blog post covering general power and water impact, and an overview of power and water impact. Azure has a detailed guide for specific guidance on workload shifting to more sustainable regions.

Google Cloud measures grid carbon intensity, which measures how clean the electricity supply is based on how many grams of carbon dioxide (CO_2e) are released to produce a kilowatt hour (kWh) of electricity. It has a comprehensive list of all their data centers' values, allowing you to set organizational policies restricted to those.

While these tools have improved a lot recently, adding long requested features such as reporting Scope 3 emissions and longer granularity time spans, development teams wanting more detail or longer reporting windows probably still need to use some of the tools presented later in this chapter.

Consider the following points if you want to research or choose the most sustainable options from an existing provider or company-authorized list of providers.

Use or Buy Energy Star-Compliant Servers

You've probably seen Energy Star stickers on many devices, and any server with one should be about 30% more efficient than one that doesn't. The Energy Star program has a large resources section showing what compliance means and what products support it. However, unless you are building your server fleet, I couldn't find many hosts, large or small, who clearly list whether their servers are compliant.

Shift Services to More Sustainable Locations and Times

Some hosting locations have less of an environmental impact than others. For example, Scaleway, a French hosting company, reports that their Paris data center has nearly 100th of the carbon impact as their Warsaw one.

> Paris-2: 0.065 $kgCO_2e/kWh$
>
> Warsaw-2: 1 $kgCO_2e/kWh$

Most of this has to do with the power source for the data center. Poland mostly runs on fossil fuels, 70%, with a roughly equal mix of coal and oil. Meanwhile, France has 40% nuclear and 30% oil. I'm not getting into the politics of energy supply, but this makes France's CO_2 emissions lower than Poland's.

However, there's an added complexity when comparing national and regional power sources. Hyperscaler providers often have their own power generation sources, including clean energy supplies. This can mean that it's harder to compare hyperscalers to smaller hosts such as Scaleway who often use the public grid. It's further complicated if the public grid's carbon intensity is lowered by the hyperscalers feeding renewables into it, and already claiming the carbon reductions for themselves, meaning carbon reductions are double counted.

The time of day can also matter. A recent presentation from Pierre Segonne and Marcus Garsdal of electricitymaps.com showed that for the same data center in Denmark, the carbon intensity of the same data center tripled in the five hours between 7 am and 12 pm, from 54g to 156g. The location and its energy source composition definitely matter. In the same presentation, Pierre and Marcus showed that on March 4, 2024, at 2 pm, the carbon intensity in Portugal was 95g, but in Poland, it was 870g. That's a factor of nine.

Some applications or application services need to run most or all the time, but others, such as model training, deployments, or testing, could run at more optimal times. Even for those needing to run longer, it's possible to dynamically shift them between data centers for the least carbon intensity. However, the act of moving services around can introduce other impacts. As always, things are complicated.

Accommodating and adapting to data center carbon intensity is further complicated by providers reporting their credentials (or lack thereof) with different methodologies. If you trust and stick to one provider, then it's easier to evaluate, but many of you involved with cloud-native development for some time know that, generally, it's preferable to spread and move payloads between different providers for cost and redundancy reasons. While much of the data and resources are inconsistent and for guidance only, some provider-independent metrics and resources are below.

Much of the difference in this reporting relates to what metrics and measurements they use and how they represent their Scope 1, 2, and 3 emissions. If you want to dig deeper into the differences and the state of reporting, I recommend the following resources:

- Adrian Cockroft's talk from October 2023 (slide 12)
- Chris Adam's talk from February 2023 (slide 23)

Both are from around two years ago and with the recent race for AI computing power, I wonder how much still applies or how much progress has been made to improve them.

The Green Software Foundation has a repository of energy metadata for the big three hyperscale hosting providers, which is gathered regularly and somewhat standardized. The foundation also lobbies providers to release the data consistently.

Even with this data set, getting a full picture is hard. Generally speaking, the five data centers (at the time of writing) with the lowest average hourly carbon intensity consumption (based on the "provider-carbon-intensity-average-consumption-hourly" column) in 2023 were

1. Google in Quebec (2)
2. Google in France (34)
3. Google in Finland (46)
4. Google in Ontario (47)
5. Google in Brazil (56)

All Google. This is because Amazon reports power usage effectiveness (PUE). This ratio describes how efficiently a computer data center uses energy and how much energy the computing equipment uses compared to other overheads that support the equipment.

So, using PUE instead:

1. Google in Oregon (1.070)
2. Google in Eemshaven (1.070)
3. Google in Las Vegas (1.080)
4. Amazon in Melbourne (1.080)

This is a very different list, but it's hard to judge as providers report different values.

Carbon-Aware Development

If you want to build carbon awareness into an application or infrastructure, there are several options in addition to the sustainability features of each hyperscaler mentioned above.

Behind many of the tools mentioned later in this chapter is one or more of the two main data providers for electricity data. In the wider scheme of things, companies and services often use these services in smart home devices or their own energy planning.

Electricity Maps offers some endpoints for free and for one zone at a time, and a lot more if you pay. A zone is a country or part of a country, depending on Electricity Maps' sources. If you don't specify a region, it defaults to detecting the request's geolocation.

The endpoints you can use for free (and personal use) are

- `https://api.electricitymap.org/v3/carbon-intensity/latest`
  - The last known carbon intensity for the region and the date and time details for the measurement
- `https://api.electricitymap.org/v3/carbon-intensity/history`
  - The last 24 hours of measurements of carbon intensity for the region and the date and time details for each measurement
- `https://api.electricitymap.org/v3/power-breakdown/latest`
  - The last known power consumption and sources breakdown of the energy supply for the region and time details for the measurement
- `https://api.electricitymap.org/v3/power-breakdown/history`
  - The last 24 hours of power consumption and source breakdowns of the energy supply for the region and time details for each measurement.

Watttime offers something similar, with limitations for free accounts. The main negative, and a large one, is that for free, you can only acquire data for the "CASIO_NORTH" region, which is somewhere in California. Instead of power consumption and carbon intensity, the APIs return marginal operating emissions rate of carbon dioxide, average operating emissions rate of carbon dioxide, or the health impact of electricity usage (which is apparently measured in USD per MWh).

Find more details on the calculations behind these measurements on the WattTime site.

- `https://api.watttime.org/v3/forecast`
  - The next 0 to 72 hours (in 5-minute intervals) forecast for the region and type of measurement you're interested in

- `https://api.watttime.org/v3/forecast/historical`
  - The historical forecast for the specified region, date range, and measurement you're interested in. Interestingly, WattTime also provides an endpoint (`https://api.watttime.org/v3/historical`) for the actual measurements instead of the forecast.

While WattTime and Electricity Maps are the two services used by most of the other tools in this chapter, they are not the only ones. There are other options available, especially for Europe, including `https://www.energy-charts.info/` (that covers most European countries) and the UK energy provider `https://carbonintensity.org.uk/`.

Some of the tools mentioned in this chapter use these sources, or allow you to use your own sources and for determined developers, you can create custom versions that do so.

Boavizta APIs

Some of the tools in the rest of this chapter also use Boavizta's APIs to help surface other data, especially emissions not related to electricity composition and usage.

They host several covering data specific to hyperscalers, dashboards, and application impact.

`https://boavizta.org/en/tools`

Why Are These APIs Useful to an Infrastructure or DevOps Engineer?

They allow you to dynamically plan and switch infrastructure and services based on power grid data. This practice is often referred to as time and location shifting or scheduling. Shifting and scheduling workloads to run at times or in locations that suit a set of parameters better—in this case, carbon awareness. Anyone who has used Kubernetes for some time has likely done something similar but using other constraints.

For example, using the Electricity Maps' latest power breakdown API, you could move payloads based on a certain percentage of renewable energy. Let's say at least 40% of the supply.

So, at the time of writing, when I run (for Poland):

```
curl "https://api.electricitymap.org/v3/power-breakdown/latest?zone=pl" \
    -H 'auth-token: TOKEN'
```

I received the following response:


```
{
  "zone": "PL",
  "datetime": "2025-01-02T15:00:00.000Z",
  "updatedAt": "2025-01-02T14:44:14.662Z",
  "createdAt": "2024-12-30T15:46:57.427Z",
  "powerConsumptionBreakdown": {
    "nuclear": 20,
    "geothermal": 0,
    "biomass": 275,
    "coal": 10624,
    "wind": 7578,
    "solar": 7,
    "hydro": 199,
    "gas": 2267,
    "oil": 202,
    "unknown": 788,
    "hydro discharge": 84,
    "battery discharge": 0
  },
  "powerProductionBreakdown": {
    "nuclear": null,
    "geothermal": null,
    "biomass": 218,
    "coal": 10628,
    "wind": 7500,
    "solar": 0,
    "hydro": 165,
    "gas": 2160,
    "oil": 202,
    "unknown": 798,
    "hydro discharge": 65,
    "battery discharge": null
  },
  "powerImportBreakdown": {
```

```
    "DE": 738,
    "SE-SE4": 0
  },
  "powerExportBreakdown": {
    "DE": 0,
    "SE-SE4": 427
  },
  "fossilFreePercentage": 37,
  "renewablePercentage": 37,
  "powerConsumptionTotal": 22047,
  "powerProductionTotal": 21735,
  "powerImportTotal": 738,
  "powerExportTotal": 427,
  "isEstimated": true,
  "estimationMethod": "TIME_SLICER_AVERAGE"
}
```


The most important value for the example is

```
"renewablePercentage": 37,
```

That's not high enough. Let's say we can also run payloads in Germany. Let's see the renewables' composition there:

```
curl "https://api.electricitymap.org/v3/power-breakdown/latest?zone=de" \
     -H 'auth-token: TOKEN'
```

This is the response:


```
{
  "zone": "DE",
  "datetime": "2025-01-02T15:00:00.000Z",
  "updatedAt": "2025-01-02T14:44:14.662Z",
  "createdAt": "2024-12-30T15:46:44.408Z",
  "powerConsumptionBreakdown": {
    "nuclear": 1484,
    "geothermal": 26,
    "biomass": 4700,
```

```
    "coal": 15112,
    "wind": 16789,
    "solar": 569,
    "hydro": 2853,
    "gas": 11296,
    "oil": 357,
    "unknown": 390,
    "hydro discharge": 1526,
    "battery discharge": 1
  },
  "powerProductionBreakdown": {
    "nuclear": null,
    "geothermal": 27,
    "biomass": 4715,
    "coal": 15751,
    "wind": 16595,
    "solar": 165,
    "hydro": 1227,
    "gas": 11019,
    "oil": 364,
    "unknown": 312,
    "hydro discharge": 1473,
    "battery discharge": null
  },
  "powerImportBreakdown": {
    "AT": 0,
    "BE": 0,
    "CH": 0,
    "CZ": 0,
    "FR": 1879,
    "LU": 0,
    "NL": 1754,
    "PL": 0,
    "DK-DK1": 227,
    "DK-DK2": 667,
```

```
    "NO-NO2": 1357,
    "SE-SE4": 684
  },
  "powerExportBreakdown": {
    "AT": 567,
    "BE": 493,
    "CH": 434,
    "CZ": 420,
    "FR": 0,
    "LU": 463,
    "NL": 0,
    "PL": 738,
    "DK-DK1": 0,
    "DK-DK2": 0,
    "NO-NO2": 0,
    "SE-SE4": 0
  },
  "fossilFreePercentage": 51,
  "renewablePercentage": 48,
  "powerConsumptionTotal": 55102,
  "powerProductionTotal": 51649,
  "powerImportTotal": 6568,
  "powerExportTotal": 3115,
  "isEstimated": true,
  "estimationMethod": "FORECASTS_HIERARCHY"
}
```


Not only is there much more data, mostly around energy import and export values, which may or may not interest us, but you can see that the percentage is above our threshold:

```
"renewablePercentage": 48,
```

It's the correct renewable composition so that we can switch services.

For more visual planning, Electricity Maps provides an interactive map for exploring their data, which can help you identify the regions and times to include in more automated API-driven decisions later.

The United Kingdom has a Carbon Intensity API, and there's also a German one.

Several third-party tools leverage these two main data sources to provide a more flexible or integrated experience as you build applications and services.

Grid Intensity Go

For more usage in local debugging or alongside cloud-native orchestration and scheduling tools, the Green Web Foundation offers a CLI tool with some interesting integration options, including running it locally as a CLI tool but also as a Docker container within Kubernetes or with Nomad. Finally, as the tool is written in Go, you can also incorporate it as a library into your own applications.

By default, you run it to find the grid intensity of a particular region and from a particular provider, including Electricity Maps and others. You can set these values from command line arguments, environment variables, and configuration files. More interestingly, and bringing the tool firmly into the cloud-native ecosystem, it has a Prometheus exporter, meaning you can bring grid intensity data into the large suite of tools that use that format, such as Grafana dashboards for monitoring and reporting.

The Carbon-Aware SDK

Another popular option is the Carbon-Aware SDK from the Green Software Foundation. It integrates the Electricity Maps and WattTime APIs and provides a unified interface and output.

It's built in .NET, a popular and solid language that is uncommon outside certain use cases and fields. But you can run it as a CLI tool or an HTTP API, giving more flexibility. The easiest option is running as an HTTP API, which you can call using various tools and programming language libraries. It has a surprising amount of dependencies and isn't the simplest tool to get running, but I found the containerized instructions easiest to get working. I struggled to find a few key details in the documentation, including details of the API endpoints, but there is an image in the repository readme that shows what's available, no matter which data provider you use.

The SDK provides convenience wrappers to help make location checking part of common stages in the DevOps workflow. There's a GitHub action that you can use to switch deployment or build locations based on metrics and integration with Azure functions.

I did come across an option for Python programmers, but it hasn't seen much development recently and only has intensity data for the Netherlands. However, it uses the Electricity Maps API, so I would assume it would be possible to support other regions.

Monitoring Server Workloads

Let's move to an area that's easier to measure but no less complicated. The infrastructure software that runs on servers. I am seasoned enough to remember when deploying an application involved uploading a bunch of files to a server and keeping your fingers crossed. Everything server-related was expensive, and if you were a small-time operator, you continually tried to find ways to save money and resources. If you had special requirements, few companies offered what you needed, keeping prices high. But then again, most applications and needs were simpler, so it evened out.

It's hard to pinpoint exactly when it happened. It was a slow transition, but at some point, application development, deployment, and maintenance became much more complex. We added layers of abstraction to almost every step, introducing complexity, vulnerabilities, and, yes, additional environmental impact. Of course, all of these abstractions bring a lot of benefits. Like many other suggested actions in this book, I am not telling you to stop using them but to think before you do and be more considerate with their implementation as you add them.

The first part of this chapter looked at the various inputs into the impact of data center servers, but when it comes to measuring your impact, you can't track all of these. Exactly what you can measure depends on your setup, provider, and the tools you use. Generally, in a modern development stack, there are now potentially the following layers involved and measurable:

- Chips: CPU, GPU, RAM
- Host operating system
- System processes
- Virtual machines
- Containers
- Workloads in Containers

Some of these layers have more options for monitoring them than others, and some tools display more than one layer. In cloud environments, you often have limited access to all layers of the stack, making it difficult to view metrics or configure the ability to view them. So, each of the following sections presents tools but also underlying components that allow those tools to work.

Chips

Intel CPUs have shipped with the Running Average Power Limit (RAPL) feature since the Sandy Bridge architecture in 2011, which over time has provided more accurate energy consumption measurements with minimal error. AMD has an equivalent Advanced Platform Management Link (APML) feature, with extensive RAPL compatibility. NVIDIA has the System Management Interface (SMI) for its GPUs and has the NVML API for accessing the metrics it generates. Thanks to its more unique way of licensing, but not manufacturing chips, ARM has the System Control and Management Interface (SCMI), but different manufacturers report different metrics.

In each case, you need to check that a chip has the feature (probably) and often install a library or SDK so that another tool can access that data.

Host Operating Systems

If you're obsessive like me, then you have likely fired up Activity Monitor (macOS), top (Linux and macOS), or the Windows task manager to see the resource usage of a process. Or is that just me?

As far as I know, macOS's Activity Monitor uses the long-running powermetrics CLI tool under the hood, representing the results visually, but using the CLI gives you more details and is perfect for piping to other places. For some other options, take a look at this AskDifferent post that has a good summary.

For Windows, the Task Manager is the primary tool for monitoring process energy usage. You can also run it in the command line using the tasklist command.

As Linux is so prevalent on servers in data centers, it has more and more comprehensive options for power monitoring. These include various flavors of top for output to the command line, but thanks to Linux's "everything is a file" design, you can also query metrics via a series of device (/sys/devices) and process (/proc) directories. Finally, there's perf, a more recent entrant that gives deep profiling insights into Linux performance metrics, which some other tools in this chapter use.

Chapter 5 revisits this topic to look more at some of the tools that operating systems or "official" development environments provide for energy monitoring, especially if you're building applications for running on mobile devices.

What Does Infrastructure Run?

This is already a big chapter but before moving on to measuring and optimizing infrastructure, first let's define the possible workloads that infrastructure can run. Chapter 5 covers more in-depth application logic and loosely "programming backend code," but this is just one part of the modern application stack. Most modern applications can consist of some of the following ancillary services, all of which are applications with their own inherent impact, that you may or may not have any control over:

- Databases
- Other storage services
- Logging, error tracking, and observability
- Caches
- Data streaming and message queues
- Gateways, service meshes
- Security, authentication, and compliance

This book won't cover all of these in-depth apart from encouraging you look into performance best practices for whichever you use. Some require minimal optimizing, some aren't worth optimizing, and some, such as security and compliance, maybe it's risky to optimize. However, there are a couple on the lists above that tend to have greater impact and potential for optimization.

Some of these are co-located with the rest of the application using provider-managed infrastructure (one of the hyperscalers, for example), co-located by using container orchestration of the services, use external providers and services, or some combination of the above.

And the list above is just ancillary services at runtime, there are also services used during development, testing, and deployment, such as

- Service catalogues

- Infrastructure as Code (IaC) tools
- Continuous Integration and Continuous delivery
- Scheduling and orchestration

All of these, to some degree, have an environmental impact.

These different services are all essentially applications in their own right, so If it runs in a way that one of the monitoring tools covered in the chapter can measure, then it's probably possible to measure its part in your overall impact.

This should be possible if you use a cloud host provider's service or you run it yourself in some way, but this changes which tool you use to measure the energy use.

If you use an external third-party service, then it's harder to access direct metrics. If you are reading this book, I assume the sustainability of services is important to you. There are dozens, if not hundreds of vendors available for some service types, so choose those that report and act upon sustainability metrics. And if your current provider doesn't report on this, then tell them it's important to you. The customer is always right, and sometimes listened to.

Again, if developers run local versions of these, you hit the local measurement problem with some of these tools, and especially IaC tools generally as you have little insight into the impact of them. However, even in total, they are probably minuscule compared to the production versions.

Before getting to those, the first question to ask yourself and your team(s) is. Do you need it?

A recurring theme in this chapter is over-provisioning, and the same applies for services in general. The modern application stack is complex because we made it that way. Every now and then I take a look at `https://landscape.cncf.io/` to see how large it has become. That's not to say that some applications don't need to be large and complex. Some have hundreds of thousands, if not millions, if not billions of regular users and the complex web of tools and services help those run as smoothly as possible. However, most products don't. Kubernetes is wonderful, but most people don't need it. You probably don't need a service mesh most of the time.

And even with some of the services that are more essential to everyone such as error handling and logging, do you really need to log as much and keep as much for as long as you likely do? All of that over-logging (and I'm not talking about trees ☺) uses resources and more crucially, storage, and storage especially, is a hidden consumer.

Fortunately, some logging tools and services have made a business out of helping you to reduce the amount of signal to noise ratio to keep. Even if you don't use one of these services, then you can likely set retention periods on logging tools, or at least, move data past this period to cold storage, which is cheaper and/or uses less energy.

You can setup sustainable retention policies and archival strategies for your log storage and databases in general. France's Regulatory Authority for Electronic Communications, Postal Affairs and Press Distribution. `https://www.arcep.fr/uploads/tx_gspublication/general_policy_framework_for_the_ecodesign_of_digital_services_version_2024.pdf`, and point 7.2 makes exactly this recommendation and sums it up nicely with the phrase, "The goal is to relieve databases and physical servers of the burden of useless data."

If you need a greater (technical) authority than a department of the French government to convince you, then even Adrian Cockroft, who among many other things, created the microservices architecture, and is now a strong proponent of sustainable software engineering, agrees. Several of his many recent talks on the subject state, "Reduce logging" and "archive and delete data sooner."

Containers and Container Orchestrators

Containers have become something of a standard for workload, application, and service delivery in the past ten years. They bring many benefits to the development process, which I won't cover here, but first, a brief and summarized data center history lesson. In the modern era of cloud and pre-cloud computing (about the past 20 years), most workloads ran on shared machines using virtual machines that divided the physical machine between several users. Using an entire server for yourself was reserved for large enterprises or those with very specialist needs (privacy, for example), as it cost a lot of money. It was (and still is) also quite wasteful, as while we have few statistics to prove it, it's likely that many of the servers, even 10–15 years ago, also ran idle a lot of the time. Virtual machines worked (and are still widely used) well, but they add a lot of overhead, creating dozens or more small operating system instances on one machine. They were also harder for developers to replicate locally, leading to the age-old problem of "it works on my machine." While not a new concept, Docker popularized the idea of containers and container runtimes just over ten years ago. Instead of multiple instances of an operating system, container runtimes share one across multiple containers, focussing their content purely on what is important to the application or service. They add a little overhead, but in aggregate, they add far less than what came before and it's much easier to specify the resources they are allowed to use.

At scale, you or your host needs a container orchestrator to handle the potentially hundreds or thousands of containers a modern application stack might create, run, and delete on a daily basis. And these days, there really only is Kubernetes. There are alternatives to Kubernetes, but it's the most widely used and has the largest ecosystem. Some of these, such as OpenShift, Rancher, and various Hyperscaler options, are essentially most of the same components as Kubernetes under the hood. I didn't explicitly test any of the tools mentioned in this section with these tools, but I would assume that if they work with Kubernetes, they probably also work with them. The few remaining complete alternatives are Nomad and Apache Mesos, which are far less active than they used to be. I struggled to find any active and functioning sustainability monitoring tools specific to them.

General Kubernetes Optimization Advice

I don't want to state the obvious, but Kubernetes is big and complex and used in many different ways and with many different combinations of tools. The first step to making Kubernetes more efficient is to ask yourself if you need it. It's widely overused, almost worn as a badge of honor, than actually needed. If you run only a handful of containers or have a mostly predictable usage pattern, you probably don't need it.

But there are some common principles to try to optimize usage, and thus reduce energy consumption. This chapter can't cover everything as it's a large topic, but I recommend looking at cast.ai. They are a commercial product, but their website also has a lot of good resources, and you can use their free tier to get a general idea of further action you can manually act upon.

This chapter mentions over-provisioning as a common problem and presents tools to help you scale more effectively in the next section. However, a subset of scaling is "bin packing," the practice of effectively scheduling pods into nodes, so you don't need to overprovision as much.

A quick Kubernetes refresher. For the most part, a container maps to a single pod, but not always, for example, in the case of a sidecar container. A node is a physical or virtual machine that can run workloads, and it runs one or more pods based on resources. The nodes are typically what you might over-provision, and the various Kubernetes scaling options work with.

As someone interested in energy efficiency, you'd probably want to pack as many "bins" (which are containers, I don't know why they are called "bins") as possible into one node. This chapter is not the place to discuss exactly how you do that, but this blog post is a great starting point. Fewer nodes equal less power consumption? Well, as always, maybe. First, you may have other considerations to consider, such as distributing workloads across different nodes for redundancy, data protection, or application code spiking resource usage and affecting other workloads. The entire point of Kubernetes is to distribute workloads. Have you gained anything if you pack them all into the same node? Should you even be using Kubernetes? There is, of course, a wider conversation on whether you should be in the first place, but I assume you've had that for now.

Thanks to the large-scale usage of Kubernetes, many have created options to help you operate it more sustainably. However, this can also mean that some of these options languish in GitHub graveyards, long since updated and non-functioning. As I step through the options, I'll only identify those that had some degree of activity in the past two years and that I could mostly get to work. As with anything technical, your mileage may vary depending on your technology stack and ability to experiment.

Before getting stuck into tools, first, here is a quick word about Kubernetes scaling (there are two types, horizontal and vertical), as many of the tools work in conjunction with scaling or make recommendations for scaling. And remember, one of the biggest wastes of energy is over-provisioned servers. Based on your settings, Kubernetes can scale workloads and resources up or down to suit what Kubernetes thinks is the best combination. First, it's important to note that this is based on your settings, and second, you need to use the feature. It's not something Kubernetes does automatically by default.

Both scaling types use the Kubernetes Metrics Server, which you need to add first. The scaling types use the Metrics Server to collect resource metrics across a cluster to fuel the algorithm scaling uses. Many of the sustainability-specific tools mentioned later in the chapter also use Metrics Server.

Horizontal scaling automatically tries to resize the number of pods in workloads, such as a Deployment or StatefulSet, to match demand based on resource usage across the resource.

You set a `resource` section in the workload definition so the scaler knows the base resources to work with. This determines the behavior of the horizontal pod autoscaling controller, which periodically adjusts the desired scale of its target (e.g., a Deployment) to match resource metrics such as average CPU or memory utilization or any other custom metric you specify.

You then use the `kubectl autoscale` command to define the minimum and maximum number of replicas to balance the resource usage you want across those replicas. For example, this could help you balance CPU usage across replica locations that are more or less carbon-intensive or try to achieve a higher CPU usage per replica, thus using fewer replicas.

```
kubectl autoscale deployment redis --namespace benchmark --cpu-percent=70
--min=1 --max=10
kubectl autoscale deployment stress-ng --namespace benchmark --cpu-
percent=20 --min=1 --max=10
```

However, manually issuing scale commands isn't particularly practical, and this is where the Metrics Server becomes useful as it exposes other resource information sources. For example, you could set scaling based on always using 90% of the CPU. There are many other interesting metrics sources, but this isn't the place to go into detail on them. However, as mentioned earlier, other tools in this chapter use or create their own.

Vertical scaling is a newer, disabled by default, and separate feature that instead adjusts the resources of individual nodes to match demand. You use it to create CustomResourceDefinitions (CRDs) for workloads that define the how, when, and method for autoscaling. As of version 1.27 of Kubernetes, it can also resize a workload in place without restarting the underlying Pod or Containers.

Instead of setting resources for a collection of containers in pods across a Deployment or StatefulSet, with vertical scaling, you can define minimum and maximum resources for individual containers and autoscale between those values based on demand. For example:

```
resourcePolicy:
  containerPolicies:
    - containerName: '*'
      minAllowed:
        cpu: 100m
        memory: 50Mi
      maxAllowed:
        cpu: 1
        memory: 500Mi
      controlledResources: ["cpu", "memory"]
```

This is useful to us, allowing for micro levels of control on containers running certain jobs in certain locations. Again, you can combine vertical scaling with sources from the Metrics Server.

You can combine the scaling methods with external events, getting closer to reacting to changes in a region's electricity composition.

KEDA and Carbon Awareness

Kubernetes Event-driven Autoscaling (KEDA) is a general tool for auto-scaling Kubernetes using the default vertical and horizontal scalers but triggered by certain events such as incoming message queues or log messages.

KEDA uses triggers supplied by available scalers to trigger scaling. For example, this could be based on a Prometheus metric reaching a certain threshold.

Despite the project's home page stating that you can use KEDA to reduce environmental impact, nothing in the documentation tells you how. However, the Microsoft Azure team created a Kubernetes Operator from 2023 that uses KEDA with carbon awareness, again using WattTime and ElectricityMaps APIs. Sadly, it hasn't had much activity since the team behind it delivered a presentation at KubeCon in 2023.

Getting it working requires a reasonable amount of back and forth and fiddling, but it is possible, following these instructions with changes needed if you want to set it up on your infrastructure and not use Kind to create the Kubernetes cluster. With all this in place, you can do some interesting things. Take, for example, this KEDA scaler:

```
apiVersion: carbonaware.kubernetes.azure.com/v1alpha1
kind: CarbonAwareKedaScaler
metadata:
  labels:
    app.kubernetes.io/name: carbonawarekedascaler
    app.kubernetes.io/instance: carbonawarekedascaler-sample
    app.kubernetes.io/part-of: carbon-aware-keda-operator
    app.kubernetes.io/managed-by: kustomize
    app.kubernetes.io/created-by: carbon-aware-keda-operator
  name: carbon-aware-word-processor-scaler
spec:
  kedaTarget: scaledobjects.keda.sh
  kedaTargetRef:
```

```
    name: word-processor-scaler
    namespace: default
  carbonIntensityForecastDataSource:
    localConfigMap:
      name: carbon-intensity
      namespace: kube-system
      key: data
  maxReplicasByCarbonIntensity:
    - carbonIntensityThreshold: 437
      maxReplicas: 110
    - carbonIntensityThreshold: 504
      maxReplicas: 60
    - carbonIntensityThreshold: 571
      maxReplicas: 10
  ecoModeOff:
    maxReplicas: 100
    carbonIntensityDuration:
      carbonIntensityThreshold: 555
      overrideEcoAfterDurationInMins: 45
    customSchedule:
      - startTime: "2023-04-28T16:45:00Z"
        endTime: "2023-04-28T17:00:59Z"
    recurringSchedule:
      - "* 23 * * 1-5"
```

The most interesting parts are at the bottom of the YAML. They define a replica count based on a carbon intensity threshold, reducing the replicas as the intensity increases. The ecoModeOff section defines the "default" state when carbon intensity doesn't manage the replica count. This ties in with the schedule section below, which disables carbon-aware scaling at certain times.

As a precursor to this work, Bill Johnson of the Azure team wrote a blog post in 2020 discussing carbon-aware Kubernetes. Before that, two researchers at the University of Bristol dug into the algorithms that could be (and maybe are) behind a carbon-aware Kubernetes scheduler.

Kube-green

Actively maintained by a small group of maintainers, kube-green's main purpose is to suspend pods when they aren't in use. It's a little different from default Kubernetes autoscaling features and also uses a CRD to let you define sleep and wake conditions. Sleeping means that kube-green reduces replicas to 1 for Deployments and StatefulSets and can also suspend CronJobs from running.

For example, to sleep Deployments and StatefulSets between 19:00 and 08:00 every weekday (by default, the sleep condition always applies at weekends) for a particular time zone, you use the following YAML:

```
apiVersion: kube-green.com/v1alpha1
kind: SleepInfo
metadata:
    name: working-hours
spec:
    weekdays: "1-5"
    sleepAt: "19:00"
    wakeUpAt: "08:00"
    timeZone: "Europe/Rome"
    suspendCronJobs: true
    excludeRef:
        - apiVersion: "apps/v1"
          kind: Deployment
          name: api-gateway
```

You can exclude specific Deployments or StatefulSets from sleeping by adding them to the `excludeRef` section.

Peaks

Another Kubernetes scheduling option, but still in the discussions and prototype phase, Power Efficiency Aware Kubernetes Scheduler (PEAKS), aims to introduce optimizing the aggregated power consumption of the entire cluster at the scheduling time. This would replace some of the other tools in this list with a more "official" Kubernetes-default option. I don't see too much recent activity in the repository, but there has been some in the past six months, so it's enough to include it here.

By default, Kubernetes mostly focuses on scheduling by resource allocation. The main justification for PEAKS is that the maintainers witnessed power consumption is often higher (relatively speaking) on underutilized nodes. When utilization is higher, power consumption efficiency is better, to a point, and while there's no loss in efficiency, it stabilizes. This isn't an uncommon observation, and among others, was made by Rahkonen and Dietrich in 2023 who noted that server efficiency increases by about 50% when processor utilization is doubled from low levels of 20% to 30%.

This chapter reiterates that many development teams over-provision resources for an anticipated but often unrealized demand. PEAKS aims to demonstrate and prove this by collaborating with the Kubernetes working groups to add power scheduling as an in-built option.

Kepler

Perhaps one of the first projects people interested in running more sustainable cloud native projects are likely to find, the Kubernetes-based Efficient Power Level Exporter, or Kepler for short, extracts and exports power consumption data in real time.

Digging deeper, it uses Extended Berkeley Packet Filter (eBPF), a relatively old but increasingly popular technology, to collect its data from various low-level hardware and software components it can access, from bare metal to containers and orchestrators. After processing the data collected, Kepler exports the values as Prometheus metrics, which you can consume in different ways, including visualizing them in Grafana dashboards.

Read the project's blog post for more details on Kepler's technical and mathematical aspects.

Some other tools in this chapter use Kepler, and Chapter 5 uses it to benchmark and compare different techniques, so it's worth digging into it in more detail now.

Adding Kepler to Kubernetes with manifest files, a helm chart, or an operator is fairly straightforward. What you then do with the metrics it gathers is more complex. The metrics Kepler can extract depend on the hardware or virtualized hardware (container, virtual machine, etc.) it's running on.

To get a quick impression of how Kepler works, I recommend following the local setup instructions for the green reviews tooling (a working group of the cloud native computing foundation I'm slightly involved with) in their public repository. There are a lot of steps, but it sets up the recommended Kepler, Prometheus, and Grafana dependencies and also adds Falco (another CNCF project) with some benchmarking tests you can run to simulate high load and generate enough data for Kepler to send to Grafana for visualization.

As is common with any Prometheus and Grafana relationship, Kepler exposes a series of metrics, which you can find more about in the documentation. You can consume these metrics through any other Prometheus-compatible tool, which is what the Grafana dashboard does. It takes these metrics and builds visual dashboards of them.

The Kepler Grafana dashboard has five main sections.

The top and most noticeable is the overall carbon footprint, measured in pounds per kWh per day for a Kubernetes namespace and/or pod. Three gauges show the carbon footprint when using coal, petroleum, and natural gas, with the calculations for the power generation provided by the US Energy Information Administration. The gauges use the kepler_container_joules_total metric, the aggregated energy consumption of CPU, memory, GPUs, and other host components for a given container tracked over 24 hours.

The second section shows Pod/Process Power Consumption (W) in a namespace, displayed sorted by the mean value and tracked over time in a bar graph. It is broken down by CPU, memory, GPUs, and other host components for a given container. Four metrics are used for these calculations to match each component.

- `kepler_container_package_joules_total` measures the cumulative energy consumed by the CPU, including all cores and related components such as cache, integrated GPU, and memory controller.
- `kepler_container_dram_joules_total` measures the total energy spent in memory by a container.
- `kepler_container_other_joules_total` measures the energy consumption on other components besides the CPU and memory.
- `kepler_container_gpu_joules_total` measures the total energy consumption on the GPUs that a certain container has used. Currently, Kepler only supports NVIDIA GPUs.

The third section shows the total power consumption for a namespace in watts per minute, displayed and sortable by the mean and max values. It is also tracked over time in a bar graph and broken down by CPU, memory, GPUs, and other host components. It uses the same four metrics as the previous panel but doesn't break them down by container.

The fourth section shows the total power consumption for a namespace in kWh per day, displayed and sortable by the mean and max values. It is tracked over time in a bar graph and broken down by CPU, memory, GPUs, and other host components. It uses the same four metrics as the previous panel but doesn't break them down by container and displays them in a different resolution for the day range.

The final section shows the Total Power Consumption of all namespaces present by Namespace in kWh per day, displayed in a bar gauge, with each namespace's consumption shown relative to the others. Again, it uses the kepler_container_joules_total metric but doesn't filter by namespace and displays it in an appropriate resolution for the day range.

Kubernetes Emissions Insights Tool (KEIT)

KEIT is an open-source tool that estimates the carbon emissions of a Kubernetes cluster, currently supporting Kubernetes on bare metal, AWS, EKS, and Azure, which is coming soon. On the surface, KEIT sounds similar to Kepler, but Kepler is (only) a data collector and exporter with a Grafana dashboard for visualizing the data it collects. You could do other things with the data it collects and exports. KEIT also uses Kepler to collect and export the data and again uses Grafana to visualize the data, but is more opinionated in the visualization using the Electricity Maps API and the grid intensity Go project to calculate carbon intensity and to add one more feature that none of the other tools mentioned here do: show embodied carbon thanks to the Boavizta API. While the project is in its early days and requires a fair bit of configuration wrangling to get working, the full suite of statistics it provides is promising.

Scaphandre

An alternative to Kepler is Scaphandre. In many ways, it seems similar to Kepler, but in addition to Kubernetes energy monitoring, it also supports monitoring the energy consumption of other sources, such as bare metal hosts and virtual machines, and exporting metrics to sources other than Prometheus. Because of this, device and operating support has more prerequisites and is more complex.

However, while I could install Scaphandre on my Linux testing machine (it has no ARM or macOS support), I could not get any data into the Grafana dashboards, so I am not sure of its effectiveness yet. This is a shame, as I have a local virtual machine and container processes running on my test machine, and it would be interesting to get an overall impression of the impact of every process.

Should you have more success or are happy to dig around the projects' demo dashboards, the result is a comprehensive dashboard (if you follow the Prometheus and Grafana path) that breaks down power consumption into each component it can monitor, tracked from the current hour to a year of data.

Karpenter

Not explicitly for energy monitoring, but relevant to keeping workloads as right-sized as possible, Karpenter provides just-in-time nodes for Kubernetes clusters. The serverless section below provides a more detailed explanation of just-in-time. The concept is a common, if broad, one in computing, involving the scheduling of resources as needed. It's maintained by Amazon, which makes me wonder if it's used behind the scenes for AWS Lambda. It's a replacement for the Kubernetes Cluster Autoscaler, but only works with certain hosting providers, including the three hyperscalers.

Karpenter adds several new Custom Resources, the most common of which is called a NodePool, which sets constraints on the nodes and pods that can run it. Most relevant to energy efficiency, Karpenter monitors system resources more closely than other autoscalers, triggering scaling based on the Pod's actual needs and sizing new nodes to match. You can also set termination and expiry times on nodes in NodePools to keep Pods as fresh as possible.

Impact framework

`https://if.greensoftware.foundation`

On initial read, it's not completely clear what impact framework is, and it's not explicitly an infrastructure monitoring tool. Instead, you use the framework to measure the Software Carbon Intensity (SCI) of your hardware, giving you a baseline to work from for other measurements.

CloudAssess

`https://github.com/kleis-technology/cloud-assess`

Similar to Impact Framework, CloudAssess is another option for assessing the environmental impact of the resources you run on cloud providers. It works slightly differently, providing an API that provides endpoints for various resources that you call and pass a JSON payload describing the resource. The API then returns a result that contains a full life cycle assessment.

Measuring Infrastructure As Code (IaC)

OpenCost

As mentioned throughout this book, sometimes, the best way to motivate those around you who aren't as concerned about the environmental impact of services is to take the cost angle. Generally, resources that consume more energy cost more money. The "FinOps" community has existed for some time and even has its own foundation.

One of the more popular tools in the FinOps space is OpenCost, which aims to introduce good cost management to cloud infrastructure. It has existed for a while to help infrastructure planners see the costs and potential costs of decisions. It planned to add carbon cost to its metrics using Thoughtworks' Cloud Carbon Footprint to bring the monitoring into OpenCost. Unfortunately, it looks like this work stopped at some point, but if someone is willing to continue, there is a history of the work in GitHub.

Crane

Also, in the FinOps landscape, Crane is another general-purpose tool for analyzing the costs of Kubernetes-based infrastructure and using Kubernetes scaling to react to those costs. While it's not mentioned in the documentation (or I couldn't find it), a carbon cost component appears as a section in the cost insights section. It gives an overview over time of carbon emissions in g/h and energy consumption in watts/h. The carbon and energy values calculation isn't that clear, but you can dig into the code to see the basic numbers it uses.

Infracost

For those who use Terraform or OpenTofu to create the infrastructure applications needed, Infracost has existed for some time to estimate the cost of the infrastructure you're deploying. It doesn't currently show carbon cost, but a long and active thread discusses adding the feature. However, it hasn't seen much activity since August 2024.

Terracost

Another Terraform and OpenTofu tool that shows an indicative cost of an infrastructure rollout, terracost doesn't have any carbon impact metrics, but the company behind it, Cycloid, does have a cloud carbon footprint module. As mentioned in Chapter 1, this book wasn't going to mention many commercial tools. One reason to mention Cycloid's offering is that while many of its other modules are optional, the carbon impact module is enabled by default. You can't disable it, forcing all their customers to at least think about carbon impact.

ecoinfra

`https://github.com/eco-infra/ecoinfra`

Another option for assessing the impact of a Terraform plan in a variety of CI/CD environments. The company behind the tool provides a commercial option that adds smarter prediction and optimization suggestions over time, but you can also use the tool to output to JSON files, and the tools that you install in your CI/CD are open source and free. Currently it only supports Terraform, not OpenTofu, and only AWS.

Carbonifier

Carbonifier explicitly measures the potential carbon impact of a Terraform rollout. It is a separate tool you can run over .tf files and estimate the emissions. Its functionality is limited, but it does mean that you can get details on carbon impact without needing a more complex tool.

Spruce

If you use AWS and already use Apache Spark for data processing, then `https://github.com/DigitalPebble/spruce` processes AWS cost and usage reports to calculate the following `https://opensourcegreenops.cloud/methodology.html`:

- Estimation of embodied emissions from the hardware
- Estimation of energy used
- Application of PUE and other overheads
- Application of carbon intensity factors

Outside of Kubernetes

Kubernetes is popular, but not everyone uses it for running application and service workloads. Indeed, in many cases, it's overkill. To reiterate, over-provisioning and unnecessary complexity are among the biggest sustainability impacts in modern computing.

Cardamon

It's challenging to know where to include Cardamon, as it's a general-purpose tool that can monitor the energy consumption of almost any process running on a machine, making it equally relevant in this chapter as in Chapter 5. You define a series of processes, scenarios, and observations. Processes are the things that Cardamon starts, stops, and measures. Scenarios represent a use case to put a process under scrutiny. Observations define how to take a measurement, typically a scenario or a process. When you first run Cardamon, it creates a configuration file that includes your CPU's information and the average power consumption, based on Boavizta data. When you first run an observation, it tries to fetch carbon intensity data to give more accurate local results. By default, Cardamon outputs results to the CLI, but also has a web UI. I tried running the Docker example in the repository several times, and Cardamon even shows trends over successive runs.

The main negative is that while Cardamon supports Docker containers and binary executables, it doesn't support Kubernetes. Still, that makes it a great tool for monitoring local systems outside of Kubernetes.

cAdvisor

cAdvisor from Google, as it's a long-standing option for monitoring container resource usage. Extracting energy usage values would involve extra work, but it gives a general idea of resource usage, and it's likely that a lot of traditional performance monitoring teams and tools already have it installed.

EnergiBridge

Cross platform and with broad CPU and GPU support, if you can run a command in a terminal, then `https://github.com/tdurieux/EnergiBridge` can provide information on the CPU and memory usage that you can output into a variety of formats and then perform calculations on.

Tracarbon

Tracks device energy consumption metrics across macOS, Linux, AWS, and containers when running on Linux. `https://github.com/fvaleye/tracarbon` uses some of the sources covered in this book (ElectricityMaps, the EEA, and others) to translate those metrics into carbon impact. More interestingly for infrastructure engineers is that you can export the metrics to common observability tools like Prometheus and Datadog.

Compute Energy & Emissions Monitoring Stack (CEEMS)

`https://ceems-dev.github.io/ceems/`

Another option for anyone with an existing Prometheus setup who wants to add energy consumption data with minimal infrastructural overhead, CEEMS consists of a Prometheus exporter and a REST API you can use to aggregate the metadata and metrics from the exporter. It supports a wide variety of CPUs and GPUs and resource orchestrators. If you want to get a similar level of detail to Kepler, then it's a good alternative to consider.

Powerjoular

`https://github.com/joular/powerjoular`

Another Intel only Linux options that monitors power consumption of bare metal and virtual machine CPUs and GPUs. In both environments, it can show the power consumption of individual processes and export them to terminal or CSV files. It can run as a systemd service, meaning it's one of the easier options to install and leave running, continuously monitoring in the background.

Energy Monitoring Tool (EMT)

`https://github.com/FairCompute/energy-monitoring-tool`

From the Phillips responsible AI team, EMT is a tool providing energy consumption at a process level with support for Intel CPUs and NVIDIA GPUs. Right now the feature set is minimal, but has some interesting features on the roadmap.

Cloud Carbon Footprint

From the venerable technology consultants Thoughtworks, Cloud Carbon Footprint is where I began my journey into sustainable computing. I was an early entrant into the space, leveraging cloud providers' billing information to give carbon impact indications long before any of the providers did directly. It's a fairly large, complex, and configurable tool that shows overall usage across clouds, carbon equivalence values, a breakdown by region, and a carbon intensity map. If you're not already using Prometheus and Grafana, then it's a great alternative to tools like Kepler and KEIT for giving an overview of the impact of cloud services.

GitHub Actions

For GitHub actions, Carbon runner aims to shift workflows to the lowest CO_2 regions. As far as I can see, it's still in a closed preview and seems to plan to charge for its usage, so I am not sure how well it does or will work.

Eco CI

It's easy to overlook "throwaway" processes and infrastructure used in CI, but some can be intensive and run so frequently that I imagine the energy impact can add up quickly. From a different perspective, Eco CI gives energy consumption estimates for CI jobs. It's regularly maintained and supports CI processes running in GitHub, GitLab, Jenkins, and other platforms by using Docker containers.

Serverless and Function As a Service

While it's a misleading marketing term, as everything still needs to run on a server, serverless and function as a service (FaaS) computing is designed to be as transient and "as needed" as possible, which does, in theory, sound more efficient. Conceptually it takes the container to a further level of abstraction, but sadly with less standards and ways for developers to test and move payloads between providers. This is perhaps my biggest issue with the concept, it's very vendor dependent, managed, and locked in.

Much of this chapter noted that a lot of money and energy is wasted on people over-providing machines that sit idle for much of the time. So running functions and services as and when you need them means that there should be fewer over-provisioned servers sitting idle. Reports such as this one from the team behind Firecracker, a lightweight virtualization framework initially designed for AWS' Lambda, but now also used by other providers, show that while not as performant as a bare metal machine, virtualization optimized for serverless, at scale, can have significant performance benefits.

Other Approaches

I come from the cloud-native CI/CD pipelines world. When I think of actions and outcomes I want to accomplish, I tend to think in terms of workflow jobs and some form of configuration for them, probably in YAML. Many of the tools and approaches presented in this chapter followed a similar approach, as that's the one I know.

However, another approach I've seen mentioned a few times, especially in more academic or research-based teams or projects, is using digital twins for modeling. In this case, modeling the environmental impact of certain changes. I don't pretend to understand how digital twins work fully, how someone sets up and uses one, or how they compare in usefulness to the other approaches this chapter presents, but they're worth mentioning.

Digital Twins for Sustainability Modeling

In essence, using a digital twin to model and measure the impact of changes isn't so different from automated processes running in cloud, container, or local environments and using metrics and dashboards to view the results. They both take inputs, run them, and present the outcome. But the way they handle them is quite different, and both approaches could learn from each other.

A digital twin is a virtual representation, simulation, or model of a physical system or thing. It is often fed data from sensors in real-world objects that the two use to simulate and predict certain scenarios. Digital twins are popular with city planners, factory managers, and energy system planners, among others. They often take the form of a 3D virtual environment, but not always.

I had heard of them before, especially in the context of urban planning, but it wasn't until a fascinating conversation with Dr Dwayne Spiteri of Deutsches Elektronen-Synchrotron (DESY), the German equivalent of CERN, that I realized they could also simulate a data center.

He created a simulation of the data center at Glasgow University, including as much detail as he could acquire on modeling that data center, from the server components to the cabling, power supplies, cooling, and lighting. He then feeds this into data sets such as the UK National Grid ESO or German Co2 Monitor to simulate grid performance and monitor what effect some of the principles covered in this chapter, especially the impact of running clocked-down machines, could have. The outputs of a digital twin look more like the results I am used to seeing (a table) rather than some virtual data center. I am not sure what that would even look like anyway. Data centers don't change much visually as they work.

During his experiments, he noticed a small percentage change based on changing the server CPUs to more efficient models, generally no more than 2% decrease in energy consumption. However, the Glasgow University data center is relatively small. More interesting is that with something like a digital twin, it's "easier" to factor in the embedded carbon of manufacturing the servers and other components, even as you swap them back and forth.

Dwayne is not the only one using digital twins to model data centers. Data Center Infrastructure Management (DCIM) software for planning data centers, already exist, such as AKCPro Server, but this is more for live data, and not many use them for scenario planning. I found an IEEE publication from September 2024 and an article on the Intelligent Data Centres website from February 2025, but they are also still at a principles level. The only more practical tool I found was from Cadence's Reality Digital Twin Platform. As with any large-scale enterprise tool, it's often challenging to figure out exactly what the software does from the website.

Summary

This chapter provided ideas, resources, and tools for developers, DevOps, and infrastructure engineers to plan, move, and measure the impact of monitoring and shifting workloads to meet sustainability goals.

However, like many aspects of engineering in a team or company of teams, the choices engineers want to make won't matter if they don't have the support, empowerment, or direct requirement from leadership to implement them. In much the same way many engineering leaders require teams to follow metrics and standards for testing, performance, security, or uptime, they also need to define sustainability goals the same way and treat a red gauge on an energy consumption dashboard with the same importance as a red gauge on error rates. As Max Kovtun, chief innovation officer for Sigma Software, told me in a sunny cafe in Lviv in late 2024.

> "We used to have to convince people that writing unit tests mattered, and over time, this shifted. The same will happen for software sustainability eventually, too. In our work developing for clients around the world, we tell them, 'we provide technical excellence', and whether that also includes ways to reduce energy consumption as well as doing everything else properly, well, 'you have to (and can) trust us.'"

CHAPTER 5

Back-end Development

Chris Chinchilla[1]
[1]Berlin, Germany; https://chrischinchilla.com/

Most end users of an application or service experience it through some form of front end. Whether that's a native application, web front-end, command-line interface, or using an HTTP API, they have an idea of how well it performs. Is it slow to respond? Does it use a lot of device resources? Does it cause the device to overheat and activate the fans to cool it down? In short, if a front end isn't performing and thus probably has a reasonable environmental impact, a user can feel it.

While most of us have minimal direct exposure to a data center, we know what they are and, at an abstract level, what happens in them. We know that bank after bank of servers and their flashing, blinking lights consume an awful lot of electricity. They need cooling systems and water to keep them running smoothly, which also requires a large amount of electricity. Chapter 4 covered this in detail. My point is that while we're not always sure what to do about it, the environmental impact of data centers is a known problem. It's talked about a lot. It's probably the most talked-about aspect of sustainable computing and the one with the largest overall impact. Again, Chapter 4 covered advice for making what runs on servers in data centers more efficient. What about the next level above that? Front-end code typically runs on end user machines, but most complex applications also have code running behind the scenes, running on servers in data centers.

Developers call this code different things, but this chapter sticks to the term "back-end." Code that serves as the business logic, API code, services, connectors, and glue code between services, among other components, depending on your application architecture. Generally speaking, code that end users never interact with directly, but powers the interactions they do have. Without this backend, the infrastructure and (maybe) front-end code have little to do, so optimizing it has an impact on resources running in data centers.

C. Chinchilla and I. Akrap, *Building the Sustainable Web*, https://doi.org/10.1007/979-8-8688-2521-7_5

Poorly written and architected backends can lead to system crashes, CPU spikes, memory leaks, and other issues. All of which have the potential to cause excessive energy consumption and poor performance for users.

There's less written about the direct impact of backends, as it's typically factored into the payloads running on infrastructure. Depending on whether the code is compiled or interpreted, it's also hard to gauge the impact. Many frameworks and libraries exist for debugging and logging individual code components and parts, but fewer exist for gauging the environmental impact of these components.

The line between backend and infrastructure is grey, but this chapter also includes interactions with some of the ancillary infrastructure services mentioned in Chapter 4, as well as "packaged" applications such as content management systems (CMS). There is some crossover with other chapters with regards to the aspects of the full stack covered and the tools used to measure them, but that is the nature of modern software development.

Finally, this chapter covers the effect of software architectural patterns and alternative options for running applications such as WebAssembly (WASM).

Back-end Code

Back-end code is a broad subject covering dozens of programming languages, application architectures, and approaches. To have any kind of benchmark, you need common reference points to demonstrate the differences that changes make. This section draws on the work of several researchers and projects, all of which have experienced the same issues. Different languages are suited to different tasks and have different performance characteristics. Some languages run better in certain contexts or hardware combinations. The general advice is to choose the language most suited to the task and follow all its best practices for optimal performance and efficiency.

Over time, I intend to maintain a library of more production-level applications to benchmark energy impact. Still, I'm one person, writing a book, and I don't have the resources to do that right now. Some common examples used are create, read, update, delete (CRUD) applications, Fibonacci sequence generators, and the computer languages benchmark game (CLBG). None are perfect for measuring the energy impact of all languages effectively. However, in combination with measurement tools in this chapter and Chapter 4, they can help you benchmark changes you make to code.

The first and perhaps most cited comparison of energy efficiency in programming languages is the "Energy Efficiency across Programming Languages" paper from researchers at the University of Minho, Lisboa, and Coimbra, Portugal.

They ran a handful of different tests from the CLBG for 27 languages, picking three of the tests that existed for each language (See Figure 5-1). These were (including the variable input data)

- **Binary-trees**: Allocate, traverse, and deallocate 21 binary trees
- **Fannkuch-redux**: Indexed access to a 12 integer sequence.
- **Fasta**: Generate and write 25M DNA sequences

binary-trees				
	Energy	Time	Ratio	Mb
(c) C	39.80	1125	0.035	131
(c) C++	41.23	1129	0.037	132
(c) Rust $\Downarrow_2$	49.07	1263	0.039	180
(c) Fortran $\Uparrow_1$	69.82	2112	0.033	133
(c) Ada $\Downarrow_1$	95.02	2822	0.034	197
(c) Ocaml $\downarrow_1$ $\Uparrow_2$	100.74	3525	0.029	148
(v) Java $\uparrow_1$ $\Downarrow_{16}$	111.84	3306	0.034	1120
(v) Lisp $\downarrow_3$ $\Downarrow_3$	149.55	10570	0.014	373
(v) Racket $\downarrow_4$ $\Downarrow_6$	155.81	11261	0.014	467
(i) Hack $\uparrow_2$ $\Downarrow_9$	156.71	4497	0.035	502
(v) C# $\downarrow_1$ $\Downarrow_1$	189.74	10797	0.018	427
(v) F# $\downarrow_3$ $\Downarrow_1$	207.13	15637	0.013	432
(c) Pascal $\downarrow_3$ $\Uparrow_5$	214.64	16079	0.013	256
(c) Chapel $\uparrow_5$ $\Uparrow_4$	237.29	7265	0.033	335
(v) Erlang $\uparrow_5$ $\Uparrow_1$	266.14	7327	0.036	433
(c) Haskell $\uparrow_2$ $\Downarrow_2$	270.15	11582	0.023	494
(i) Dart $\downarrow_1$ $\Uparrow_1$	290.27	17197	0.017	475
(i) JavaScript $\downarrow_2$ $\Downarrow_4$	312.14	21349	0.015	916
(i) TypeScript $\downarrow_2$ $\Downarrow_2$	315.10	21686	0.015	915
(c) Go $\uparrow_3$ $\Uparrow_{13}$	636.71	16292	0.039	228
(i) Jruby $\uparrow_2$ $\Downarrow_3$	720.53	19276	0.037	1671
(i) Ruby $\Uparrow_5$	855.12	26634	0.032	482
(i) PHP $\Uparrow_3$	1,397.51	42316	0.033	786
(i) Python $\Uparrow_{15}$	1,793.46	45003	0.040	275
(i) Lua $\downarrow_1$	2,452.04	209217	0.012	1961
(i) Perl $\uparrow_1$	3,542.20	96097	0.037	2148
(c) Swift		n.e.		

fannkuch-redux				
	Energy	Time	Ratio	Mb
(c) C $\Downarrow_2$	215.92	6076	0.036	2
(c) C++ $\Uparrow_1$	219.89	6123	0.036	1
(c) Rust $\Downarrow_{11}$	238.30	6628	0.036	16
(c) Swift $\Downarrow_5$	243.81	6712	0.036	7
(c) Ada $\Downarrow_2$	264.98	7351	0.036	4
(c) Ocaml $\downarrow_1$	277.27	7895	0.035	3
(c) Chapel $\uparrow_1$ $\Downarrow_{18}$	285.39	7853	0.036	53
(v) Lisp $\downarrow_3$ $\Downarrow_{15}$	309.02	9154	0.034	43
(v) Java $\uparrow_1$ $\Downarrow_{13}$	311.38	8241	0.038	35
(c) Fortran $\Downarrow_1$	316.50	8665	0.037	12
(c) Go $\uparrow_2$ $\Uparrow_7$	318.51	8487	0.038	2
(c) Pascal $\Uparrow_{10}$	343.55	9807	0.035	2
(v) F# $\downarrow_1$ $\Downarrow_7$	395.03	10950	0.036	34
(v) C# $\uparrow_1$ $\Downarrow_5$	399.33	10840	0.037	29
(i) JavaScript $\downarrow_1$ $\Downarrow_2$	413.90	33663	0.012	26
(c) Haskell $\uparrow_1$ $\Uparrow_8$	433.68	14666	0.030	7
(i) Dart $\Downarrow_7$	487.29	38678	0.013	46
(v) Racket $\Uparrow_3$	1,941.53	43680	0.044	18
(v) Erlang $\Uparrow_3$	4,148.38	101839	0.041	18
(i) Hack $\Downarrow_6$	5,286.77	115490	0.046	119
(i) PHP	5,731.88	125975	0.046	34
(i) TypeScript $\downarrow_4$ $\Uparrow_4$	6,898.48	516541	0.013	26
(i) Jruby $\uparrow_1$ $\Downarrow_4$	7,819.03	219148	0.036	669
(i) Lua $\downarrow_3$ $\Uparrow_{19}$	8,277.87	635023	0.013	2
(i) Perl $\uparrow_2$ $\Uparrow_{12}$	11,133.49	249418	0.045	12
(i) Python $\uparrow_2$ $\Uparrow_{14}$	12,784.09	279544	0.046	12
(i) Ruby $\uparrow_2$ $\Uparrow_{17}$	14,064.98	315583	0.045	8

fasta				
	Energy	Time	Ratio	Mb
(c) Rust $\Downarrow_9$	26.15	931	0.028	16
(c) Fortran $\downarrow_6$	27.62	1661	0.017	1
(c) C $\uparrow_1$ $\Downarrow_1$	27.64	973	0.028	3
(c) C++ $\uparrow_1$ $\Downarrow_2$	34.88	1164	0.030	4
(v) Java $\uparrow_1$ $\Downarrow_{12}$	35.86	1249	0.029	41
(c) Swift $\Downarrow_9$	37.06	1405	0.026	31
(c) Go $\downarrow_2$	40.45	1838	0.022	4
(c) Ada $\downarrow_2$ $\Uparrow_3$	40.45	2765	0.015	3
(c) Ocaml $\downarrow_2$ $\Downarrow_{15}$	40.78	3171	0.013	201
(c) Chapel $\uparrow_5$ $\Downarrow_{10}$	40.88	1379	0.030	53
(v) C# $\uparrow_4$ $\Downarrow_5$	45.35	1549	0.029	35
(i) Dart $\Downarrow_6$	63.61	4787	0.013	49
(i) JavaScript $\Downarrow_1$	64.84	5098	0.013	30
(c) Pascal $\downarrow_1$ $\Uparrow_{13}$	68.63	5478	0.013	0
(i) TypeScript $\downarrow_2$ $\Downarrow_{10}$	82.72	6909	0.012	271
(v) F# $\uparrow_2$ $\Uparrow_3$	93.11	5360	0.017	27
(v) Racket $\downarrow_1$ $\Uparrow_5$	120.90	8255	0.015	21
(c) Haskell $\uparrow_2$ $\Downarrow_8$	205.52	5728	0.036	446
(v) Lisp $\Downarrow_2$	231.49	15763	0.015	75
(i) Hack $\Downarrow_3$	237.70	17203	0.014	120
(i) Lua $\Uparrow_{18}$	347.37	24617	0.014	3
(i) PHP $\downarrow_1$ $\Uparrow_{13}$	430.73	29508	0.015	14
(v) Erlang $\uparrow_1$ $\Uparrow_{12}$	477.81	27852	0.017	18
(i) Ruby $\downarrow_1$ $\Uparrow_2$	852.30	61216	0.014	104
(i) JRuby $\uparrow_1$ $\Downarrow_2$	912.93	49509	0.018	705
(i) Python $\downarrow_1$ $\Uparrow_{18}$	1,061.41	74111	0.014	9
(i) Perl $\uparrow_1$ $\Uparrow_8$	2,684.33	61463	0.044	53

***Figure 5-1.** Programmning language results for binary-trees, fannkuch-redux, and fasta*

And the normalized results across the tests are the following (See Figure 5-2):

Total					
	Energy		Time		Mb
(c) C	1.00	(c) C	1.00	(c) Pascal	1.00
(c) Rust	1.03	(c) Rust	1.04	(c) Go	1.05
(c) C++	1.34	(c) C++	1.56	(c) C	1.17
(c) Ada	1.70	(c) Ada	1.85	(c) Fortran	1.24
(v) Java	1.98	(v) Java	1.89	(c) C++	1.34
(c) Pascal	2.14	(c) Chapel	2.14	(c) Ada	1.47
(c) Chapel	2.18	(c) Go	2.83	(c) Rust	1.54
(v) Lisp	2.27	(c) Pascal	3.02	(v) Lisp	1.92
(c) Ocaml	2.40	(c) Ocaml	3.09	(c) Haskell	2.45
(c) Fortran	2.52	(v) C#	3.14	(i) PHP	2.57
(c) Swift	2.79	(v) Lisp	3.40	(c) Swift	2.71
(c) Haskell	3.10	(c) Haskell	3.55	(i) Python	2.80
(v) C#	3.14	(c) Swift	4.20	(c) Ocaml	2.82
(c) Go	3.23	(c) Fortran	4.20	(v) C#	2.85
(i) Dart	3.83	(v) F#	6.30	(i) Hack	3.34
(v) F#	4.13	(i) JavaScript	6.52	(v) Racket	3.52
(i) JavaScript	4.45	(i) Dart	6.67	(i) Ruby	3.97
(v) Racket	7.91	(v) Racket	11.27	(c) Chapel	4.00
(i) TypeScript	21.50	(i) Hack	26.99	(v) F#	4.25
(i) Hack	24.02	(i) PHP	27.64	(i) JavaScript	4.59
(i) PHP	29.30	(v) Erlang	36.71	(i) TypeScript	4.69
(v) Erlang	42.23	(i) Jruby	43.44	(v) Java	6.01
(i) Lua	45.98	(i) TypeScript	46.20	(i) Perl	6.62
(i) Jruby	46.54	(i) Ruby	59.34	(i) Lua	6.72
(i) Ruby	69.91	(i) Perl	65.79	(v) Erlang	7.20
(i) Python	75.88	(i) Python	71.90	(i) Dart	8.64
(i) Perl	79.58	(i) Lua	82.91	(i) Jruby	19.84

Figure 5-2. *Normalized global programming language results for Energy, Time, and Memory*

Both images from Rui Pereira, Marco Couto, Francisco Ribeiro, Rui Rua, Jácome Cunha, João Paulo Fernandes, and João Saraiva, 2017. Energy Efficiency across Programming Languages: How Do Energy, Time, and Memory Relate? In Proceedings of 2017 ACM SIGPLAN International Conference on Software Language Engineering (SLE'17). ACM, New York, NY, USA, 12 pages. `https://doi.org/10.1145/3136014.3136031`.

The results aren't that surprising. Compiled languages are generally more energy efficient than interpreted ones. Possibly the only results that surprised me were how energy efficient Java is and how inefficient Swift, C#, and Go are. What I found most disappointing was how inefficient TypeScript is compared to JavaScript, despite my assumption that the better practices TypeScript encourages would make it more efficient. TypeScript does, however, add dependencies to a project, and unnecessary code bundled into an application increases inefficiency.

However, different languages are suited to different purposes, so this isn't completely unexpected. This is where the problems with benchmarking lie, and the team behind the paper references "The computer language benchmarks game's speed page" to illustrate some of the problems.

As Maxim Kovtun, in his "Creating Green Software Development Program for IT Outsourcing" thesis (shared privately), which first introduced me to the paper above pointed out, "The selection of programming language on a project does not come only to the energy efficiency, there are many other factors that should be taken into account, such as experience of the team using the programming language, existing ecosystem of infrastructure and tool, customers' preferences, development time, etc."

He continues with more practical advice when choosing a language for energy efficiency. "It might not be practical to write each piece of software using C, but it might make sense to limit the usage of outliers, as the majority of common and powerful programming languages have an energy efficiency factor up to 5 when compared to C."

There are further criticisms and solutions of the original "Energy Efficiency across Programming Languages" paper in the "It's Not Easy Being Green: On the Energy Efficiency of Programming Languages" paper from the University of Massachusetts. It has a handful of criticisms, most of which are reasonable and Maxim and I mentioned above. It was also written in 2024, so far more recent than the original paper. This is one of the main issues I found with existing research on the topic. The materials are generally created to coincide with a thesis and then not maintained beyond that.

1. Different programming languages are optimized for different use cases and have multiple language variants. Rust and Go, for example, have a single, widely used implementation. Other languages, such as Ruby and Java, have many different implementations, and the original report didn't factor these into benchmarks.

2. The benchmarks used don't necessarily take advantage of the programming languages' best practices or ways of working.

3. There are unaccounted anomalies in the resulting data, like some of those I noted above, such as TypeScript, and the difference between C++ and C.

4. They may not factor in optimization details such as just-in-time (JIT) compilers, or languages that run faster after an initial warm-up period, etc. For example, the paper shows a five times energy saving when using LuaJIT compared to Lua.

These criticisms aside, the writers follow a similar setup, but limit themselves to 11 languages across 13 implementations: C, C#, C++, Go, Java, JavaScript, Lua (including LuaJIT), PHP, Python (including CPython and PyPy), Rust, and TypeScript. These are 11 of the top 12 most popular general programming languages in the 2024 StackOverflow survey. They attempted to factor in CPU core usage more into the benchmark, as well as address other concerns raised in the above criticisms (See Figure 5-3).

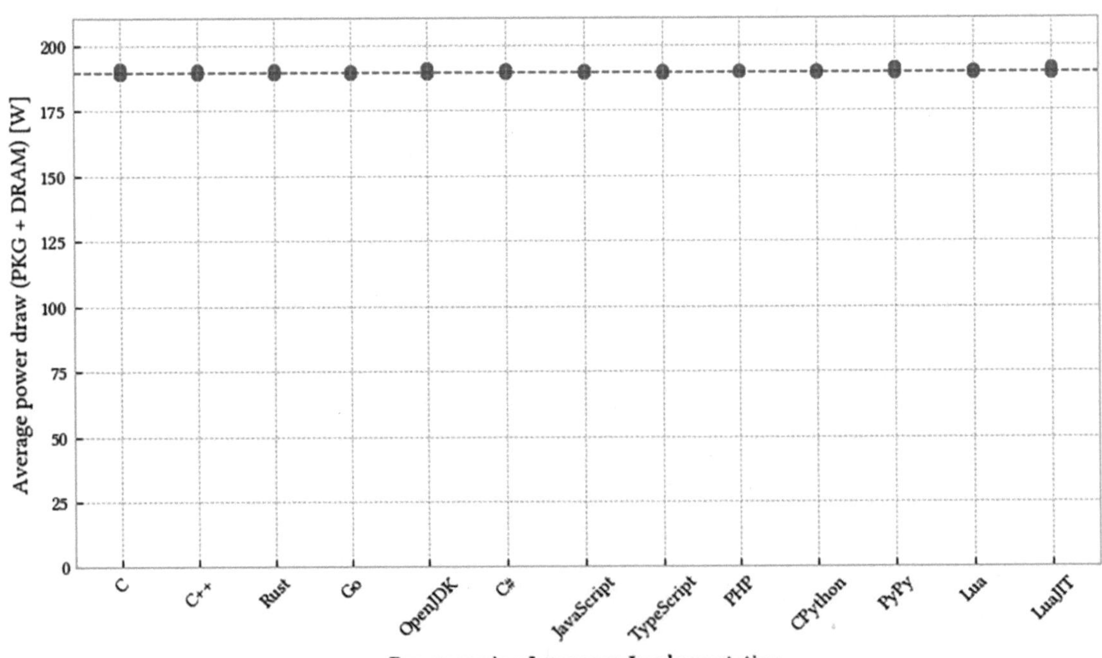

Figure 5-3. *Average power draw (package (PKG) + DRAM)*

arXiv:2410.05460 [cs.PL] (or arXiv:2410.05460v3 [cs.PL] for this version)

`https://doi.org/10.48550/arXiv.2410.05460`

Which benchmark do you believe, if any? It should be clear by now that "it depends" is the answer (as it always is) to which programming language is best for energy efficiency. And much the same applies to writing efficient code. It depends on the language, what you're trying to achieve, and other external constraints. However, here's a list of some of the more common ideas and patterns to consider and try.

Caching As Much As Possible

Using caches to reduce the amount of data transfer isn't a new concept, and it's one that I would imagine anyone working on any reasonably high-traffic application or service already uses. But as seen in chapter 4, data transfer can also be one of the most energy-intensive tasks in typical application infrastructure. While caches add their own energy overhead, they typically reduce overall energy overhead by reducing the need for transfer when not required. You can use caches at various levels of the application stack from the browser and front end, to the back end, and all the way down to CPU caches.

Most modern programming languages support use case-appropriate caching and MojoAuth (`https://mojoauth.com/implement-caching/`) maintain a good getting started guide for most programming languages.

Energy consumption as low-level as the CPU is far more complex and not something many need to worry about, but should you ever want to, there are fascinatingly detailed reports from the Advanced Computer Architecture Laboratory, University of Southern California and the IEEE.

For all other levels, identify the most frequently accessed information and place it behind a cache with cache invalidation. This is a perfect task for time and location shifting as mentioned in Chapter 4, set the invalidation at a time that achieves the right balance of freshness and carbon shifting.

Furthermore, in an (old now) example of using caching in front of a NoSQL database, researchers at Texas State University found that using optimized queries with caches can make their power usage even more efficient. Anything up to 50%. This makes sense, as you are requesting data which is already in the cache, instead of creating it. Again, this ties to well-implemented time and location shifting to populate cache misses. The same research demonstrated that while indexing doesn't always improve performance much, it does help reduce energy consumption by 47%. The reason why isn't explained, but it could be due to less storage access.

Loops

Computers and programming languages excel at performing repetitive tasks, typically with loops. Increasing the efficiency of loops can start at a high level and get to a low level quite quickly. The higher-level recommendations create more efficient code, which can lead to more efficient energy use. From a high level, make sure you choose the right loop type for the right task and that your language supports, reducing unnecessary operations.

For example:

- **For Loops**: When you know the number of iterations beforehand.
- **While Loops**: When the number of iterations is tied to a state or condition.
- **Functional Loops such as ForEach, Map, and Filter**: For iterating over collections of arrays or objects.

Other high-level advice, which I won't go too deeply into, as I am sure you can find a lot of advice like this in most programming language tutorials.

- You should reduce the number of operations inside each loop iteration.
- Avoid nested loops as much as possible, as they can rapidly escalate complexity and inefficiency.
- Use loop flow control keywords such as break, continue, and return to exit, skip, and return from unnecessary loop iterations.
- Loop over appropriate data structures and avoid calling the database in loops.

Moving to a lower level, typically more suited to lower-level languages, such as C and C++.

- Pre-increment iterators, for example, ++i over i++, avoid creating a temporary copy of the variable.
- Counting down to zero in a loop uses fewer CPU registers than counting up.

- Use loop unrolling to reduce iterations by performing more operations in each iteration. For example, deleting more than one item at once from an array during each iteration instead of one item at a time per iteration. Fethullah Goekkus's paper on Energy Efficient Programming shows the potential power saving of loop unrolling over time.

The image below shows the results of the research. Energy Delay Product (EDP) is another measurement method that considers both energy and run-time. EDP = Energy x Run-time (See Figure 5-4).

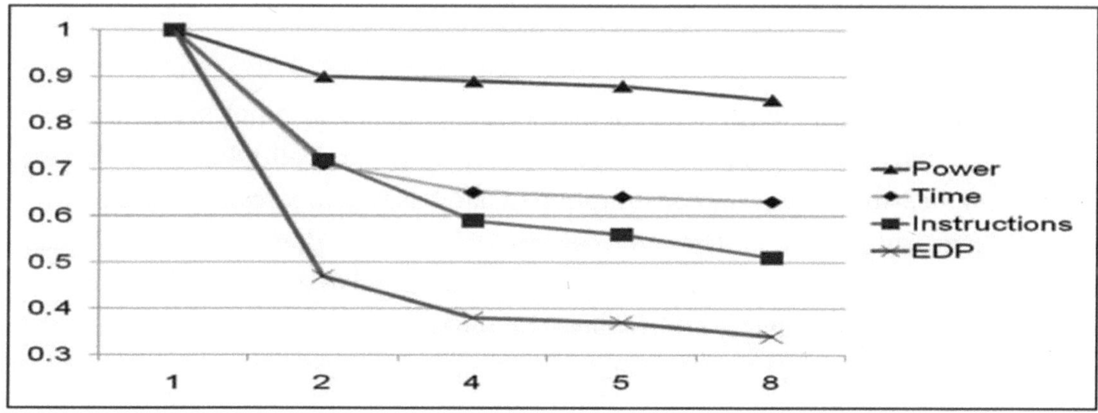

Figure 5-4. *The effect of unrolling factor on the power, execution time, and instruction count*

Energy Efficient Programming: An Overview of Problems, Solutions and Methodologies, bachelor thesis, Fethullah Goekkus

The same paper also mentions avoiding loops that constantly check if a condition is true, typically called spinning or polling loops. The energy efficiency comes from a CPU thread running the loop remaining active but not performing any useful work until the condition is true.

Databases

When I first started looking into computing sustainability, my initial experiments with Thoughtworks' Cloud Carbon Footprint tool showed that 98% of the carbon emissions were from Google's Cloud SQL. This was an unoptimized database, but it still showed how significant the impact of databases can be.

Every database engine has its own suite of advice for performance optimization, and it's been a while since I had to maintain any database backend at scale. Below is a list of resources to try, which follow a lot of the patterns you would expect and also apply in many other areas of engineering. They present resources for the top 5 database engines according to DB-Engines ranking for February 2025.

- Oracle's database performance hub
- The MySQL Optimization manual
- Microsoft's SQL Server performance tools
- PostgreSQL's performance tips
- MongoDB's performance guide

In terms of the most energy-efficient database engines, some reports rank them, such as this report from the Indian Institute of Technology Tirupati, which created DBJoules to measure the energy consumption of databases. DBJoules also has its own report from the same authors. The same caveats for benchmarking databases apply as with programming languages. Different databases are suited to different tasks and data structures. Accessing databases is also reliant on the programming language and the connector library used to access the database. For all the benchmarks, the authors used Python, but the connector libraries could bring their own inefficiencies. Still, here are their results from using the Netflix userbase and SMS spam datasets from Kaggle. It's interesting that both the most and least energy-efficient are NoSQL databases. While the time taken differences are minimal, much like with languages, fastest is not always most efficient (See Figure 5-5).

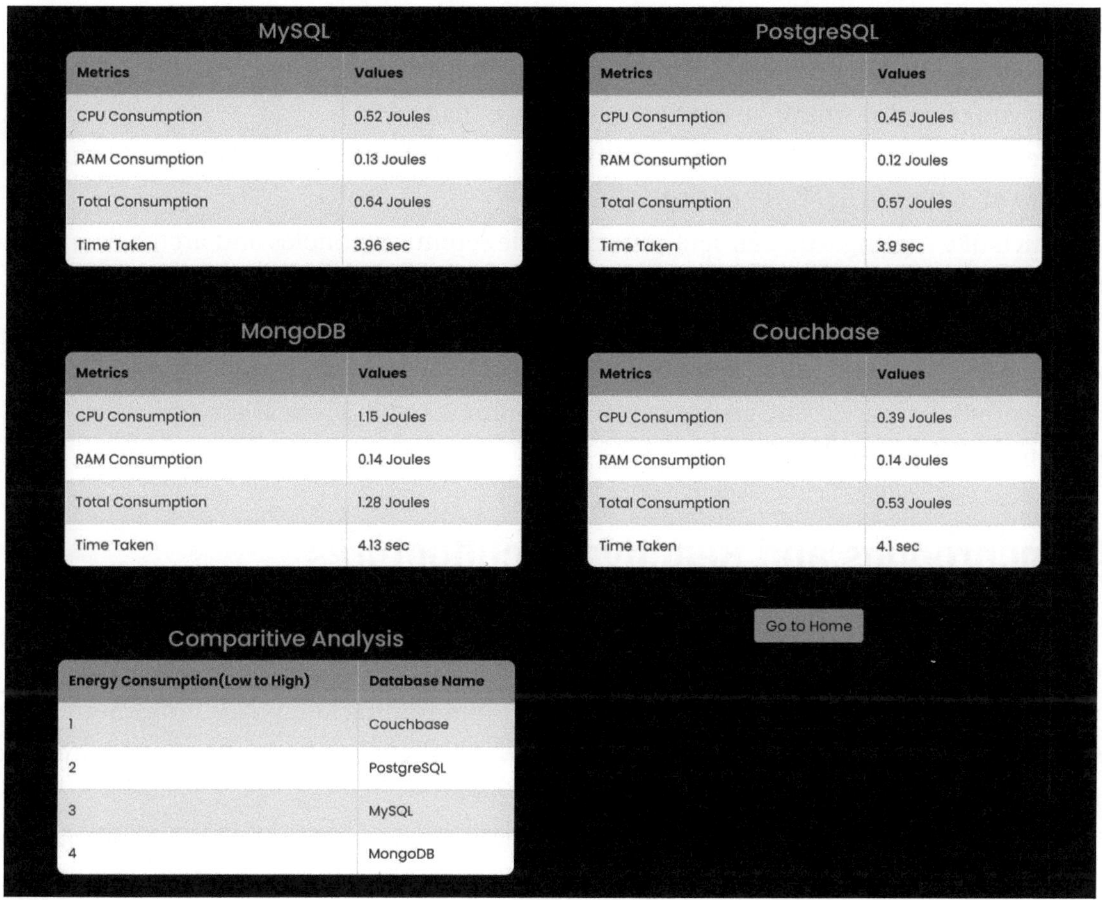

Figure 5-5. *Results for executing a select query in all 4 databases using the Netflix Userbase dataset (`https://rishalab.github.io/DBJoules/`)*

Another report from Texas State University demonstrates increasing energy efficiency of relational and NoSQL databases through query optimization. And if you want to get detailed, then this report from Xinjiang University, China, discusses energy-efficient database design.

However, the most efficient database application design is one that minimizes the use and querying of databases, particularly when storing data that is no longer needed or when querying more records or fields than necessary. Some of this efficiency comes within application logic when you query or write data, but also during application design and with how you design the schema. With relational databases, this comes from reducing the number and usage of joins, which combine rows from one or more tables, potentially leading to querying even more unnecessary fields and rows. If the database system you use allows for it, use indexes to reduce reads.

Ideally, you use right size databases to meet needs with a caching layer to reduce the number of database queries needed.

Much like logging, you can set up sustainable retention policies and archival strategies for your data. France's Regulatory Authority for Electronic Communications, Postal Affairs and Press Distribution (ARCEP) published a framework for the ecodesign of digital services, and point 7.2 makes exactly this recommendation and sums it up nicely with the phrase, "The goal is to relieve databases and physical servers of the burden of useless data."

Asynchronous and Reactive Architectures

Chapter 4 spoke about reactive and functional infrastructure, which goes some way toward reducing the sizing and idle time of servers, but application code can also be more reactive. The exact details depend on the programming language, and generally, writing code this way is more complex, but it is worth the effort in terms of application performance, user experience, and energy efficiency.

Asynchronous programming is fairly well established, meaning tasks in application code don't block threads (a sequence of commands sent to a CPU core). With the advent of multicore processors, asynchronous programming is more possible and popular. It also means that fewer machine resources sit idle, as they are doing more at the same time. The energy efficiency calculation is a little more complex as you potentially offset the increased energy consumption of multiple running tasks with the wastage of idle time. With modern CPU architectures and programming languages, asynchronous is likely the better option.

Reactive programming is most suited to areas of application code that react to changes in data, such as sensors and IoT devices, triggering relevant code in response. Event-driven programming is similar in concept, but the "event" can be broader, and not just data. In both cases, the application remains mostly idle until the trigger occurs, consuming some power, but less than the code and network traffic that periodically polls to check for changes instead. However, event-driven programming often needs additional services to manage event traffic, which adds energy consumption.

Monoliths vs. Microservice Architectures

Out of all of the possible patterns and practices I considered covering in this chapter, this was one of the comparisons I was most interested in evaluating and was probably the hardest to evaluate. Almost everything I read says that using microservices is most efficient, as it's easier to scale parts of an application as needed. But a lot of the content making that recommendation was written by cloud vendors, so it's hard to know how pragmatic and balanced that recommendation is. In principle, that advice is correct. A large monolith consumes a lot of resources, no matter what it's doing, and microservices give the opportunity to scale only what's needed.

But in practice, as you can see in Chapter 4, I wonder how many teams take this opportunity and instead just multiply the idle and over-provisioned servers. Instead of one large over-provisioned monolith, you have dozens of medium-sized over-provisioned microservices. You also have to factor in the overhead of microservices, which could be anything from a series of containers effectively running on the same server to a vast mesh of Kubernetes clusters plus all the related network and monitoring infrastructure required.

And the task of switching from a monolith to microservices is also long, hard, and expensive, requiring completely different ways of thinking about your application, it's not a quick change.

There are, of course, other architectures that combine elements of others, such as self-contained systems and micro-front-ends which attempt to bring the flexibility of microservices, but reduce the amount of infrastructure and connectivity required. In theory, these could be more energy efficient, but they are less popular patterns with less research.

Mobile Applications and Native Development Environments

Nowhere is performance and energy efficiency more important than on mobile devices. And while mobile app development overlaps with front-end development, some topics don't fit neatly into any category, and depending on the programming language, desktop or backend developers can often use the same profiling tools for energy and performance analysis. Profiling and tracing applications for various performance bottlenecks aren't new practices and are still applicable for general performance improvements, but this section specifically focuses on tools that report energy usage.

JetBrains make a series of popular developer tools based on the IntelliJ platform. None of their tools support energy profiling, but Android Studio (also based on IntelliJ) does when connecting Pixel devices (which is a fairly limited set of conditions, but still).

XCode provides Power Profiler, again, only for connected mobile devices. While there are less tools for macOS apps, Apple does provide some comprehensive documentation on energy optimization for macOS. Though it does feel fairly old as it talks about "OS X," which was changed in 2016.

Visual Studio used to have an energy profiler back in the days when Windows was still pushing hybrid mobile and desktop applications, but it's since been deprecated.

Web Assembly (WASM)

In many of the programming language benchmarks, Rust does well, and as a compiled, modern, and popular language, this isn't surprising. Web Assembly (WASM) is a newer technology that follows the dream of many projects before it, to create a write once, run anywhere programming option. Coming from the same origins at Mozilla, Rust has excellent support for WASM, but so do many other programming languages now.

Like many of the languages presented earlier in this chapter, WASM also runs in a virtual machine, but as a binary format, potentially making it as efficient as native compiled code.

Stuart Harris of Red Badger put together a proof of concept benchmark repository for comparing a Java Spring Boot microservices application to an equivalent built in Rust. He also compared the Rust version running in Kubernetes and in WASM. You don't need me to tell you that the Rust version created smaller and more efficient containers than the Java Spring Boot version. The WASM binaries were hundreds of kilobytes in size instead of hundreds of megabytes and ran in fractions of a second. On his local test setup (an M1 MacBook Pro), he was able to process over 2,300 orders to the application per second.

Granted, WASM doesn't suit every application type and to make something like Stuart's example application, you need a handful of ancillary services that need to run somewhere, but still, if you have a use case that can target the WASM runtime, it's well worth looking into and can require minimal changes to existing codebases.

Evaluating Off-the-Shelf Software

Like many of my age, my professional development journey began with PHP-based CMS like Drupal, WordPress, and Joomla back in the early 2000s. And I remember how much optimization we needed to do to make sites built with them run optimally on the limited resources at the time. While these days, those CMS pale in comparison to many modern applications, the nature of providing software that most people with a modicum of knowledge and time can install and use means that they aren't always running in the most optimal state. Wordpress still runs over 40% of sites on the web, although it's not clear if that means the hosted or open source version. If Wordpress runs inefficiently, a lot of the web is also running inefficiently. Many of the general principles in other chapters also apply, but naturally, there are efforts the Wordpress core team and community can also take to improve the performance out of the box.

Sadly, in a slew of questionable decisions in the past year or so, the Wordpress sustainability team (for the commercial hosted version) has been disbanded. The sustainability team for the community project continues, and among other activities, is creating a more "official" fork of a carbon footprint plugin for WordPress sites.

While none have the presence of WordPress, many of the other CMS projects and products have sustainability statements and efforts, including

- Drupal
- Wagtail
- Umbraco

These are all great resources for sustainable software development in their own right.

And these are just a handful of the thousands of off-the-shelf software products people use on an hourly basis. All of the above are a mix of open source, in which case you can manage and track their impact yourself, and commercial offerings, where tracking depends on the vendor. Many of their impacts are counted in the general overall impact of data centers, but as they're not "your" services, it's too easy to ignore them.

As Arwel Owen mentioned in Chapter 4.

> "90% of the world's largest companies run SAP, and 85% of carbon emissions come from (the business of) SAP customers."

Here are a couple more, specifically frequently used in the backends of application stacks, and their energy impact, if I could find them:

- **Salesforce**, market cap of $270B: I feel like they used to be one of the better SaaS companies with regards to sustainability. They still issue a sustainability report as part of their general yearly report. But there are also reports, like many other companies, of rolling some of these back. Salesforce reports emissions and their 2025 financial year emissions for data centers were roughly 19% of 2.2Bkg CO2e or 418M kg CO_2e. That's roughly equal to 87,109 homes' electricity use for one year.
- **Shopify**, market cap of $80B: Most recent sustainability (they call it "climate") report was issued in 2024, and a lot of their messaging is around their carbon offsets, funds, and sustainable product shipping service. Shopify doesn't report its carbon emissions.
- **Snowflake**, market cap of $50B: No real information.
- **Datadog**, market cap of $40B: Started publishing emissions data in 2023, but there hasn't been one since. In 2023, they reported 30.1M Kg of CO_2e, equivalent to the annual electricity use of 6,285 homes.

You could make some estimates for the others based on their market cap. If a company reports they have bought offsets or green energy, it's also worth factoring in when you compare services and providers.

My point is not that you should avoid using these services or anything like them, as often using their services is more efficient than building and running your own from a financial and environmental perspective. My point is that if you're serious about tracking your own carbon footprint, you need to factor in the third-party services you use and also follow as many of their sustainability and performance best practices as possible.

Tools to help you measure code impact during development

If nothing else is clear from this chapter, it's that as you make changes to application code that you hope will impact energy use, you need to measure that impact. Some of the tools listed in this section are the same as those listed in Chapter 4, but in a different context, while others are new.

Perun

`https://perun.readthedocs.io`

Perun calculates the energy consumption of Python scripts by sampling usage statistics from Intel, Nvidia, or AMD hardware components. It can handle Message Passing Interface (MPI) applications, and gather data from hundreds of nodes, and accumulate it efficiently. You install perun as a package and use it as a command-line tool or as a function decorator in Python scripts.

For example, to monitor an entire script, use

```
perun monitor app.py
```

Or to monitor individual Python methods, use

```
@perun.perun(data_out="results", format="json")
def main():
```

Tracarbon

https://github.com/fvaleye/tracarbon

Also covered in Chapter 4, tracks device energy consumption metrics across macOS, Linux, AWS, and containers when running on Linux. It uses some of the sources covered in this book (ElectricityMaps, the EEA, and others) to translate those metrics into carbon impact. You can also use it in Python code, to track the impact of certain functions or lines of code, connecting to the running instance of the CLI tool in Python code, to track the impact of certain functions or lines of code, connecting to the running instance of the CLI tool.

For example:

```
from tracarbon import TracarbonBuilder, TracarbonConfiguration

configuration = TracarbonConfiguration() # Your configuration
tracarbon = TracarbonBuilder(configuration=configuration).build()
tracarbon.start()
# Your code
tracarbon.stop()

with tracarbon:
    # Your code

report = tracarbon.report() # Get the report
```

Energy Monitoring Tool (EMT)

`https://github.com/FairCompute/energy-monitoring-tool`

Another option for Linux hardware running Intel or AMD processors with RAPL (see Chapter 4) support is primarily designed for monitoring the energy consumption of Python code, with plans to implement support for a command line option in the future. As it also supports monitoring NVIDIA GPUs, it's a great candidate for those building machine learning applications in Python.

CodeCarbon

`https://codecarbon.io`

Mixing carbon intensity awareness with measurement, if you use Python, you can use the library to measure the carbon impact of sections of code based on where they run.

grid-intensity-go

`https://github.com/thegreenwebfoundation/grid-intensity-go`

If writing Go code, you can use the library to fetch carbon intensity data of grid locations. This doesn't help you measure the impact of code decisions, but as many infrastructure tools (e.g., Kubernetes) are written in Go, it makes sense.

Carbon Aware SDK

`https://carbon-aware-sdk.greensoftware.foundation`

Similarly, if you code in C#, you can use the Carbon Aware SDK to fetch carbon intensity data of grid locations.

Carbon Aware Computing

`https://github.com/bluehands/Carbon-Aware-Computing`

For .NET developers, the Carbon Aware Computing library leverages a series of other underlying libraries (Including the Carbon Aware SDK) to allow you to shift application workloads around based on the renewable energy composition of the power grid.

OpenTelemetry Java Agent Extension

https://github.com/RETIT/opentelemetry-javaagent-extension

For Java developers already (or wanting to) use OpenTelemetry traces and metrics, then this extension adds the ability to calculate the carbon emissions of individual calls in an application. It follows the same methodology as Thoughtwork's Cloud Carbon Footprint (CCF) tool featured in Chapter 4. For anyone looking to keep data in a cohesive OpenTelemetry format, this is compelling. Hopefully someone creates versions for other languages.

JoularJX

https://github.com/joular/joularjx

For Java programmers targeting Intel processors, this cross platform (if you're still running intel macs) agent displays power consumption of runtime methods running on bare metal or in virtual machines.

PyJoules

https://pypi.org/project/pyJoules/

Another Python option, but not updated for a while, it's simpler than CodeCarbon and only measures the energy impact of code sections.

Oaklean

https://www.oaklean.io

For JavaScript and TypeScript developers; has a suite of tools for measuring the energy consumption of lines of code. The Oaklean suite of tools includes a VSCode extension that can show energy impact inline and the ability to run measurements during tests, both of which are compelling for during development. Oaklean uses the host operating system's default energy profiler to produce the metrics, but it's not clear how the project then calculates energy impact based on those default energy profilers to produce the metrics.

Coppers

https://github.com/ThijsRay/coppers

For any Rust programmers compiling for Intel, Coppers takes a slightly different approach to some of the other tools in this section, as it's designed to run at a test stage. You then use the results of the tests to track and visualize the energy consumption of an application between builds, seeing if there has been any change.

Creedengo

https://github.com/green-code-initiative/creedengo-rules-specifications

Recently rebranded from ecoCode and in the early stages of development, Creedengo uses SonarQube to perform static code analysis, and based on series of rules highlights code structures likely to be energy inefficient. It uses a plugin architecture, which means it can support Java, JavaScript, Python, PHP, C#, Android, and iOS and output all results to a common dashboard. Due to the recent changes, the project is a little confusing to navigate and documentation is mixed between French and English, but in theory it's a promising idea and approach.

Summary

If there's one thing to take away from this chapter, it's that designing, optimizing, and monitoring backend code is a big and complex topic. This chapter looked at some ideas and principles that can affect code efficiency. Each of them is an entire chapter or book in itself, but I hope they provided starting points for further thought, research, and experimentation.

Even if it couldn't provide directly actionable changes relevant to your exact use case, the code monitoring tools will help you assess the energy and sustainability impacts of changes you make to code. As with many practices that aim to improve code, metrics, and the ability to prove (or disprove) an assumption are key to making effective changes.

CHAPTER 6

Designing Sustainable Experiences

Ines Akrap[1]
[1]Munich, Germany; inesakrap.com

These days, I do most of my shopping online. During one of my recent browsing sessions, I came across a webshop for a clothing brand I hadn't heard of before. The moment I opened their site, I felt seriously overwhelmed by everything flashing in my face. I focused for a few seconds and realized that not only the main hero element, but every single teaser in the viewport was switching its background between an image and a full block of color. Not in sync, in case you were wondering. I closed the site almost immediately and continued browsing for clothes, a big question lingering in my mind. Why would someone do that?

That question stayed with me for hours. Eventually, I went back to the page, not to buy anything, but to understand what was going on. It didn't take long to notice the link to their sustainability statement. As someone who increasingly prefers sustainable slow fashion, I realized that this brand actually excels in that area. Under different circumstances, they could have been a perfect fit for me. But the flashing design had already pushed me away. So I kept wondering. Why did the design team make these choices? What were they trying to achieve?

The Importance of Designers

In Chapter 3, which focuses on the ideation of sustainable websites and web applications, we discussed the importance of stakeholders and the impact of very early-stage decisions, as well as the consequences of every new feature added along the way. It is worth repeating that web sustainability is a highly horizontal topic. It requires involvement from every role in the process.

C. Chinchilla and I. Akrap, *Building the Sustainable Web*, https://doi.org/10.1007/979-8-8688-2521-7_6

Product owners can decide what gets built and what does not, and they can push products in a particular direction. Designers, however, are in a unique position. They shape both the visual language of a product and the way people navigate, understand, and interact with it. A well-designed website or web application can increase engagement, retention, and conversion, often leading to better commercial outcomes. But design decisions also influence inclusivity, efficiency, attention, and trust. Those choices shape whether a product feels respectful, usable, and sustainable over time.

It is easy in any role to say, “I am just following instructions.” But every role also has the ability to question, to advocate, and to educate. Designers are no exception. With the decisions they make every day, often in small and seemingly harmless ways, they define what users see, what they are encouraged to do, and what gets loaded, animated, or ignored. These decisions matter, and their impact should not be underestimated or dismissed.

Sustainable UX Design

Traditionally, user experience (UX) design has focused on fulfilling the needs of the end user while aligning with business objectives. Adding the word sustainable in front of it slightly shifts that perspective.

To consider our UX design sustainable, we need to move beyond the needs of a single target user and expand our scope to include everyone around them. That means being aware of the impact of our decisions and making deliberate choices, not only about usability and conversion but about what our designs demand from people, systems, and the environment. This requires doing one of the hardest things in any field: finding balance. It may sound intimidating to introduce yet another set of considerations into an already complex process. However, it is often a constraint that drives creativity and innovation.

Adding Sustainability to the Principles of UX Design

If sustainable UX is about expanding our perspective, the next question is how that perspective fits into the principles designers already use every day. Good user experience design rests on core principles that make websites and applications intuitive, inclusive, and grounded in real user needs. When we introduce sustainability into the picture, those foundations don’t disappear. They expand.

It's no longer only about helping users complete tasks efficiently. It's also about understanding the wider consequences of our design decisions: how they affect people beyond the primary user, how they shape behavior over time, and how much they demand from devices, infrastructure, and the environment.

In the following sections, we'll look at familiar UX principles through this sustainability lens. To keep the discussion practical, each principle will be applied to a simple example: a website launched by a small city to help residents discover local cultural events.

Understanding Users

To design something truly useful, we begin by learning how people actually behave: what they need, what they prefer, and how they interact with similar products in their everyday lives. This often means observing real usage, listening to their frustrations, and asking thoughtful questions through interviews, surveys, or co-creation sessions. We then synthesize that information into personas or journey maps to guide our design decisions and ensure the product fits smoothly into the real-world context it's meant to serve.

Sustainability lens:

A sustainable approach expands this understanding beyond the immediate user to consider the broader contexts and long-term impacts of their interactions. We can ask questions such as

- How does the product affect users' well-being over time?
- Could it inadvertently harm users' mental health or social connections?
- What environmental impact do the behaviors encouraged by this design create?
- Are there ripple effects on families, communities, or ecosystems?

This also means including people who are often left out of traditional research, such as those with limited Internet access, older devices, or temporary disabilities, and taking their constraints seriously in the design process.

Example: While designing a local event finder website, research revealed that many older residents accessed the Internet through public library computers running outdated browsers. Others, including recent immigrants, faced language barriers. Taking this into account, the team created a lightweight version of the site optimized for older hardware, added multilingual support, and offered a simplified event list view that avoided loading heavy maps by default. The result was a more inclusive experience that also reduced energy use and helped extend the lifespan of existing devices.

Usability

Usability is about ensuring that people can interact with a product easily, efficiently, and without unnecessary friction. A well-designed interface guides users toward their goals intuitively, reducing confusion, errors, and the time it takes to complete tasks. This means lowering cognitive load through clear language, logical layouts, consistent patterns, and timely feedback. When usability is done well, users feel in control and confident, even on their first visit.

Sustainability lens:

Usability is not only about user effort; it also has a direct impact on resource use. Confusing interfaces lead to repeated actions, unnecessary page loads, and longer sessions than intended. Designing interactions that reduce clicks, trim page weight, and avoid redundant content loading results in fewer server requests, shorter load times, and lower energy use. This is especially important for people on limited data plans or older devices, and it contributes to a lower environmental footprint overall.

Example: On the event site, the team reduced the number of steps needed to discover relevant events. Decorative animations and heavy widgets were removed, significantly lowering page weight and improving performance. Users reached what they were looking for faster, while the site transferred less data and consumed less energy with every visit.

Accessibility

Accessibility in user experience design means creating products and services that can be used by people with a wide range of physical, sensory, and cognitive abilities. This includes compatibility with assistive technologies like screen readers, full keyboard navigation, meaningful alternative text for images, and clear, inclusive language. It also means avoiding patterns that can cause harm, such as flashing elements that may trigger seizures, and ensuring that content remains understandable and operable in different contexts. At its core, accessibility is about equitable access: giving every user the ability to engage independently and with confidence.

Sustainability lens:

Accessibility is a fundamental part of ethical and social sustainability. When products are designed to work across abilities, devices, and environments, fewer people are excluded by default. Offering low-bandwidth or offline modes, supporting dark mode to reduce eye strain and battery use, and ensuring layouts function well on older hardware all help extend the usable life of devices. These choices reduce forced upgrades, lower energy demand, and support more inclusive access to digital services.

Example: The local events website was designed with accessibility as a baseline. It fully supported screen readers and keyboard navigation, used clearly labeled controls and descriptive alt text, and allowed users to adjust font sizes and contrast. By avoiding heavy graphics and unnecessary visual effects, the site remained usable on older devices and slower connections, supporting both social inclusion and lower resource use over time.

Navigation and Consistency

Good navigation helps users understand where they are, where they can go, and how to get there efficiently. Clear menus, logical page structures, and intuitive pathways reduce the chance of getting lost or making mistakes. Consistency reinforces this by ensuring that similar elements behave the same way throughout a product, such as buttons appearing in predictable locations or using the same language across screens. Together, these principles lower the learning curve, build trust, and help people complete tasks without confusion or hesitation.

Sustainability lens:

Consistent navigation patterns reduce the need for one-off design solutions, which makes digital products easier to maintain and evolve over time. Reusing layout structures and interface components limits duplication in both design and development, lowering the ongoing cost of changes and updates. A well-structured information architecture also supports efficient caching, faster page loads, and fewer unnecessary backend computations. Over the lifetime of a product, these small efficiencies add up, reducing resource use and environmental impact.

Example: On the local events website, the team used a modular design system with reusable components like event cards, category filters, and date selectors. These patterns were applied consistently across pages, reducing the need for custom development and simplifying future updates. The site's structure followed a clear hierarchy that supported effective caching and avoided unnecessary dynamic content loading. This not only helped users find events quickly but also minimized backend processing and energy use, making the platform more efficient to run and maintain over time.

Feedback

Feedback keeps users informed about the results of their actions. Whether it's a button changing state, a message confirming a submission, or a loading indicator, good feedback builds confidence, reduces uncertainty, and helps users stay oriented. It reassures people that the system is responsive and that their input has been received, which in turn reduces frustration and hesitation.

Sustainability lens:

Not all feedback is equal from a sustainability perspective. Feedback mechanisms that trigger unnecessary network requests, run continuous polling, or animate purely for aesthetic reasons all consume energy on both the server and the device. The most sustainable feedback is also the most purposeful: it fires only when it genuinely informs the user, uses the lightest mechanism available, and avoids creating work the system doesn't need to do.

Example: On the local events website, filter changes triggered instant updates without reloading the page, giving users clear visual confirmation that their input was registered. Forms included inline validation that flagged issues before submission, helping users avoid errors early. These feedback mechanisms reduced frustration and avoided unnecessary page loads, and with that saved bandwidth, improving performance and lowering the platform's overall energy use.

Error prevention

Preventing errors is more effective than helping users recover from them. Good UX anticipates where mistakes might happen, such as entering invalid data or selecting the wrong option, and designs to guide users gently toward success. This includes things like input constraints, clear instructions, smart defaults, and confirmation steps.

Sustainability lens:

Avoiding errors limits repeated actions, corrections, and unnecessary backend processing, all of which consume time, energy, and computational resources. It can also reduce the need for customer support or manual intervention later on. By designing interfaces that help users get things right the first time, we create smoother experiences with less waste, both human and technical.

Example: On the local events website, the event submission form used dropdowns, calendars, and smart defaults instead of open-ended input fields. Required fields were clearly marked, and submissions were blocked until issues were resolved. These design choices helped local organizers submit accurate listings on the first attempt, reducing follow-up edits, support requests, and system-side processing, saving both effort and energy.

These six core UX principles are likely familiar to most designers. When viewed through a sustainability lens, however, they take on new depth. Grounded in foundational frameworks such as Nielsen's usability heuristics and Norman's design principles, this perspective shows how thoughtful user experience design can reduce environmental impact while supporting long-term resilience.

In the next section, we'll move even earlier in the process and look at how to apply this thinking from the very beginning, embedding sustainability considerations directly into early ideation.

Considering Sustainability in Early Ideation

The best time to think about sustainability is before anything has been designed or built. Early ideation isn't just about brainstorming features or sketching interfaces; it's about defining what kind of impact we want the product to have on users, systems, and the world around them. At this stage, the decisions made are far-reaching: they shape the scope of the product, its technical foundation, its design constraints, and its eventual environmental footprint.

In Chapter 3, we looked at how sustainability principles can guide product thinking from the outset, such as questioning whether a product should exist at all, or whether its goals could be met through simpler, less resource-intensive means. We are continuing our journey with that same mindset. In the ideation phase, designers have an opportunity to ask foundational questions that align functionality with ethics, inclusion, and environmental responsibility.

One powerful approach is establishing a carbon budget early in the design process. Just as teams set performance budgets for page load times or accessibility budgets for compliance, carbon budgets provide a concrete framework for making sustainable design decisions. This might mean setting targets for total page weight, limiting the number of third-party scripts, or defining maximum energy consumption per user session. With clear carbon constraints established up front, design decisions become easier to evaluate and defend.

Some helpful prompts at this stage might include:

- What would be a bare-bones version of this product, offering just the necessary?
- Can this experience be simplified or reduced?
- What devices, bandwidth levels, and abilities should we assume or avoid assuming?
- Will this feature encourage overuse, distraction, or unnecessary interaction?
- Can this experience be designed with a strong baseline, and enhanced progressively as user conditions allow?
- What user behaviors will this design promote, and are they sustainable?

By embedding these questions into workshops, sketching sessions, or sprint planning, we begin to shift the culture, not just of individual projects but of the design process itself. We normalize considering marginalized users, longer-term consequences, and the invisible environmental cost of each new interaction or asset. These small shifts early on can prevent much larger sustainability compromises later in the development cycle.

The sooner these conversations happen, the easier it is to act on them. And the more often they occur, the more natural and expected they become. Sustainable design begins with how we think, not just what we build, and it belongs at the core of every design conversation.

Look Both Ways: Expanding the UX Perspective

When designing digital products, UI and UX teams often focus on target users and stakeholders. But time and resource limits can lead to generic personas and skipped user interviews. Sometimes, “make it fun” or “make it sexy” become the main design “requirement.”

If we’re lucky, there’s time for proper user research, which traditionally focuses on a specific end user and their needs. How can we solve their problems? How can we make their life easier or more enjoyable?

The challenge is that this often means designing for a narrow, simplified version of a user. Let's say this middle-class, employed woman in her 30s is a persona for a high-street fashion brand. We assume she'd love a personalized banner on the homepage, showing the newest seasonal trends. But do we consider that she most likely works in an office and spends about an hour commuting on the metro every day? What better to do on the metro than browse her favorite brand's catalog? But what if the page doesn't load properly? She sees the logo and header, waits a bit, and then gives up, puts on a podcast, and moves on. Maybe she's lost as a user, possibly for good if this happens daily. **So, does it make sense to design that personalized banner if she never gets to see it?**

Or what if this woman is a new mom, browsing during late-night feeds? Maybe she'd appreciate a dark mode or the ability to navigate one-handed. But if we never consider those situations, we miss key user needs. Understanding users' real-life contexts and designing to include everyone isn't just ethical and good practice. It's smart business.

Recent accessibility laws have helped bring more attention and resources to designing for all users, including those in low-bandwidth areas, using old devices, or with different language needs. Designing with these realities early on reduces costly redesigns later.

But even when we consider all users, there's a bigger question: who else might be affected by our design? Sometimes the side effects aren't apparent to both users and product teams. We need to uncover and make those potential harms visible.

Use at Your Own Risk

The year is 2016. As you walk down the street, you notice more people looking at their smartphones than usual, unless you are one of them. In that case, you are also trying to find the next stop, catch your next Pokémon, or get an egg to hatch by walking around the block for hours. Pokémon Go was one of the first widely popular augmented reality games, which quickly turned out to be a dangerous activity. What was supposed to be fun and even fitness-simulating (encouraging users to walk more) ended up flooding news headlines with many accidents that users got into while playing the game. A study found that in the first five months of its release, Pokémon Go was estimated to be responsible for approximately 145,000 car accidents. Of those car accidents, approximately 29,000 people were injured, and 250 people were killed.

On top of that, there are many other cases of injuries and deaths of game players caused primarily by a lack of awareness of their surroundings while being immersed in the game (from attackers and robbers choosing players as targets due to their distraction to several fatal falls onto railway tracks, from cliffs, etc.). So, a digital product created for entertainment that was doing its primary job wonderfully turned out to have some quite severe side effects. It was causing apparent physical harm to its users. And yet, nothing much changed. Figure 6-1 shows some of the warning screens added to the interface, which, I am pretty sure, most users simply ignored.

Figure 6-1. *Pokémon Go warning screens*

Despite lawsuits and concerns about safety, Niantic, the creators of Pokémon Go, were never held legally responsible for these incidents. Courts recognized the risks but placed the responsibility on the players themselves. Sure, users should be responsible for how they use a product. But as designers, shouldn't we try to minimize foreseeable harm? You may be wondering how we can possibly predict every way people might misuse what we build? The truth is, digital product teams often come from similar backgrounds and perspectives, and testing can be an afterthought. One way forward is diversifying our teams by bringing in varied experiences to spot potential problems early and then doing what we can: test, test, test, and test again, with a wide range of users.

Using at Others' Risk

Let's take that a step further. We design a product to do its purpose amazingly. It solves our target user-specific problem in such a nice, convenient way that they never considered possible. However, it turns out it also has some negative side effects. Sometimes, our users are directly affected, which causes them to become aware of the issue and decide on their future use of the product. However, often there is a third party that neither the end user nor the product team is aware of. It is time for this part to change, and we should start thinking about who or what else is being put at risk by our product and/or service.

In his talks about Sustainable UX Design, Torsten Jonas, Founder of the SUX Network, says:

> *Too often it is the convenience to the user that overrules the well-being of the other actors in the system. Someone else pays the price for the good UX for the user.*

You may already be thinking of the non-human personas we mentioned in Chapter 3, at least I hope you are, and that is a great start. The other actors in the system can be anyone, not just non-human personas. It can often be people closest to the user, like their family and friends, who experience side effects. These can range from the user stopping to engage and interact with them due to their constant presence in the digital world to the user spending family budget on unnecessary shopping sprees. It can also be a delivery person who, due to doorstep delivery options, now has to work much longer hours, affecting their well-being and family relationships. Then, we can delve into the ecosystem, the planet, the woods, the lakes, and everyone who considers them home. **None of them receives the warning, nor the convenience or enjoyment of the product or service. They don't have the choice to close or delete; they often just have to suffer the side effects. We see a very common pattern: many suffer for the enjoyment and convenience of a few**. Luckily, there is a way to change that.

Rethinking User Research

User research has always been about understanding who you're designing for. But when you apply a sustainability lens, the focus expands from user needs alone to the broader impacts of the digital experiences we create. Instead of simply asking what our users want, we begin to question what constraints they live with, what ripple effects our design might have, and how we can meet needs without wasting resources or creating unnecessary harm.

We can start with ethical, privacy-respecting data collection: anonymous analytics, voluntary feedback, and inclusive surveys. These tools help avoid generalizations that often lead to overbuilt features and bloated interfaces. Fewer unnecessary features mean reduced development overhead, less server load, and lower emissions.

Take, for example, a user research finding: many of your users rely on older smartphones or use your product on slow or limited mobile connections. That insight can drive decisions like simplifying the interface, avoiding heavy JavaScript, or providing low-bandwidth modes, making the product not only faster and more accessible but also more sustainable. When a product continues to work well on older devices, users don't need to upgrade hardware as frequently, reducing e-waste.

This line of thinking should also extend beyond the end user. Does the delivery traffic generated by your service regularly impact neighbors? Do data-heavy features put unnecessary strain on global infrastructure? By identifying these hidden or indirect consequences early, your team can address them before they become costly problems or ethical liabilities.

Involving a broader set of stakeholders, such as users with disabilities, those in underserved regions, and those who may be unintentionally affected by the product, gives you a clearer picture of the real-world impact. Even adding one or two diverse voices in user testing can highlight constraints your core team may never have considered.

Sustainability-minded research also pushes you to ask questions such as

- Are my users relying on limited bandwidth or old devices?
- Do they interact with my service in places or times where energy is scarce or expensive?
- Are there ways to meet their needs using less data, fewer screens, or simpler flows?
- Who else might this design affect (directly or indirectly)?

The aim isn't perfection, it's progress. By embedding care, clarity, and accountability into our research, we can make design decisions that support real people in real conditions, while reducing harm wherever we can.

Designing for User Preferences

Paul Coldren, an IT infrastructure professional, spent approximately 14.5 months deployed to Antarctica in 2022–2023 as part of the US Antarctic Program. During that time, he shared personal observations about logistics, infrastructure, and daily life on the ice on his blog *brr.fyi*. One of my all-time favorite articles comes from his blog, and it is called "Engineering for Slow Internet." It reflects Paul's frustration as a user of multiple apps on an extremely slow, satellite-based Internet Connection. It may sound extreme (Antarctic), but is it really? Do we think that everyone always has access to high-end devices and a high-speed network? In this article, Paul comments:

> *Does this webapp really need to be 20 MB? What all is being loaded that could be deferred until it is needed, or included in an "optional" add-on bundle? Is there a possibility of a "lite" version, for bandwidth-constrained users?*

Here, he is (desperately) asking for something that should be a default expectation for user experience: an alternative (lightweight) version of the product. Adapting experience to respect users' conditions, preferences, and choices should be a cornerstone of a well-designed, sustainable app. So, what choice can we give them?

Respecting Users' Conditions

We can start by acknowledging that users arrive under very different conditions. Device type, connection quality, available memory, and processing power all affect how a website or application is experienced. During product design, it is not necessary to understand every technical detail, but it is important to avoid assuming fast networks, new devices, or unlimited resources by default.

There is also a growing conversation around environmental conditions, such as the carbon intensity of electricity powering a user's device. Today, this data is still imperfect and often very broad. From a design standpoint, the important point is not precision, but direction. We can already design interfaces that can adapt. Experiences that make heavier features optional, that delay non-essential loading, or that allow users to choose a lighter mode are better prepared for a future where environmental signals become more reliable and more widely used.

Respecting users' conditions is ultimately about humility. We accept that we do not control the context in which our products are used. We design for difference, not for the ideal case. And when we do that well, we create experiences that are not only more inclusive and resilient but also more sustainable over time.

Giving Users a Choice

Very few websites or web apps I use take my preferences into account, let alone actively offer me choices. In the same way we can account for users' current conditions, we can also respect their stated preferences, such as tracking settings, data-saving modes, reduced motion, or preferred color schemes. Respecting these signals should be standard practice. Ignoring them can be harmful for users and, in some cases, illegal.

Tracking users can often be illegal or tightly regulated. Since tracking strategies are usually planned and managed by marketing teams, we explore this topic in more detail in Chapter 8. From a design perspective, other preferences are just as important. Many animations, especially when misused, can trigger symptoms ranging from vertigo, migraines, and anxiety to epilepsy. Respecting requests for reduced motion is therefore essential, not optional.

Color schemes may seem less critical, but they still shape how usable and comfortable a product feels. Poor contrast, forced light modes, or designs that fail in very dark or very bright environments can frustrate users, especially those with limited color perception or situational constraints. Frustration often leads to abandonment.

So how do we ensure that user conditions and preferences are respected across all contexts, from fast high-end smartphones to slow satellite connections? The answer lies in how we structure our design from the start.

Progressive Enhancement

One of the most effective ways to design with user conditions, preferences, and constraints in mind is to follow a **progressive enhancement approach**. This approach starts with a strong, accessible foundation and adds more advanced features only when the user's environment can support them. The focus is on delivering core functionality and meaningful content first, while treating animations, interactivity, and visual effects as optional layers rather than requirements.

In other words, we make sure the product works well before making it work beautifully. This naturally leads to lighter, faster, and more inclusive interfaces that adapt to a wide range of devices, connections, and abilities. It also avoids unnecessary waste by not forcing every user to download and process scripts, assets, or effects they may never benefit from.

One of my favorite ways to explain progressive enhancement is by comparing it to making a cake (illustrated in Figure 6-2). We start with the cake itself. A good sponge and a solid filling are the foundation. Then we might add a layer of icing to improve both taste and appearance. After that, we can add decorations, details, or candles if it is a birthday cake. The cake can look spectacular, but at its core it is still food. If the base cake is bad, no amount of decoration will create that moment of delight when you take the first bite. Digital products work the same way. If the core experience fails, enhancements cannot save it.

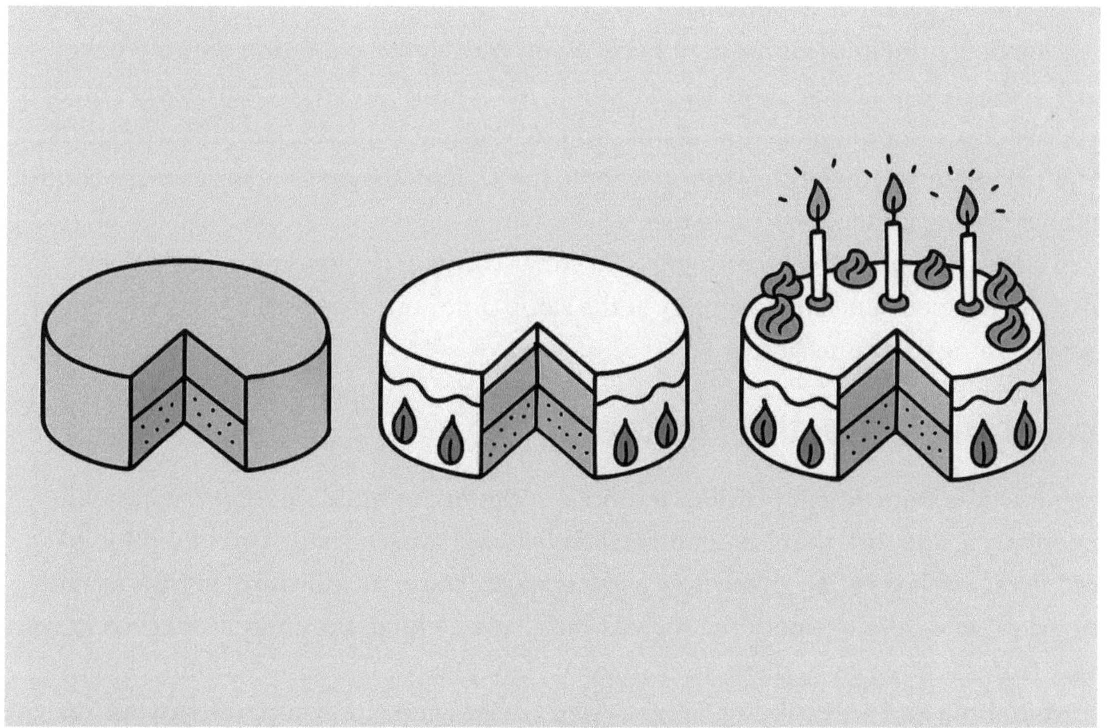

Figure 6-2. *Concept of progressive enhancement*

Progressive enhancement encourages us to think in layers and to be honest about what is essential. Let's apply this thinking to the local events website we introduced earlier.

First, we define the core functionality. In this case, it is delivering event information. Each event needs a title, location, date, and time. That is enough for the product to be useful. As the list grows, basic search and filtering become important, so they belong in this foundational layer as well. With simple styling, sufficient contrast, and support for both light and dark color schemes, this baseline experience works for everyone.

From there, enhancements can be added progressively, depending on user preferences and conditions. Event images can be lazy-loaded to enrich the listing. Filters and sorting can update dynamically without full page reloads. A map view can be introduced to visualize locations. Subtle transitions can help guide interaction without overwhelming or distracting the user. Nothing essential is hidden behind advanced features. If someone disables JavaScript, prefers reduced motion, or accesses the site from a public library computer with an older browser, the core experience still works. At the other end of the spectrum, users on fast devices and reliable connections can enjoy a richer, more interactive experience.

One final principle is important here. When we detect a condition or preference, such as data-saving mode or reduced motion, and choose to serve a lighter version of the experience, we should make that visible and offer user a choice. A simple message like "You're in data-saving mode. Do you want to load event images?" keeps users in control without forcing unnecessary data use.

That is the real strength of progressive enhancement. It allows us to design with flexibility, respect, and sustainability at the same time, and it creates a solid foundation for everything that comes next.

Optimizing Interactive Features

Progressive enhancement provides a solid foundation for building robust, adaptable experiences. But once that foundation is in place, we must also turn our attention to the interactive layers that shape how users engage. These include form inputs, motion behaviors, and interface patterns such as carousels. Though they may seem secondary, these features often carry disproportionate weight when it comes to usability, energy consumption, and accessibility. Their design choices can either support or work against our sustainability goals. Let's look at how we can design them in ways that are both user-friendly and resource conscious.

Forms

Most of us fill out a digital form almost every day. They are a critical part of many digital interactions, from signing up for a newsletter to completing a purchase or submitting content. But they can also be a source of friction, frustration, and waste when poorly designed. Sustainable form design means balancing usability, accessibility, and ethical data collection with performance and environmental impact.

We can start by minimizing form content. That is one of the simplest and most effective ways to improve both UX and sustainability. By collecting only the vital information, we can reduce users' cognitive load and shorten completion time, resulting in lower data transmission and processing demands. Less transmission and less processing can mean lower emissions.

Ethical responsibility matters, too. Requesting excessive or sensitive data when it isn't needed not only undermines trust but may also violate regulations such as GDPR. By clearly explaining why the form exists, how long it takes to complete, and what the user's data will be used for, we show transparency and respect for our users.

Every form should be accessible. That means clearly labeled, keyboard-navigable with a sensible tab order, and compatible with assistive technologies. They should perform well on a wide range of devices, including those with limited processing power or older operating systems. Inclusive form design, including proper focus handling, intuitive error messages, and input validation, not only supports accessibility but also improves completion rates and reduces frustration.

Auto-complete and autofill features can further support efficiency, especially when integrated with password managers or browser tools. These small conveniences reduce repetitive typing and help users complete forms faster. However, we should avoid implementing unnecessary auto-suggestions that may duplicate native browser behavior, increase processing load, or distract from the primary task, especially on lower-powered devices or slower connections.

The most sustainable forms are the ones users hardly notice.

Animations

The same rule can work for animations. When used well, animation can enhance digital experiences by guiding attention, indicating transitions, or providing feedback. But animations are also a double-edged sword: they can be resource-intensive, distracting, or even harmful, both to people and to the environment.

From a sustainability perspective, motion should always serve a purpose. Does it help the user understand a transition? Clarify system status? Reinforce a key message? If not, consider whether it's worth the resource and attention cost. Since animations often require extra CPU and GPU power, they can increase memory usage, slow down performance, and drain battery life. When implemented carelessly or used decoratively, animations can contribute to unnecessary energy consumption and reduced accessibility.

We already touched upon ethical and inclusive considerations and why it is crucial always to respect users' requests and preferences. Continuous motion can cause discomfort for people with vestibular disorders or concentration challenges. Flashing or rapid animations can trigger seizures in users with photosensitive epilepsy and even distract or overwhelm other users, such as that image flashing did for me. Offering controls to pause or turn off animations, and avoiding unnecessary movement altogether, ensures the experience remains accessible, comfortable, and usable for everyone.

Designing sustainably with motion includes

- Using animation only when it adds clear value
- Avoiding autoplaying or looping decorative motion
- Respecting user settings for reduced motion
- Making all animated content controllable (pause, stop, start)
- Testing how animations perform on lower-end hardware or poor connections

Subtle, well-timed animation can improve understanding and even support engagement or conversion. But overdone or unnecessary motion creates noise, slows performance, and increases energy use. In sustainable design, animation should be seen as a tool and not a decoration.

Carousels

This may be very personal, but I have been fighting a war against carousels for many years now, and I need as much backup as I can get. There are many layers to this topic. I understand they're often included for commercial reasons, such as eCommerce sites selling slide positions to brands. But here's the irony: carousels are frequently shown to hurt the very commercial goals they're meant to serve, while also damaging user experience and site performance.

My war began in 2018. I was working on an eCommerce website, cleaning up a few-years-old codebase to improve performance. One day, the product owner came to me with a request for assistance. Stakeholders have realized the site is performing much worse than the competitors' and wanted to know why. I knew straight away where the issue was. The carousel. There was a 5MB heavy carousel sitting there at the top of the page. Yes, 5MB. According to the 2024 HTTP Almanac Page Weight Chapter, an average website has around 2.5MB. **So this carousel alone was as heavy as two whole average pages.** This was not a very usual case I have seen with carousels; however, they do tend to be quite heavy. So what was so extreme in this one? I was expecting a regular issue of a not-optimized asset; however, it ended up being much worse than that. Every slide was generated by an external templating tool to include current product prices dynamically. I can understand the commercial aspect. Still, in this case every slide was around 1 MB, and all five slides (four of which weren't even visible on load) were loaded immediately as the first thing on the page. For anyone without high-speed Internet and a powerful device, the result was a blank page for an average of 30 seconds. I don't know about you, but unless I'm waiting for my bank statement or in the Ticketmaster's waiting room, I'm not sticking around for that. If there's an alternative, the business has just lost me as a customer, and I am positive most users feel the same. So what can we do about it? Is there a more sustainable alternative?

The most common alternative is a **hero image or banner**, usually with a call-to-action button. Those types of components are much more lightweight and straightforward to implement. They allow us to highlight one specific product or display one key message, reducing distractions and overwhelm. One thing to note here is that these types of components often have video as a background. We will discuss videos later in the chapter; however, in the context of this component, it is good to apply the principle of progressive enhancement and play the video only when conditions are appropriate and the user would like it.

Another common alternative is to **display slides in a grid** as shown on Figure 6-3. You can play with sizes and positioning to make them all fit in the viewport. This offers good accessibility with clear structure, easy keyboard navigation, and accessible labels, and allows users to scan through content without waiting for the slide swap.

Figure 6-3. *Example of hero grid layout*

These alternatives are just some we can use to replace a carousel. But what if business requirements mean you can't avoid it? Follow this quick checklist to make it as sustainable and user-friendly as possible:

- **Keep the Slide Count Low**: 3–4 slides are more than enough
- **Give Users Full Control**: No autoplay and clear, accessible controls
- **Make sure it is fully accessible**: Clear focus handling, accessible controls, and proper semantics for assistive technologies
- **Limit Motion and CPU/GPU Load**: Keep animations subtle, avoid flashy or rapid transitions

In sustainable UX, less really is more. The most sustainable carousel is the one you never designed.

Educating Our Users

Design choices can go a long way toward making a product more sustainable. But responsibility does not end with removing heavy components or optimizing assets. Sustainability is also shaped by how people use the products we build. Just as we design for efficiency and accessibility, we can design to support understanding, helping users make informed choices without overwhelming them or demanding extra attention.

Education in this context does not mean constant feedback or real-time dashboards. In fact, those approaches can easily backfire. Continuously updating indicators come with their own processing cost and can encourage unnecessary interaction, especially if users start exploring the interface simply to watch numbers change. From a sustainability perspective, that is rarely desirable.

Instead, impact information works best when it is contextual and tied to meaningful decisions. For example, showing the relative impact of different delivery options at checkout, or providing a lightweight comparison between alternatives when a user is already choosing between them. This kind of feedback supports decision-making without adding background noise or encouraging extra clicks.

Clarity is essential. A raw number like "20 g of CO_2" means very little to most people. Providing context, such as simple comparisons to familiar activities, helps users understand scale and consequences. At the same time, it is important to avoid misleading metaphors like "number of trees offset," which can reinforce the idea that emissions can simply be cancelled out later. The goal is reduction, not justification.

There is also a temptation to use gamification to drive sustainable behavior. This needs to be handled with care. Sustainability should not become another engagement loop. Gentle cues, occasional feedback, or positive reinforcement at key moments can be effective, but they should never push users to interact more than necessary. The aim is not to maximize time on site, but to support better choices and then let users move on.

When done thoughtfully, educating users becomes an extension of calm, respectful design. It makes sustainability visible without turning it into a spectacle, and it reinforces the broader principle that good digital experiences help people do what they came to do, efficiently and with minimal waste.

Avoiding Deceptive Patterns

Educating users about sustainable choices is only effective when those choices are genuine. Some design patterns are intentionally crafted to push people toward actions they did not intend to take. They may increase engagement metrics in the short term, but they damage trust, harm user autonomy, and create unnecessary environmental impact.

Patterns such as infinite scroll, autoplaying videos, preventing text selection, or requiring an account just to make a purchase all interfere with the user's control over their own experience. At the very least, we should avoid actively interfering with people's ability to use our products. From a sustainability perspective, many of these patterns encourage overconsumption of data and attention. Infinite scroll keeps loading new content whether the user wants it or not, increasing bandwidth usage and device processing. Autoplay forces media to load and play even for people who may never watch it. These choices consume more energy on both the user's device and the servers delivering the content. Take the decision by a popular music streaming platform to replace static album artwork with short video loops by default. This change significantly increases data usage and battery consumption, while the option to disable it is buried deep in the settings. As a result, most users consume more resources unless they actively search for a way to opt out.

It is important to acknowledge that design always nudges behavior in some way. Showing consequences, highlighting options, or ordering choices are all forms of influence. The ethical line is not whether nudging exists, but whether it is transparent, reversible, and aligned with the user's interests. In many cases, the most responsible approach is to make the lower-impact option the default, while keeping alternatives clearly available. Defaults are powerful, and when chosen carefully, they can reduce environmental impact without removing user agency.

Ethically, deceptive patterns undermine informed consent and often collect more personal data than necessary. Some are designed to make opting out of tracking deliberately difficult, leading to additional data transfers between analytics and advertising systems. Each of these transfers carries a carbon footprint and erodes user privacy. Avoiding such patterns means designing with honesty, transparency, and respect for the user's goals. Let people choose when and how they receive information. Replace infinite scroll with pagination so users request more content only when they want it. Avoid unnecessary interface restrictions that force workarounds and waste energy.

The result is a faster, cleaner, and more trustworthy experience. By removing manipulative elements and choosing responsible defaults, we reduce confusion, lower the risk of mistakes, and help users achieve their goals efficiently, benefiting both people and the planet.

Designing for Non-Visual Interactions

As we explore ways to educate users, empower them to make sustainable choices, and avoid manipulating those choices, we should also question the assumption that visual interfaces are the default or only way to interact with a product. Many people interact with digital services using non-visual methods like screen readers, voice assistants, or other audio-based tools. Some users may depend on these modes out of necessity. Others may choose them for convenience, such as asking a voice assistant for a train schedule rather than opening a web app. Either way, offering robust support for non-visual interaction not only increases usability but also contributes to digital sustainability.

Designing with this in mind means ensuring content is well-structured, labeled clearly, and navigable using semantic HTML. It means making key functionality accessible via voice and keyboard, and avoiding patterns that rely solely on visuals to communicate meaning. In other words, it's not just about access, it's about designing with awareness that not every experience begins or ends on a screen.

By reducing reliance on heavy visual elements, we lower the processing demands on devices and make products work well across more contexts, for more people, with less environmental cost. Supporting non-visual interactions is both an inclusivity win and a sustainability gain.

And when we zoom out, these considerations are not isolated. They're part of the larger flow of how a person experiences a product from start to finish, which brings us to the user journey, where all these design choices converge into a complete, real-world experience.

Sustainability in User Journeys

The user journey is where everything we've discussed so far comes together. This is where principles like usability, accessibility, feedback, and error prevention stop being theory and start shaping real-world interactions. Sustainable design in this context isn't about adding more features; it's about removing friction, excess, and waste so that users can move through a product efficiently, comfortably, and with minimal environmental cost.

A frictionless journey means reducing the number of steps, distractions, and dead ends between a user and their goal. Whether it's finding an event, signing up for a newsletter, or completing a purchase, the path should be smooth, predictable, and respectful of both the user's time and their device's resources. That means clear progress indicators, realistic expectations for how long a process will take, and no decision fatigue caused by too many unnecessary options.

Streamlining benefits everyone. Less time spent waiting, reloading, or navigating means lower device energy use, reduced data transfer, and faster, more responsive products. This is particularly important for those on older hardware, slower connections, or limited data plans, but even users with the latest devices benefit from faster, cleaner experiences.

Removing unnecessary elements is key. Modals, auto playing videos, overly complex navigation, and surprise chatbots don't just frustrate users; they also increase load time, CPU usage, and energy consumption. In sustainable UX, we respect users' attention by presenting only what is necessary and valuable at each stage of the journey, and we let users opt into extra content rather than forcing it.

Familiarity also plays a role in efficiency. Established design patterns help users instantly recognize where they are and what to do next, reducing cognitive effort and making interactions faster. Clear layouts, predictable actions, and consistent visual cues support both usability and low-energy environments.

We can even extend efficiency beyond navigation by giving users control over how and when they receive updates. Configurable notifications, for example, can replace constant page refreshes or background polling, saving bandwidth and reducing server load while creating a more respectful experience.

The culmination of these efforts is a journey that feels effortless for the user but is intentional in its design. Every click removed, every shortcut offered, every distraction avoided makes the product lighter and faster, which makes it better for the user, their device, and the planet.

We've shaped how users move through a product, but what about what they see, touch, and experience on the surface? Let's explore how we can design user interfaces that put people and planet first.

Sustainable User Interface (UI) Design

User Interface design is where sustainability becomes visible. It's where the abstract concepts of usability, accessibility, and ethics are translated into color palettes, button shapes, image sizes, and font stacks. While UX considers how things work, UI is about how they look and feel and those visual decisions can have a very real environmental cost.

The Weight of Aesthetic Decisions

Well-crafted visual design improves usability, accessibility, and user trust, but overly decorative, resource-intensive interfaces can slow down performance, shorten device lifespan, and exclude users on limited bandwidth or older hardware.

One slightly extreme situation I was in is when the design team decided to include an animated character, drying its hair on the hero element. The file with the animation in question was around 4MB. Character was cute and funny, but, as you may imagine, it was a site loading nightmare. It took me showcasing website loading videos with and without the animation, side-by-side, to showcase how bad of an idea that was for anyone who is not a power-user.

Sustainable UI design doesn't mean "ugly" or "boring." It means being intentional:

- Choosing visuals that serve a purpose, not just fill space or be cute
- Avoiding trends that degrade usability (e.g., ultra-light text, low contrast)
- Being mindful of the performance and carbon impact of design decisions
- Offering alternative or lighter versions of visuals to meet different user requirements.

Layout and Visual Hierarchy

Clear visual hierarchy helps users find what they need faster, with fewer page loads or unnecessary clicks. Sustainable layouts avoid clutter, prioritize essential content, and guide users naturally through their journey. This reduces time-on-task without sacrificing engagement, saving energy and bandwidth.

Using design systems or modular components also promotes sustainability. Reusable UI patterns not only improve consistency and accessibility, they also lower development overhead, reduce redundant code, and make future updates more efficient.

Color and Contrast

Color choice affects far more than branding, it shapes legibility, accessibility, usability, and even energy use. For example, dark mode on OLED and AMOLED screens can reduce battery drain by powering fewer pixels, which is particularly beneficial for mobile users. It's important to note that dark mode is not an energy-saving feature in itself, but a user preference that should be respected. Any energy savings depend on the display technology and how people use their devices. Supporting dark mode gives users control and enables efficiency where it is technically meaningful, without assuming or enforcing behavior. High-contrast themes improve readability, reduce eye strain, and make interfaces more usable for people with low vision or in challenging lighting conditions.

When designing with people and planet in mind, we use color intentionally. Information needs to be clear, accessible, and efficient to display, and not just visually appealing. We can achieve that by choosing palettes that work in both light and dark contexts, maintaining sufficient contrast between text and background, and avoiding combinations that exclude users with color vision deficiencies. It also means resisting unnecessary gradients, shadows, and high-saturation visuals when they don't serve a functional purpose, as these can increase file sizes and rendering effort.

Color should work for the user and the device, supporting both accessibility and performance while contributing to a lower environmental footprint.

Typography

While color sets the tone and ensures content is visible, typography carries the message. The two work together: color draws the eye, while type delivers the words. In sustainable UI design, we need to make sure that text is easy to read across devices and environments while keeping performance overhead low. When typography is chosen well, it ensures that information is accessible, efficient to render, and inclusive for all users.

Clear, well-structured type reduces cognitive strain, shortens time on task, and improves comprehension. This means prioritizing legibility, supporting assistive technologies, and avoiding unnecessary font weight that increases load time and energy use.

Legible typography starts with appropriate sizing and spacing. Use a minimum of 16px for body text to ensure readability across devices and user preferences. Ensure strong contrast between text and background and maintain clear line height and letter spacing that support comfortable reading without causing eye strain.

Accessibility considerations should guide typeface selection. Choose fonts that work well with screen readers and assistive technologies, avoiding ambiguous letterforms where "I," "l," and "1" might be confused. Design with respect for users who adjust their text size preferences, ensuring your typography hierarchy remains clear at different scales.

Font efficiency directly impacts sustainability. Limit the number of fonts and weights to reduce load times and energy consumption. Prefer system fonts when possible since they render immediately without requiring downloads. When custom fonts are necessary, subset them to include only required characters and serve them in efficient formats like WOFF2.

It's not unusual to find projects loading dozens of font files, many of which are never used. Every extra font carries a hidden cost in load time, bandwidth, and energy use. Thoughtful typography avoids that waste, while also making content easier to read and faster to deliver, saving effort for both the user and their device.

Design Systems

The same principle of doing more with less applies at a larger scale when we think about design systems.

Design systems are more than just a style guide or a pattern library; they are powerful frameworks that enable teams to build consistent, efficient, and scalable digital experiences. By formalizing reusable components and patterns across an application or website, design systems help avoid the need to reinvent the wheel, saving time, effort, and emissions.

From a UI perspective, design systems create visual consistency by standardizing components like buttons, forms, and layouts, maintaining brand coherence while reducing clutter and avoiding performance costs from redundant styling. From a UX perspective, consistent patterns make interfaces easier to learn and navigate, lowering cognitive load, reducing frustration, and improving success rates for all users, including those on assistive technologies or less powerful devices.

Sustainability benefits follow naturally:

- **Efficiency**: Reusing prebuilt, optimized components reduces code redundancy and file sizes.
- **Accessibility**: Systems with accessible components built in make inclusive design the default.
- **Reduced Development Waste**: Shared design decisions lower design and engineering effort across teams, saving time and resources over the product life cycle.

- **Environmental Responsibility at Scale**: When environmental criteria are baked into the system, they propagate across every feature that uses them.

Well-maintained design systems result in better long-term product quality, fewer inconsistencies, and a smoother user experience. They can also contribute to lower bounce rates by creating interfaces that feel familiar and easy to use. When used thoughtfully, a design system becomes a tool not just for faster delivery but for more ethical, inclusive, and sustainable product development at scale.

Assets

Visuals, media, and downloadable content can elevate a digital experience—but when overused or poorly implemented, they also become one of the biggest sources of unnecessary emissions and exclusion. From oversized images to autoplay videos, excessive asset use slows performance, drains energy, and disproportionately impacts users with older devices or limited connectivity.

Sustainable asset design isn't about stripping your site of beauty. It's about being strategic—ensuring every asset serves a clear purpose, delivers value, and minimizes waste.

Keep It Clean, Keep It Efficient

Decorative images and graphics should only be used when they meaningfully enhance user experience. As web design pioneer Jeffrey Zeldman wisely noted: "Content precedes design. Design in the absence of content is not design, it's decoration." Unnecessary flourishes increase page weight and rendering time, which negatively affects both usability and sustainability. Prioritize clarity over clutter and avoid visual noise that distracts or delays, especially on the homepage or key conversion flows.

Where images are essential, design with optimization in mind. Plan for multiple sizes since desktop hero images must also work on mobile. Design layouts that function before images load and consider whether high-fidelity photography is necessary, or if illustrations could work instead. Question purely decorative imagery and explore whether CSS could achieve the same visual effect more efficiently.

Media with Meaning

Video and audio require more bandwidth and processing power than most assets. Without thoughtful integration, they can undermine performance and create barriers for many users. Avoid autoplay and give users the choice to engage instead. Design meaningful poster images that work as stand-alone content even if the video never loads. Always include text alternatives like transcripts and captions for accessibility and efficiency.

When presenting video options, display the file size or estimated data usage so users can make informed decisions about whether to load content, especially valuable for users on limited data plans or slower connections. Consider how often users actually engage with embedded videos on websites: research suggests engagement rates are surprisingly low. Rather than assuming rich media is the default experience, offer it as an enhancement, not a requirement.

Documents and Downloads

For downloadable documents, clearly communicate what users are getting before they commit to a download. Include file type, size, and content summary so users can make informed decisions. Consider web pages instead of PDFs for content primarily read online and provide plain text alternatives when possible. Make downloads optional rather than required to access key information, ensuring the core experience doesn't depend on heavy file transfers.

Always Offer Alternatives

Not every user wants or can engage with media-heavy content. Sustainable design ensures content is accessible in multiple ways. Write alt text for all images that work as a stand-alone experience, going beyond mere description to convey purpose and meaning. Provide captions and transcripts for multimedia and offer text equivalents for complex visual information. Allow users to opt into resource-heavy elements rather than forcing them to opt out.

This approach reduces both cognitive and computational load, improves accessibility, and ensures digital experiences don't exclude or overwhelm users with different needs or constraints.

Sustainable assets are intentional ones. When assets are essential, make them count.

In Chapter 7, we'll explore the technical implementation of these asset strategies, including responsive image delivery, efficient video loading, and performance measurement tools that help validate these design decisions.

Testing and Measurement

In Chapter 2, we explored the complexity of measuring digital sustainability and carbon emissions. As designers, we need practical ways to validate whether our design decisions create better experiences while reducing environmental impact.

Core Web Vitals: A Designer's Starting Point

Google's Core Web Vitals provide measurable proxies for user experience that connect directly to sustainability. Largest Contentful Paint (LCP) measures how quickly key content loads. Designs that prioritize essential content and optimize critical assets naturally improve this score while also reducing energy consumption. Interaction to Next Paint (INP) reflects how responsive a page feels during user interactions over time, capturing delays caused by heavy scripts, complex layouts, or poorly structured interactivity. A progressive enhancement approach, with a strong baseline and optional enhancements, directly supports good INP by ensuring interactions remain responsive across devices. Cumulative Layout Shift (CLS) measures layout stability while loading. Thoughtful design prevents unexpected shifts that force users to reorient, increasing frustration, cognitive effort, and unnecessary interaction.

These metrics don't capture everything about sustainable design, but they provide concrete targets that align well with both user experience and resource efficiency goals. When Core Web Vitals scores improve, it often indicates a more inclusive, more resilient, and more sustainable experience.

Testing in Real Conditions

The most valuable testing happens outside ideal conditions. Test your designs on older devices and slow connections to ensure they don't exclude users or waste resources through excessive loading times. Check how experiences work with JavaScript disabled to validate your progressive enhancement approach. Verify that designs function when images load slowly or fail entirely, and test with different accessibility settings to ensure broad usability.

Monitor how your design decisions impact actual performance by tracking asset weight and Core Web Vitals scores before and after changes. The goal is to ensure design choices create inclusive, efficient experiences rather than digital barriers.

Making Measurement Actionable

Focus on questions that drive better design decisions. Do Core Web Vitals scores improve with your design changes? Can users complete tasks effectively across different devices and connections? Are you reducing resource consumption while maintaining or improving usability? When measurement serves design improvement rather than just data collection, it becomes a tool for creating more sustainable, inclusive digital experiences.

Chapter 7 will cover technical tools like Firefox Power Profiler that provide deeper performance insights to validate these design approaches.

Laws and Regulations: The Changing Landscape for UX

Sustainable UX is often framed as a matter of good practice or ethics. But increasingly, it is also becoming a legal issue. Laws and regulations are increasingly recognizing that design choices can actively harm users and that responsibility does not stop at content or data handling. Interface design itself is now under scrutiny.

The European Union is currently leading this shift. Some manipulative interface patterns, often called dark patterns, are already restricted under existing laws such as the Digital Services Act (DSA). The DSA explicitly addresses designs that mislead users, limit their ability to make informed choices, or push them into actions they did not intend to take. This is an important change: design is no longer treated as neutral presentation, but as something that can cause real harm.

More regulation is likely to follow. The European Parliament has called for stronger protections around digital well-being, and the European Commission is working toward a Digital Fairness Act. While this law is still in development, the direction is clear. Features that exploit attention, encourage compulsive use, or rely on manipulative personalization are becoming harder to justify, both legally and ethically.

What's Being Questioned

Regulators are paying closer attention to patterns that keep people engaged longer than they intend. These include infinite scroll and pull-to-refresh interactions that remove natural stopping points, auto playing videos that consume data without consent, and notification systems designed to pull users back in constantly.

Personalized feeds that rely heavily on behavioral tracking are also under review, especially when they prioritize engagement over user well-being. Gamified elements such as streaks, badges, and urgency cues are increasingly seen as pressure mechanisms rather than neutral features. Even seemingly small design decisions, like hiding opt-out options or making settings hard to find, are part of this conversation.

These patterns are not only questioned for their psychological impact, particularly on children and vulnerable users, but also for their environmental cost. More scrolling, refreshing, and media consumption mean more data transfer, more server activity, and more energy use. Design choices that demand more of users' attention usually demand more resources as well.

Design for Compliance and Ethics

As discussed in Chapter 2, measuring impact is rarely simple. Just as it is difficult to attribute precise carbon emissions to a single feature, it can be hard to prove direct harm caused by a single interface pattern. But the overall trend is clear. Designers are expected to support transparency, user control, and informed choice.

For UX professionals, this means designing experiences that respect attention by default. Clear stopping points instead of endless feeds, optional rather than automatic media loading, and calm interfaces that do not constantly interrupt the user are becoming safer choices. These approaches reduce legal risk, improve user trust, and often lead to lower energy use at the same time.

The overlap between regulation, user well-being, and sustainability is not accidental. Interfaces that respect people's time and autonomy are usually lighter, calmer, and more efficient. As regulations evolve, sustainable UX design is likely to shift from "nice to have" to something teams are expected to do as standard practice.

Conclusion

The flashing fashion site from the chapter's start is a vivid reminder: good intentions aren't enough. Even mission-driven brands risk losing users when their online shops are overloaded with brightness and motion. What we build on-screen directly affects who can use it, how fast it loads and whether it earns trust or frustration.

Grace Everts conducted a small study for Branch magazine in which users were shown three versions of a website: original, moderate, and stripped-down. They were asked for their preference: first without any emissions data, then again after learning how much carbon each variation produced. Before seeing the emissions, most preferred the visual richness of the original. After learning the carbon impact, preference flipped: most chose the more sustainable version, and some even favored the stripped-down model over the original. The takeaway is clear: users are willing to choose more sustainable digital experiences when those choices are made visible, understandable, and comparable.

Sustainable design isn't about sacrificing creativity or usability. It's about making deliberate, ethical choices that serve both people and planet. The responsibility should not be placed on users to make "the right choice constantly" but should be carried by the design itself through sensible defaults, lightweight foundations, and respectful enhancements. From progressive enhancement and accessible UI patterns to intentional assets, efficient typography, and lean client-side experiences, every decision shapes a web that's faster, fairer, and of lower-impact. And makes our users' smartphone batteries last a little longer.

Don't forget to document the reasoning behind your sustainable design decisions so future team members understand why certain choices were made and can maintain these approaches during updates and iterations. Sustainable design practices only remain effective when they persist beyond individual projects and designers.

In the next chapter, we'll turn these principles into action by exploring development strategies, tools, and performance measurements that bring sustainable design philosophy into code.

Summary

This chapter explored how user experience and interface design play a central role in building more sustainable digital products. Sustainability in design is not an abstract ideal or a visual style; it is the result of everyday decisions about structure, interaction, content, and defaults.

We examined how core UX principles, such as usability, accessibility, feedback, and error prevention, take on greater depth when viewed through a sustainability lens. By designing for real user conditions, respecting preferences, and avoiding assumptions about devices, networks, and attention, teams can create experiences that are more inclusive, resilient, and efficient.

Progressive enhancement was introduced as a foundational approach for sustainable design, ensuring that products work reliably for everyone before layering in richer features. We saw how this mindset influences forms, motion, carousels, non-visual interactions, user journeys, and interface elements, reducing unnecessary resource use while improving clarity and usability.

The chapter also addressed the environmental and ethical impact of visual design choices, from color and typography to assets and media. Thoughtful design systems and efficient UI patterns help scale sustainable decisions across teams and products. Testing and measurement, including Core Web Vitals, provide practical ways for designers to validate the impact of their work in real conditions.

Finally, we looked at the evolving regulatory and ethical landscape around manipulative design patterns and attention-heavy interfaces, highlighting how sustainable UX aligns with emerging legal expectations for transparency, user control, and digital well-being.

Taken together, these practices show that sustainable UX and UI design is not about doing less for users, but about doing better: designing experiences that respect people's time, devices, and contexts, while reducing waste and supporting a healthier, more responsible web.

References

UX Foundations and Design Principles

- Nielsen, Jakob. "10 Usability Heuristics for User Interface Design." Nielsen Norman Group, 1995.

  `https://www.nngroup.com/articles/ten-usability-heuristics/`

- Usability.gov. "User Experience Basics."

  `https://www.usability.gov/what-and-why/user-experience.html`

- Norman, Don. *The Design of Everyday Things*. Revised and Expanded Edition. Basic Books, 2013.

Sustainable UX and Responsible Design

- Sustainable UX Network (SUX):

  `https://sustainableuxnetwork.com/`

- Jonas, Torsten. "Imperfect Design for a Better Future." *Branch Magazine,* Issue 8.

  `https://branch.climateaction.tech/issues/issue-8/imperfect-design-for-a-better-future/`

- W3C Sustainable Web Guidelines—User Experience Design

  `https://www.w3.org/TR/web-sustainability-guidelines/#user-experience-design`

- The Calm Web (Calibre):

  `https://calibreapp.com/blog/calm-web`

- Deceptive Design Patterns:

  `https://www.deceptive.design/`

Performance, Page Weight, and Sustainability Measurement

- HTTP Archive Almanac 2024—Page Weight:

  `https://almanac.httparchive.org/en/2024/page-weight`

- Chudley, James. "Decarbonising User Journeys."

  `https://jameschudley.co.uk/2025/01/23/decarbonising-user-journeys/`

- *Branch Magazine*, Issue 9. "Design Constraints in Grid-Aware Web Development."

  `https://branch.climateaction.tech/issues/issue-9/design-constraints-in-grid-aware-web-development/`

User Constraints and Low-Bandwidth Experience

- Coldren, Paul. "Engineering for Slow Internet."

  `https://brr.fyi/posts/engineering-for-slow-internet`

Case Studies, Harm, and Safety

- Pokémon Go and traffic injuries, Harvard T.H. Chan School of Public Health:

  `https://www.hsph.harvard.edu/news/hsph-in-the-news/pokemon-go-accidents/`

Law, Regulation, and Policy

- European Parliament. "Addictive Design and Consumer Protection."

  `https://www.europarl.europa.eu/doceo/document/A-9-2023-0340_EN.html`

CHAPTER 7

Front-End Development

Ines Akrap[1]
[1]Munich, Germany; inesakrap.com

It is easy to fall in love with front-end development. Realizing that with just one line of code, you can instantly change something on the screen can seem like magic and get you hooked right away. However, if you have ever tried it, you also know that the front-end honeymoon phase usually lasts until you have to center a "div" for the first time. Or perhaps set up a code build. Or you start looking into many, many frameworks. Falling in love with the front end is easy; staying in love can be the challenging part.

Today's front-end work is far more complex than ever before. We have multiple languages, frameworks, design systems, build pipelines, and libraries. They come and go quickly, causing developers to spend more time wrestling with tooling than delivering real value to the end user. In the middle of this complexity, it's easy to forget the basics: that every line of code we ship will eventually be executed on a real person's device, consuming energy, draining batteries, using data, and shaping their experience.

As front-end developers, we are not just implementers of design. We are gatekeepers of performance, accessibility, and efficiency. The choices we make determine how quickly a page loads, how much data is transferred, how long a battery lasts, and whether someone with an older device or slower connection can even access the service.

The front end is the crucial part of sustainable websites and web applications. This chapter will explore how we can build them to be not only beautiful and interactive but also efficient, inclusive, and mindful of their environmental impact.

The Foundations of Front End

We usually consider the front end to be everything the user sees and interacts with in the browser, the presentation layer of a digital product. In Chapter 6, we discussed the design of user experiences and user interfaces. The front end is where those designs come alive, where we use code to bring those pixels and interactions to life.

C. Chinchilla and I. Akrap, *Building the Sustainable Web*, https://doi.org/10.1007/979-8-8688-2521-7_7

Every digital product starts with a foundation. For the front-end part, that foundation is built from three core layers: HTML for structure, CSS for presentation, and JavaScript for interactivity. These building blocks have been a part of the web since its early days. While the ecosystem surrounding them has expanded in complexity, they remain essential to every site and application.

HTML: The Structure

Everything needs its base, its skeleton: our bodies, buildings, and our websites. The fundamental block for building web pages and web applications is HTML, or Hypertext Markup Language. It provides structure and content that the browser then displays on the screen for users.

With tags like `<h1>`, `<p>`, or `<ul>`, we define different types of content and their roles. HTML5 introduced semantic elements, such as `<header>`, `<footer>`, and `<article>`, making the intent clearer to both browsers and assistive technologies. This small step improves accessibility for users and visibility for search engines.

One of the most powerful ideas behind HTML is linking. The "hypertext" part refers to those connections between pages, whether within one site or across the entire web. That simple feature is what turned static documents into today's interconnected Internet.

HTML can also embed multimedia such as images, audio, and video, and link to scripts and styles to extend functionality. This is where it all starts; every site you've ever opened began here.

CSS: The Presentation

Humans are visual beings living in a visual world. A good foundation with well-structured content is essential, but it also needs to be presented in a way that appeals to the person using it. Writing just a few lines of code and instantly changing the look and feel of a page is what makes CSS, or Cascading Style Sheets, feel like magic.

CSS defines how HTML elements are displayed, giving precise control over colors, fonts, spacing, alignment, and responsiveness. Due to its cascading nature, styles are applied based on specificity, inheritance, and order, making CSS flexible but sometimes tricky to manage.

Styles can be added inline with the style attribute, included within the page, or linked in external files. Developers usually rely on IDs for unique elements and classes for reusable patterns, keeping presentation consistent across a site.

JavaScript: The Interactivity

For quite some time, websites were primarily focused on displaying content. We would structure them with HTML, style them with CSS, and connect them through links. But as the Internet grew into a platform for communication, entertainment, and commerce, users needed to do more than consume; they needed to participate.

That's when JavaScript stepped in. Running directly in the browser, it responds to clicks, mouse movements, and keyboard inputs, enabling real-time interaction. With a single button press, users can submit data, load new content, or complete a purchase.

Back in 2019, I did a web development workshop for school-age girls, and I created this visual on Figure 7-1 to explain these three fundamental building blocks of the web. I still like to use it, and I'll take the opportunity to add it here as well.

Figure 7-1. *HTML, CSS, JS progression*

Where It Gets Complicated

Structure with HTML, beautify with CSS, and add some interactivity with JavaScript, and there you have it, the front end of your website. Not so fast. As the web evolved to support communication, shopping, banking, and entertainment, projects grew in complexity. Technology has evolved not only to provide users with more powerful applications but also to enhance the developer experience, making the job easier (or at least less painful).

I still remember the day I read a LinkedIn job ad for a front-end developer role and, for the first time, I understood all the abbreviations in the list. I was far from being an expert in all of them, but at least I knew what each one was. I felt like I was on top of the world. Well, the world of LinkedIn, at least.

An average front-end job posting requirement looked something like this (still does), and as a bonus, you get a live commentary from my mind during my early front-end career:

- **HTML**: All good, basics. I've known that one since high school.
- **CSS**: Yeah, classes, styles, colors, got that one covered.
- **CSS Preprocessors**: Check, SASS, LESS, make my life easier.
- **JavaScript**: Still good, another one of the usual suspects. I can always search for syntax. It may be time to re-watch those Wes Bos videos. Should I read a book on this?
- **jQuery**: Well, JavaScript, check.
- **Package managers**: npm/yarn: uf, those node versions always end up taking me much more wasted time than expected, but I do like re-using good code.
- **Version control system (such as Git)**: I am still not sure how to properly revert pushed commits, and sometimes merge conflict resolution explodes my code, but as long as it is less than once a week, I guess I am good.
- **Responsive design**: Occasional media query and test on iPhone view, can do that.

- **Front-end Build Tools (e.g., Webpack, Gulp, Parcel)**: Yep, Webpack is all everyone talks about these days, but I'm still not entirely sure what it does. I will leave it to my FE lead and go through those 12 open tabs with videos and articles about them next week. I will, for sure (spoiler alert: she did not until she had to do an FE build herself for the first time)
- **RESTful APIs and AJAX:** I do know what an API is. Isn't AJAX a football club? Well, API, check.
- **Cross-Browser Compatibility**: Are they finally going to deprecate IE ?!?! Pleaseee!!!
- **Testing and Debugging Tools (e.g., Chrome DevTools, Jest, Cypress)**: Do we really need these tools? What is wrong with good old console.log ?! I will figure it out, I guess, or just keep pretending I know them while keeping debugging by logging messages to myself (ten years later, she still does that, it is a lifestyle).
- **Accessibility (a11y) Standards**: Yees, we should all do that !!! A shoutout to Natalia Venditto for introducing this topic to me in the 2nd week of my Front-end developer career.

You get the point. It is fascinating how we often view the front end as a straightforward HTML/CSS/JS scenario, and in reality, this is just a piece of a much larger puzzle. You may also notice that in this list, we are still on jQuery, and modern front-end frameworks, such as React, Angular, and Vue, are nowhere to be seen.

When I started as a front-end developer, my first assignment was a "basic" project for a big Swiss bank. It used only the fundamental trio (with some gulp magic I never really understood). It had a strong focus on accessibility, which I am forever grateful I learned about so early in my career. At the time, most teams were working on the maintenance and upgrade of older codebases with jQuery, and then there was this one "the-cool-kids-on-the-block" (more accurately, "the-cool-kids-in-the-open-office") team that got to implement an app with Angular. I admit I had 0 idea what Angular was until I joined the second "cool-kids" team a year later, but I knew it was new and cool, and everyone wanted to work with it. Fast-forward to today, and I seriously struggle to find a website that uses basic JavaScript instead of one of the frameworks.

The Cost of Complexity

As the front end grew more complex, so did the weight of the average website. According to the 2024 HTTP Archive Web Almanac, the median desktop page weight in October 2024 was about 2.65 MB, while the median mobile page was around 2.31 MB. In both cases, it is far higher than in previous years. From the graph on Figure 7-2 we can see that both figures are significantly larger than earlier benchmarks, and the overall median page weight continues to increase year over year, showing that heavier pages remain the norm rather than the exception.

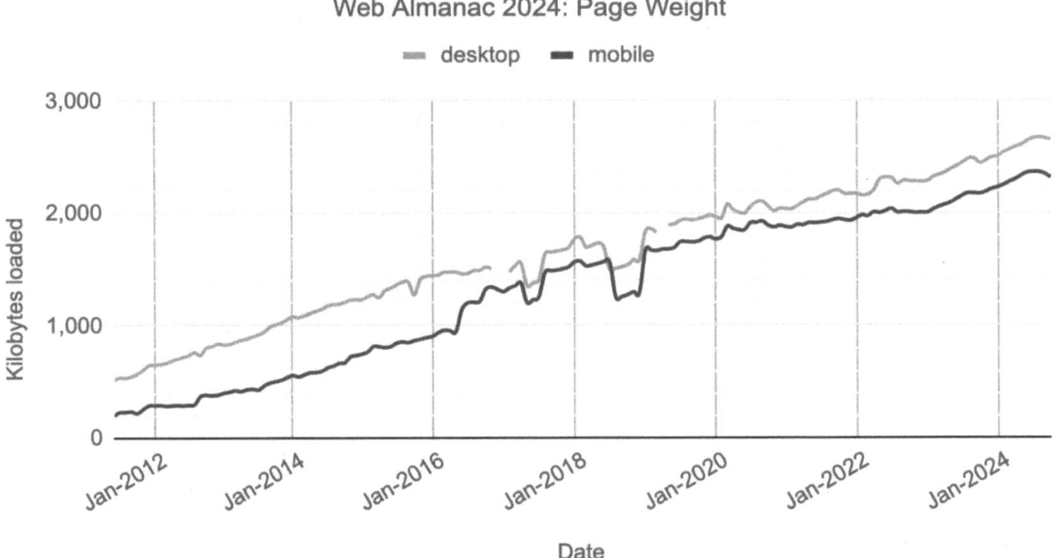

***Figure 7-2.** Median page weight over time from 2024 Web Almanac*

Every extra kilobyte has a cost. It has to be stored on a server, transferred over networks, and rendered by a browser on someone's device. Rendering large JavaScript bundles is particularly expensive: it delays the time to first interaction, drains battery, and wastes energy. On less powerful devices, the site can feel sluggish or even unusable.

This is the part that is easy to forget when we're knee-deep in the latest framework or shiny new tool. Every dependency we add, every extra library we import, every kilobyte of unused CSS shipped to production, all of it eventually lands on a real user's device. Those users are paying not only for electricity, battery life, and data plans. They're also paying with their time and patience.

This is where sustainability and usability align. A lighter, more efficient front end not only reduces carbon emissions but also makes sites faster, more accessible, and more enjoyable to use.

Sustainable Front End

So what would make the front end of an application sustainable? The short answer: designing and developing with both people and planet in mind.

A sustainable front end isn't just about squeezing kilobytes out of JavaScript bundles or compressing images, though those are important. It is also about ensuring that the experience works for everyone across devices, connection speeds, and abilities. Efficiency and inclusivity go hand in hand.

Several principles can guide us here:

- **Interoperability**: Making sure websites work across browsers, operating systems, and devices so that people don't need to buy new hardware just to access services
- **Openness**: Relying on open standards and common technologies (HTML, CSS, JavaScript) instead of proprietary formats that can lock users out
- **Accessibility**: Building sites that are usable for people of all abilities, from semantic HTML to proper contrast ratios to keyboard navigation
- **Security**: Protecting users' data and interactions at the client side, which is part of building trustworthy and sustainable digital ecosystems

These aren't "nice-to-have" extras. They are the foundations of a sustainable web. Each of them reduces barriers, extends the lifetime of devices, and increases the usefulness of the services we build.

Interoperability

At its core, interoperability means that our sites work the way they should for everyone, no matter which browser, device, or network they use. It sounds obvious, but anyone who has spent late nights fixing CSS hacks for Internet Explorer or debugging mobile layout glitches knows that this has never been guaranteed.

When a site doesn't work on someone's device, there are usually two outcomes: either they give up and leave, or they feel forced to upgrade to a newer version. In the first case, we lose a user. In the second, we contribute to e-waste and embodied carbon, all because the service wasn't built to support older hardware. Neither is a good outcome.

The best way to avoid this is to stick to web standards. Semantic HTML, CSS written according to official specifications, and widely supported JavaScript features form a strong baseline. Modern browsers have made significant progress toward alignment, but checking resources like *Can I Use* remains part of the everyday toolkit. Testing across a realistic range of devices and browsers, not just the latest MacBook on high-speed Internet, makes a big difference.

Interoperability is also closely tied to performance. A 4 MB JavaScript bundle that runs fine on a high-end laptop might grind a five-year-old Android phone to a halt. Code splitting, progressive enhancement (explained in detail later in this chapter), and avoiding unnecessary libraries all help keep our sites usable for more people, on more devices, with less frustration.

In short, interoperability is about building for resilience. Devices vary, networks drop out, and browsers evolve. By embracing standards and keeping things lightweight, we make the web more reliable, more inclusive, and a little bit kinder to the planet.

Openness

Openness in front-end development means building with technologies and practices that are available to everyone. When we rely on open standards like HTML, CSS, and JavaScript, our work is compatible with all major browsers and devices. When we rely on proprietary tools or closed formats, we risk locking people out and limiting access.

Open practices also support accessibility. By using semantic HTML and following established guidelines, we give screen readers, search engines, and other tools the information they need to interpret our sites correctly. This makes the web not only more inclusive but also more robust.

There is also a community side to openness. Much of the front-end ecosystem is powered by open source libraries and frameworks. By sharing solutions, contributing back, or even just filing clear bug reports, we take part in a culture that helps all of us build better software. That collaboration is one of the reasons web development moves so quickly.

Finally, openness helps us avoid dead ends. Proprietary formats and locked-down codebases might feel convenient in the short term, but they often make it harder to adapt when requirements change or when a company drops support. Open standards and open-source tools tend to be more resilient and longer-lived, making them the more sustainable choice for both developers and users.

Accessibility

Accessibility in front-end development is about making sure the sites we build can be used by everyone, regardless of ability, device, or environment. It is not something to "bolt on" later. Remember that elevator metaphor for Chapter 3? Have you ever seen an elevator added to an older building? Not built in, but bolt-on. I can only imagine how challenging it must be to add it later instead of adding it from the beginning.

Accessibility starts in the HTML itself. Semantic elements, such as <header>, <nav>, <main>, and <footer>, provide structure and meaning to content, enabling screen readers and other tools to navigate a page effectively. Proper use of <label> for form inputs, alt text for images, and clear link text all make a huge difference. But it doesn't stop with HTML. CSS can support or break accessibility. Low color contrast, tiny font sizes, or hover-only interactions can exclude people. Using relative units (like em or rem) instead of fixed pixels helps users who zoom in on their text. Ensuring focus styles are visible makes navigation possible for users who rely on a keyboard rather than a mouse.

What about JavaScript? With all its power, JS can easily undermine accessibility if we are not careful. Dynamic content requires ARIA (Accessible Rich Internet Applications) roles and states so that assistive technologies can understand what is happening. Modal windows need to trap focus so keyboard users are not stranded behind them. Interactive widgets need to be operable with both the mouse and the keyboard. These things take a little extra thought, but they make the difference between an inclusive app and a frustrating one.

Most of us are not building features just for "someone else." Every developer is also an end user of countless websites and apps. We have all been in situations where captions were helpful because we couldn't turn on the sound, or where we wished buttons were larger because we only had one hand free. Accessibility is not just about disability; it's about designing for real people in real contexts.

The best part is, we don't need to reinvent the wheel. Standards like the Web Content Accessibility Guidelines (WCAG) provide a framework, and modern browsers come equipped with built-in tools to test contrast, tab order, and screen reader behavior. Automated checkers can catch many issues, but nothing replaces testing with real people. If possible, invite users with different needs to try out your site.

Accessibility in front-end development is really about empathy turned into code. Each <alt> tag, each label, each properly handled keyboard event is a small signal that we care about everyone using what we build.

Security

Security might not be the first thing that comes to mind when discussing sustainable front-end development but it should be. An insecure site puts people at risk, wastes resources, and erodes trust. All three undermine sustainability.

Most security threats on the client side come down to protecting users from malicious code or unintended data leaks. Cross-site scripting (XSS), cross-site request forgery (CSRF), and clickjacking are among the most common threats. These may sound abstract, but the impact is real: stolen sessions, hijacked accounts, or personal information exposed. That's not just bad for users; it's bad for everyone. Every breach generates clean-up costs, reputational damage, and wasted energy spent chasing problems that could have been prevented.

So what can we do on the front end? The first step is to never trust input. All user-provided data should be validated and sanitized, even if we believe it's harmless. Content Security Policy (CSP) headers are another robust defense: they instruct the browser on which resources are allowed to load, blocking unexpected scripts before they can run. For cookies, we can set HttpOnly and Secure flags so session data isn't exposed to JavaScript or plain-text connections. And of course, HTTPS is non-negotiable for encrypting all traffic.

We also need to monitor the code we import. Most front-end projects rely on dozens, sometimes hundreds, of third-party packages. If those aren't kept up-to-date, they can become a severe liability. Regular dependency audits, automated updates, and pruning unused libraries help reduce the attack surface. The smaller our dependency tree, the lower the risk of something going wrong and the smaller the overall footprint of the website or application.

Good security also ties back to good usability. Clear error messages, secure password practices, and avoiding unnecessary forms all contribute to safer and smoother experiences. Ultimately, sustainable security is about prevention. By keeping things lean, updated, and intentional, we protect our users and avoid unnecessary harm.

Measuring the Sustainability of the Front End

As we discussed back in Chapter 2, measuring the impact of a website is not straightforward. The system is complex, and there is a notable lack of transparency in many of its components. Still, if we want to improve, we need at least some metrics to guide us. For front-end work, those metrics usually fall into two categories: the impact on the planet and the impact on users.

Energy Use and Carbon Emissions

For the planet, the most direct metric we can observe on the front end is energy use. Carbon emissions are derived from that energy consumption, and as we discussed earlier, they are difficult to measure precisely because so many factors are involved across networks, devices, and data centers. Still, energy use gives us a practical starting point.

On the client side, we now have a few tools that can bring us closer to understanding this impact. One of the most precise is the Firefox Power Profiler, shown in Figure 7-3. It lives in the Performance tab of Firefox Developer Tools and can generate a local power profile of a website. We hit record, load the page, scroll, click, interact, and then stop the recording. The profiler displays the amount of energy the site consumed during that session. Since early 2023, and when energy profiling is explicitly enabled in the settings, it can also estimate the resulting CO_2 emissions, powered by CO_2.js and the Sustainable Web Design model.

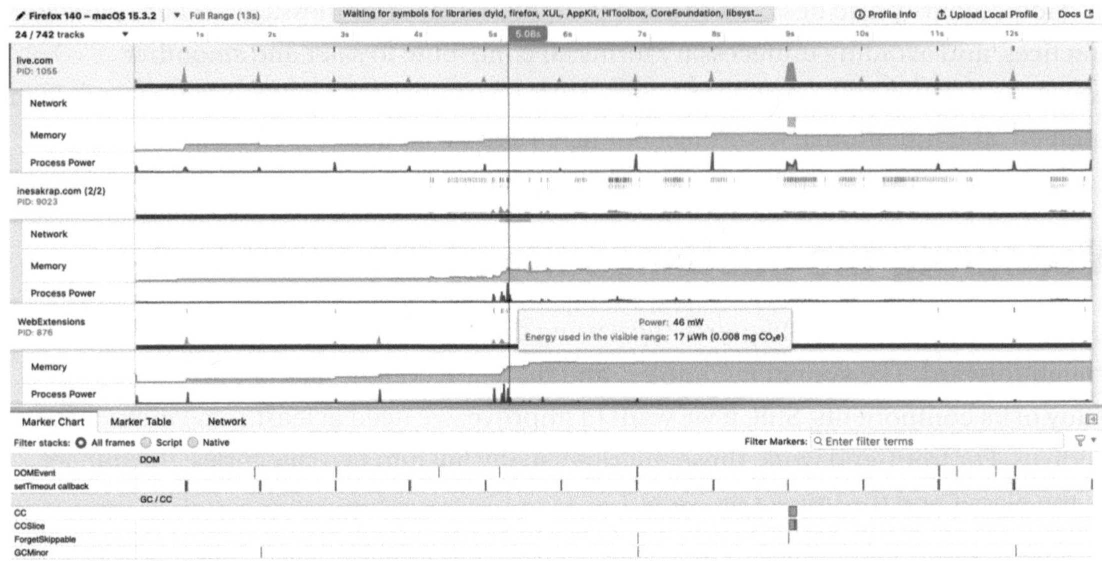

***Figure 7-3.** Firefox Power Profiler*

This is not a perfect system-level measurement, but it does provide a way to see how our front-end choices translate into energy usage on real devices. Mozilla performance engineer Florian Quèze has given several talks on the tool, and they are worth exploring if you want to understand its methodology in more depth.

Carbon emissions remain a useful proxy because they translate energy use into a single, comparable value. However, they are not the whole picture. Other planetary impacts, such as water use for cooling data centers or the material footprint of devices, also matter. These are harder to measure directly from the front end, but it is important to remember that carbon emissions are only one part of the planet's equation.

Beyond individual tools and proxies, there is growing work toward more structured models for reasoning about software emissions. One of the most influential is the **Software Carbon Intensity (SCI) specification from the Green Software Foundation (GSF).** SCI provides a general framework for expressing emissions relative to a functional unit of software, such as a request, task, or transaction, linking energy use, carbon intensity, and time. While SCI is now an accepted standard for software systems more broadly, applying it meaningfully to the web remains an open challenge.

Adam Newman and Oliver Winks, founders of Root & Branch, a consultancy specialized in web sustainability, and contributors to the W3C Sustainable Web Guidelines, are actively investigating how SCI-style thinking could be adapted for web contexts. Their work highlights a key difficulty: web experiences distribute energy use across servers, networks, CDNs, and end user devices, making it much harder to define clear system boundaries or functional units than in backend services or batch workloads.

In parallel, the Green Web Foundation is also examining how SCI concepts might inform web measurement, building on its work in grid-aware and carbon-aware web systems. These efforts are exploratory rather than prescriptive, but they point toward a shared direction: moving beyond page weight and static averages toward models that better reflect real runtime behavior and energy flows.

At this stage, SCI-inspired approaches for the web should be understood as conceptual tools, not precise measurement instruments. They do not replace practical front-end techniques such as browser power profiling or performance metrics. Instead, they offer a common language for connecting front-end decisions to system-level impact, and a foundation on which more robust, web-specific standards may emerge.

While these models help frame planetary impact, sustainability is not only about emissions.

Usability

For people, one of the strongest measures is usability. A site that frustrates users is not sustainable, regardless of its page weight. Measuring usability usually involves looking at

- **Task success rate**: Can people actually complete the task?
- **Error rate**: How often do they get stuck or make mistakes?
- **Time on task**: How long does it take them to succeed?
- **User satisfaction**: What do they say afterward?

We also have technical metrics that reflect how users experience performance in practice. The most widely used are the Core Web Vitals, which we already mentioned in Chapter 6:

- **Largest Contentful Paint (LCP)**: How quickly the main content becomes visible.
- **Interaction to Next Paint (INP)**: How responsive the page feels during user interactions.
- **Cumulative Layout Shift (CLS)**: How stable the page layout is while loading.

These metrics can be tracked using tools like Lighthouse, Chrome DevTools, or PageSpeed Insights, and monitored continuously in production with real-user monitoring (RUM). Together, they provide us with both lab and field data on how our sites actually perform for users.

Alongside task-based testing, Core Web Vitals provide a concrete way to measure how usable and efficient a front-end experience really feels. They don't just signal speed; they highlight points where users get frustrated or waste effort, which is both a user experience problem and an energy problem.

We can collect usability data through testing sessions, analytics, and monitoring tools, and Core Web Vitals can be measured continuously in production. Even lightweight testing (watching a few people try to sign up, buy something, or find information) reveals friction that leads to wasted effort and wasted energy.

Accessibility

Closely tied to usability is accessibility. A website that locks people out because of poor contrast, missing labels, or broken keyboard navigation is not serving its purpose. Automated tools like Axe, Lighthouse Accessibility, or WAVE quickly catch common problems, such as missing alt text, low contrast, and broken landmarks. But we shouldn't stop there. Manual checks are still essential:

- Navigate the site with just a keyboard.
- Try it with a screen reader.
- Zoom text to 200% and see what breaks.

And when possible, involve people with different needs in testing. No automated score beats real-user feedback.

Sustainability of Measurement Itself

It is worth pausing to note that measurement is not free. Real-user monitoring (RUM) is powerful, but it comes at a cost: the scripts we add to gather data must be shipped to every user, executed in their browsers, and the data they produce must be transferred and stored. That means increased network traffic, additional energy consumption, and often large volumes of data sitting idle in logs.

The temptation is to collect "just in case," but that mindset leads to digital hoarding. From a sustainability perspective, we should treat data collection with the same care as code: only gather what is truly useful, collect it in the lightest possible way, and clean it up when it is no longer needed.

There are practical ways to do this:

- **Sample instead of tracking everything**: Capture data from a fraction of sessions rather than every user, unless full coverage is genuinely required.
- **Use lightweight scripts**: Avoid shipping large third-party analytics packages if you only need a few metrics.
- **Limit retention**: Keep logs for as long as they are valuable, then delete or aggregate them.
- **Prefer synthetic tests where possible**: Use lab tools like Lighthouse or WebPageTest for baseline metrics, and reserve RUM for gaps that lab data cannot cover.

Measuring sustainability should not create new waste. By being selective about what we measure and intentional about how we collect it, we make sure the act of measurement supports our goals rather than undermines them.

No single number will ever tell us whether a front end is sustainable, but combining these perspectives gives us a fuller picture. Tools like Firefox Power Profiler help us see the energy impact, usability testing and Core Web Vitals show us how people experience our sites, and accessibility checks ensure no one is left out. Services like Ecograder, Website Carbon Calculator, and Digital Beacon combine multiple dimensions into simple reports, making sustainability more visible and easier to share with stakeholders. The important part is not chasing perfect scores, but making sure we are paying attention to both people and planet as we build.

Creating a Sustainable Front End

Theory and measurement are critical, but sustainability ultimately lives in the code we ship. Every dependency, every library, and every script we load has an impact on performance, user experience, and energy use. The browser doesn't distinguish between a necessary feature and a leftover plugin: it downloads, parses, and executes whatever we give it. That is why front-end developers are in a unique position to make or break the sustainability of a project.

And this is where the discipline of engineering comes in. **Engineering is about designing under constraints, and in the front end, our constraints are clear: devices of different ages and capabilities, networks that are not always fast or stable, users with different abilities, and a planet already under strain**. As Alex Russell argues in *The Performance Inequality Gap* (2024), for front-end work to truly count as engineering, we need to internalize those constraints and design within "the envelope of what's possible on most devices." Instead of viewing this as a limitation, we can see it as the source of our work's meaning. Building for users and the planet is not a restriction; rather, it defines front-end development as an engineering practice. It is what makes it creative and fun. That creativity comes through in the practical choices we make every day.

JavaScript

JavaScript powers the modern web, but it is also one of the most expensive resources we can ship. Every extra kilobyte must be downloaded, parsed, compiled, and executed. On powerful laptops, this might be a minor annoyance; on low-end phones, it can freeze the browser, drain the battery, and shorten the device's lifespan.

I had already been working in web performance for years when I watched a talk in 2020 titled "Transitioning to Modern JavaScript," by Jason Miller and Houssein Djirdeh. The technical arguments were not new to me. I was already aware that most users run modern browsers, that legacy syntax is heavier, and that shipping unnecessary code hurts performance. What changed things for me was not the information itself but how clearly its impact was visualized. One slide in particular showed how all that unused and unnecessary JavaScript, shipped by default to almost everyone, translates into real energy use and ultimately into CO_2e emissions. It made the cost visible in a way I had not seen before. That was the moment when performance stopped being just about speed or best practices and started feeling like an environmental issue. The realization was simple but uncomfortable: code that does not meaningfully help users still consumes energy, at massive scale.

Once JavaScript is seen as both a feature enabler and a source of hidden waste, it becomes easier to ask the right questions: Do we really need this dependency? Is this library worth the weight? Is this feature helping the user right now? These questions guide the way we write and manage code, and the answers usually point toward a few practical steps:

- **Audit and measure**: Tools like Lighthouse, WebPageTest, or the Coverage tab in Chrome DevTools can indicate which parts of the code are actually executed and which remain unused. It is often surprising to see how much of an imported library never gets executed, but this visibility is the first step toward reducing unnecessary code.
- **Tree shaking and bundling**: Modern bundlers can remove unused exports, but only when the code they process allows it. Tree shaking works best with ES modules, while CommonJS and side-effect-heavy dependencies limit what can be safely removed. This is why importing entire libraries, or relying on packages that ship only legacy formats, often results in far more JavaScript being delivered than is actually used.
- **Code splitting and lazy loading**: An application does not need to be delivered all at once. By splitting code into smaller chunks and loading only what is necessary for the initial view, startup is faster while deeper features remain available when requested.
- **Polyfills**: These are essential for compatibility, but serving every polyfill to every browser is a form of waste. Most modern browsers no longer need them. They should be delivered conditionally so that only older browsers carry the extra weight.

A memorable way to frame this mindset comes from a metaphor inspired by Marie Kondo, whose philosophy I am a huge fan of (Figure 7-4). If a piece of JavaScript does not bring clear value to the user, we should thank it and delete it. The point is intentionality. Every line of code has a cost, and if it does not meaningfully improve the experience, that cost is hard to justify.

Figure 7-4. *Slide from Addy Osmani's 2023 talk "The Cost of JavaScript," using a Marie Kondo metaphor to encourage removing JavaScript that does not meaningfully benefit users*

None of these techniques should sound new or revolutionary. They are about being aware of the cost JavaScript carries and being deliberate with what is shipped, ensuring each line has a purpose. Making sure that every line of JavaScript we ship sparks joy. The result is faster interactions, smoother experiences, and reduced pressure on devices and networks. By minimizing unnecessary processing, we not only save energy but also extend the usefulness of the hardware people already own. And just when JavaScript feels under control, frameworks enter the picture, magnifying the trade-offs we face and making efficiency even more critical.

Front-End Frameworks

Frameworks are everywhere in front end today. React, Angular, Vue, Svelte, Astro, the list keeps growing every year. They promise faster development, modern tooling, and the ability to scale complex applications. I have tried working with most of them, and yet I often find myself returning to basics, using vanilla JavaScript. Sustainable development requires us to adopt the mindset that frameworks are tools, not identities. They should be chosen for the job at hand, not simply because they are popular, fun to use, or we like the community around them.

According to the State of JavaScript survey and the Web Almanac, frameworks have matured significantly over the last decade. React and Angular dominate, while Vue has a steady base; newer entrants like Svelte and Astro are carving out their own space. Their popularity reflects how much they help developers manage complexity, but at the end of the day, frameworks always translate into more code for browsers to download and process.

Frameworks offer a wide range of benefits, including routing, state management, component models, reactivity, server-side rendering, and an entire ecosystem of plugins. This power comes with a cost. Even before we write a single line of code, the framework itself adds baseline weight. Once it is running, features such as virtual DOM comparison, hydration, and change detection all consume CPU cycles on the user's device. The patterns a framework imposes can also lock us in, making it difficult to switch later. And sometimes what feels convenient for the developer results in a heavier, slower experience for the person on the other side of the screen.

This tension is real. A framework can make development more enjoyable, but the user's device and connection ultimately carry the energy and performance costs. That does not mean frameworks should be avoided. It means they need to be used with care.

Practical steps to make framework use more sustainable include

- **Start with the smallest footprint**: Avoiding the use of a complete framework for a simple interface. Vanilla JavaScript or a light library may be enough.
- **Lean on the server**: Using server-side rendering or partial hydration so the browser does less work.
- **Import only what is needed**: Taking advantage of modular builds and bundlers that tree-shake unused code.
- **Measure the impact**: Using bundle analyzers, runtime profilers, and performance monitoring to understand what framework features actually cost.
- **Keep boundaries clean**: As applications grow, refactoring often to prevent monoliths that are too tightly tied to a single tool.

Frameworks succeed because they improve developer experience. But developer experience should never come at the cost of user experience. If the person on a low-end phone struggles to load the page because our project shipped an extra 300 KB of JavaScript, then we have solved a problem for ourselves while creating one for them. Sustainable front-end development means remembering that distinction every time we reach for a new tool.

Third-Party Scripts and Dependencies

If JavaScript is the code we choose to write, third-party scripts are often the code that slips in. Analytics, ads, A/B testing, chat widgets, social buttons, sometimes even entire UX testing platforms, they frequently arrive as "just a snippet," but quickly pile up into a heavy load. They bring extra JavaScript, pull in styles, open connections to other domains, and often block page rendering, while also running long after the page has loaded.

While auditing a project I worked on some years ago, I noticed a surprising amount of third-party code had sneaked in. One of the heaviest was Hotjar, a UX testing tool. As I dug deeper, I uncovered a total of 26 different third parties. I put them all in a spreadsheet and asked the product owner to assign a responsible person for each one, someone who could argue why it was needed. Within weeks, most of them disappeared. No one was using them, no one claimed them, and we were left with only a handful of scripts that actually served a purpose. And about 30% less JavaScript on the page.

That experience taught me that third parties are not just about performance. They are also about accountability. If no one "owns" a script, it probably should not be there.

Practical steps we can take include

- **Audit regularly**: Utilize tools like Request Map or WebPageTest to pinpoint which external scripts are being loaded.
- **Remove what is not needed**: If a dashboard goes unchecked or a widget is unused, cut it. A forgotten third party is pure waste.
- **Import on interaction**: Defer loading until someone actually engages. For example, load a help chat widget only when someone clicks the "Need help?" button.

- **Respect consent**: Do not load tracking or advertising code until the user opts in. Many sites use tools like OneTrust, but these often send data such as IP addresses to the vendor before consent is given. A better approach is to host a lightweight consent banner yourself and only call out to third parties after acceptance.

Handled well, third parties can be a helpful resource. Left unchecked, they quietly bloat pages, drain batteries, and compromise privacy. What stuck with me was how invisible all that waste had been. Nobody noticed it, nobody claimed it, but users everywhere were paying for it in slower load times and higher energy consumption. In the case of Hotjar alone, its scripts was adding about 77 KB gzipped, and in some setups can increase page weight by almost 0.5 MB. On this project, it was being transferred and processed on every single page of the entire site for at least a year, without anyone realizing it. Third parties are rarely questioned, which is precisely why we should question them.

And for my next party trick, bring me a font subsetter, please.

Fonts

Fonts give a site character and personality, but they can also add weight. Every custom typeface is another file to download, often hundreds of kilobytes in size, and most sites use more than one. According to the 2024 HTTP Archive Web Almanac, the median web page loads three to four font files, contributing well over 100 KB to the page. That may not sound like much in isolation, but it is more than the size of the average HTML and CSS combined just a decade ago. Many sites, however, go far beyond the median. Fun fact: the most I have personally seen in one project was 31 different font files.

Several factors influence that weight. Font files often bundle multiple weights and styles, sometimes as many as four or more in a single download. They also include thousands of characters across different languages, even if a site only ever needs Latin. Designers may hand off a beautiful type system with multiple families and weights, but by the time it hits production, users are downloading megabytes just to read a headline.

When I redesigned my personal portfolio in 2022, I ran straight into this problem. My goal was to make the site as lightweight as possible, which required me to use system fonts. But once I had a working design, I realized it lacked personality. To fix that, I added a handwriting-style font, Dancing Script, just for my name and surname. The "Get font" download from Google Fonts weighed in at 453 KB. I was aiming for as close to 0 as possible. Clearly, 453 wasn't anywhere near that.

So I started cutting. First, I realized the file contained four weights; dropping down to just "regular" weight cut it to 81 KB. It was much better, but I wasn't really happy with it. Next, I tried subsetting it to Latin only, which brought it to around 30 KB. That was finally in a range I could accept. But then I thought: what if I only include the characters I actually need? Ever since I did a student exchange in Portugal, I've been aware of how short my full name is. That awareness gave me the idea for the ultimate experiment: a version of Dancing Script that only contained the 9 letters of my name and surname: 2 uppercase and 7 lowercase. The result was my favorite personal optimization story: a 3.4 KB font file, Dancing Script (Ines Version).

I once shared that story in a conference talk, and months later at another event, someone recognized me and said: "Oh, you're the one with the 4 KB font!" It made me laugh, but it also showed me something: out of everything in that talk, what stuck with him was this small, yet impactful, detail. A reminder that optimizations don't just save bytes, they stick in people's minds.

Most projects aren't like my personal site. Many run on CMS templates, reuse fonts across multiple contexts, or depend on branding guidelines that front-end developers don't control. But that doesn't mean we are powerless. Even if we can't veto the designer's choice, we can still look critically at how fonts are delivered and optimized.

Practical steps we can take include

- **Limit typefaces and weights**: Stick to essentials. Users rarely notice whether a site uses two weights or six, but their devices will feel the difference.
- **Subset fonts**: Trim down to Latin or other relevant scripts. This alone can reduce file sizes from hundreds of kilobytes to a fraction of that.
- **Use font-display**: swap: Show fallback text immediately, avoiding the "flash of invisible text" that leaves users staring at blank spaces.
- **Prefer system fonts where possible**: For body text and UI elements, system fonts are fast, familiar, and require no additional download costs.

Handled well, fonts can support both brand and performance. Left unchecked, they quietly bloat every page load. Even if we don't have complete control over type choices, we can question the defaults, identify opportunities for improvement, and ensure that personality doesn't compromise usability and efficiency.

From a sustainability perspective, fonts matter more than they seem. Every extra kilobyte has to travel across networks and be processed on real devices. Multiply that by thousands or millions of visits, and the energy use becomes significant. Optimized fonts don't just reduce emissions; they also help older devices stay useful for longer, and they make sure users on slow connections aren't locked out of content.

This brings us to another piece of the puzzle: even optimized assets cause waste if they are downloaded over and over again. This is where caching and delivery come in.

Caching and Delivery

Optimizing code and assets is only half the story. How those assets are delivered to users matters just as much. Even the smallest font, image, or script becomes wasteful if it is downloaded fresh on every visit. The reality of the web is that users often come back to the same product page, to the same form, to the same dashboard. If our sites force their browsers to re-fetch everything from scratch each time, we are forcing them to pay the performance and energy costs again and again.

Caching and smart delivery aim to break that cycle. Once an asset has been fetched, the browser should be able to reuse it, whether the user reloads the page, navigates deeper, or comes back tomorrow. Done right, caching means fewer network requests, faster loads, and less wasted energy. Done poorly, it means duplicate downloads, higher emissions, and frustrated users.

Practical steps we can take include

- **Set proper cache headers**: Use Cache-Control, ETag, and Expires so that browsers know when they can safely reuse assets without downloading them again.

- **Use service workers for offline caching**: Service workers can store common resources locally and intercept repeat requests, making sites more resilient on flaky connections.

- **Leverage CDNs**: A content delivery network serves files from servers geographically close to users, reducing latency and backbone traffic.

- **Compress text-based assets:** Always deliver HTML, CSS, and JavaScript with gzip or Brotli. Compression often cuts transfer size by 70–80%, and modern browsers handle it out of the box.
- **Cache bust responsibly**: When assets change, version them in the filename so browsers fetch the new one, but don't force users to re-download everything on every visit.

Caching and delivery may not be glamorous, but they are among the highest-impact optimizations we can make. The payoff is immediate: faster page loads, reduced strain on servers, fewer wasted network requests, and a smoother user experience for those on limited connections.

From a sustainability perspective, this matters greatly. Data that doesn't need to move shouldn't move. Every repeated transfer is unnecessary energy burned, and every wasted request shortens the life of devices and networks. Caching is one of the simplest tools we have to make the web more efficient, reliable, and sustainable.

Constraints are not limits; they are what make front-end engineering meaningful. Designing for users and the planet pushes us to think harder, work smarter, and often be more creative than we ever imagined. **Sustainability is not a restriction on what we can build; it is a feature of how we build well.** When we choose carefully what to ship, we create faster, fairer, and more resilient experiences for everyone.

Working with Images and Video

We have talked about structuring the site correctly, reducing code, and making it accessible. We covered caching, dependencies, and third parties. But one more category remains, the elephant on the page: assets. On an average site, the largest share of weight is not the code, but the media, including images and, increasingly, video.

You probably know what Marie Kondo would suggest: start by removing anything that doesn't spark joy. However, in practice, front-end engineers rarely get to decide which images or videos are kept. Those decisions typically fall under design or content. What we can do is ensure that the included media is delivered as sustainably as possible.

If It Is Not Needed Yet, Do Not Load It

One of the simplest ideas in performance and sustainability is also one of the most effective: if something is not visible yet, do not load it. That is the principle behind the well-known pattern of lazy loading. Instead of downloading every image at once, the browser defers the request until the element is close to entering the viewport.

This has gone from a hacky JavaScript library pattern to a native browser feature in just a few years. According to the 2024 Web Almanac, about one-third of websites now use lazy loading for images. That is a remarkable adoption rate for such a new standard, demonstrating how quickly it has become an integral part of everyday development.

A few key practices make lazy loading an effective, sustainable web strategy:

- **Use native support**: Adding loading="lazy" to an <img> tag is enough in modern browsers. No extra libraries required.
- **Be cautious with above-the-fold content**: Hero images and key interface elements should never be deferred, as this can negatively impact Largest Contentful Paint and user perception.
- **Offer a placeholder**: A blurred thumbnail or background color makes the load feel intentional, rather than leaving users staring at an empty box.

Lazy loading is not a silver bullet, but it is a low-effort, high-return practice. By holding back what users have not requested yet, we reduce wasted transfers and make pages appear faster. It is one of those beautiful cases where performance, sustainability, and user experience all move in the same direction.

Responsive Images with <picture>

Even when we delay loading, the size of the asset that eventually arrives still matters. The HTML <picture> element, introduced in 2016, provides a native way to serve different images based on device characteristics, such as screen size, resolution, or media queries.

```
<picture>
  <source srcset="mdn-logo-wide.png" media="(min-width: 600px)" />
  <img src="mdn-logo-narrow.png" alt="MDN" />
</picture>
```

This allows the browser to make the choice: a smaller image for a mobile screen on a slow network, a sharper one for a large desktop display, or a fallback for an older browser. It is a way of meeting users where they are, instead of pushing the same heavy file to everyone. And the browser, which generally knows more about the user's context than we do, gets to make the choice.

But that doesn't mean the problem is solved. <picture> only works as well as the sources we provide. That brings us to the next challenge: choosing the correct sizes in the first place.

Asking for the Correct Size

The <picture> element is only helpful if we provide it with meaningful options. In practice, this usually comes down to one critical detail: the sizes attribute. It tells the browser how large an image will actually be rendered in the layout, and it should describe the container the image lives in, not the full viewport.

While working as a Sustainable Web Consultant for a client, I encountered a classic example of this problem during an audit. Many very large images were being delivered, even though only the main hero image could ever justify that level of resolution.

It did not take long to see what was happening. A common mistake had crept in: tying the viewport width (vw) directly to image size without considering the actual layout. The page used a three-column article teaser component, restricted by a maximum width on larger screens (Figure 7-5). On the widest displays, a teaser image could never be wider than about 500 px, yet the site was delivering the largest available rendition for each of the nine teaser images. One of those images alone was over 2 MB.

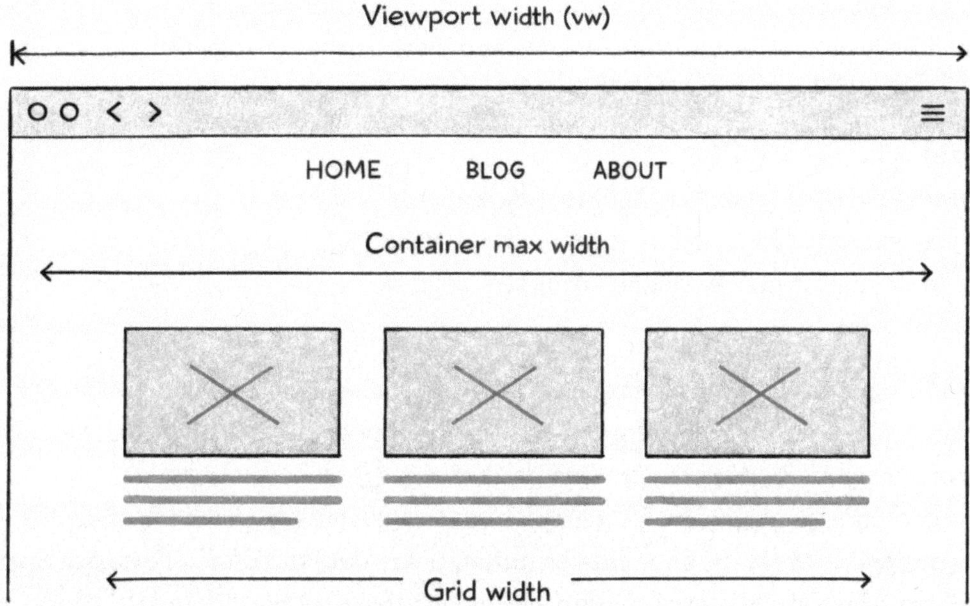

Figure 7-5. *Relationship between viewport width, container max width, and grid width*

Fixing the sizes definition to reflect the real container width instead of the viewport instantly reduced the weight of that component by roughly 90%. No redesign. No new assets. Just a single line of code corrected to match reality.

This was a good reminder that sustainability improvements do not always come from large architectural changes. Sometimes they come from noticing where our assumptions break down. Once we start looking for these mismatches between intent and implementation, we find them everywhere. And there are more techniques we can use to reduce asset sizes even further.

Choosing the Right Format

Modern image formats can dramatically reduce file size, but sustainability is not just about choosing the smallest possible format. It is about choosing formats in a way that does not exclude users or force unnecessary upgrades.

Formats like WebP and AVIF offer significant size savings compared to JPEG or PNG. Both WebP and AVIF are now widely supported, with AVIF delivering even better compression. Relying on a single format assumes too much about the user's device, browser, and update cycle.

The good news is that this does not need to be an either-or decision. The <picture> element allows us to offer multiple formats and let the browser select the most efficient option it can handle:

```
<picture>
  <source srcset="logo.avif" type="image/avif">
  <source srcset="logo.webp" type="image/webp">
  <img src="logo.jpg" alt="Our website logo">
</picture>
```

With this approach, capable browsers get the smallest, most efficient format, while older or more limited environments still receive a reliable fallback. No user is locked out, and no one is pushed toward upgrading hardware just to view an image.

This is progressive enhancement applied to assets. It respects device diversity, extends hardware lifetimes, and reduces unnecessary data transfer. A few extra lines of markup can save significant bandwidth at scale, while ensuring efficiency never comes at the cost of access.

Image Caching

Even optimized images are wasteful if they are downloaded again and again. Browser caching allows us to store assets locally, preventing repeat visits from triggering new transfers. For images, a few strategies work exceptionally well:

- **Set long cache lifetimes** for static assets like logos, icons, or brand graphics that rarely change.
- **Version filenames when content changes**, so that browsers know when to fetch a new one.
- **Use service workers** to cache frequently used images offline, especially in apps or dashboards where the same assets are requested repeatedly.
- **Leverage CDNs** to serve images from servers located near users, thereby reducing the distance traveled and energy consumption on the backbone.

To make this more concrete, consider a common setup for static images served from a web server or CDN. A logo that rarely changes can be cached aggressively using HTTP headers:

```
Cache-Control: public, max-age=31536000, immutable
```

This tells the browser it can safely reuse the image for up to a year without re-downloading it. If the logo ever changes, the filename is updated, for example, from logo.png to logo.v2.png, which forces a fresh download only when it is actually needed.

The payoff is immediate: faster reloads, fewer network requests, and less repeated energy use across the network. From a sustainability perspective, cached data is data that does not need to move again. And data that does not move does not consume energy.

Video: Handle with Care

Thank it, and... yeah, I know you can't. Streaming and social media aside, adding video to a page can be valuable for users. Hopefully, the design and content team has already agreed on which ones are genuinely needed. But once they are there, we can still minimize their impact on performance, carbon emissions, and user experience.

First things first: please do not autoplay videos. Don't offer that option, don't implement it. Autoplay can trigger seizures or other physical reactions, and most people just find it annoying, especially if it interferes with a fast load. There is more on this in Chapter 6, but it bears repeating.

In 2023, I gave a talk titled "Reducing the Carbon Footprint of Your Website." To make it concrete, I analyzed the websites of each conference where I delivered my presentation. This provided me with real-world examples to showcase on stage, and as a bonus, the audience, which consisted mostly of developers, was also the primary user group of those sites. Almost every conference site had a "summary video" from the previous year on its homepage. When I asked the audience who had actually watched it, usually only one or two hands went up. Around 98% never pressed play.

Now, not pressing play is already helpful: the video data won't be transmitted unless the player requests it. But there is still a hidden cost. Most embedded players from third-party streaming services weigh around 300 KB, and this payload is loaded on every single visit, whether the video is played or not.

Import on Interaction

Instead of embedding the entire player up front, we use a facade: a simple, optimized image styled to resemble a video thumbnail. Only when the user clicks it do we load the actual player and start playback. Figure 7-6 illustrates this import-on-interaction pattern, showing how a lightweight placeholder is rendered first and the full video player is only loaded after explicit user action. There are libraries for this, such as YouTube Lite Embed and Lite Vimeo Embed, but it can also be implemented manually with a few lines of code.

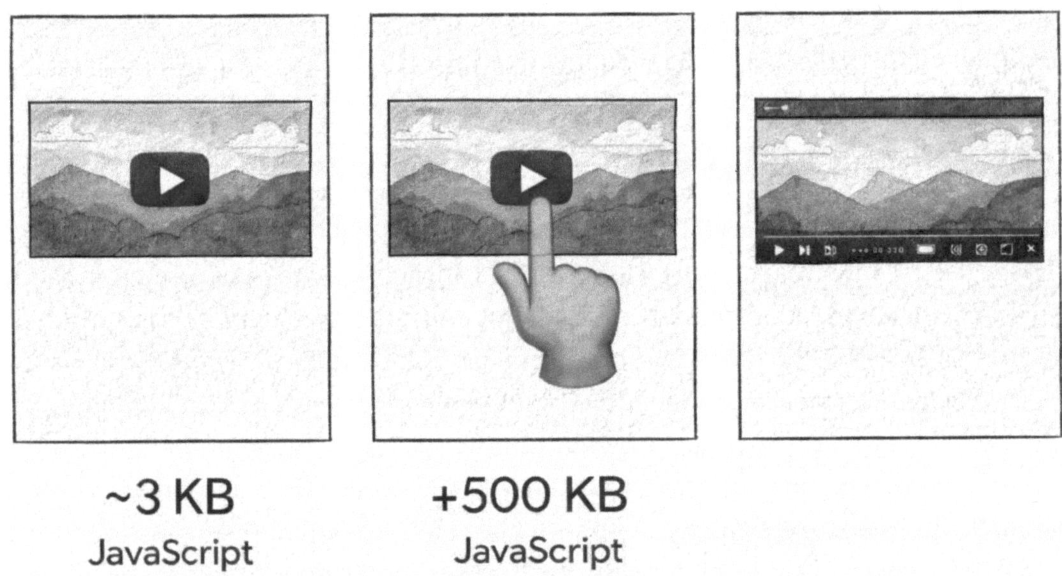

***Figure 7-6.** Import-on-interaction pattern for embedded video player*

Yes, this adds a slight delay for the minority of users who click play. But for the vast majority who never do, it avoids loading hundreds of unnecessary kilobytes. That is a trade-off worth making: better performance for everyone, lighter pages for the planet, and videos only when they are truly wanted.

Keeping Videos Lean

Beyond loading videos only when someone actually asks for them, there are other ways to reduce their footprint without removing them entirely. A few practical strategies stand out:

- **Use adaptive streaming wisely**: Most modern platforms already break video into chunks and adjust quality based on connection speed. But you can also set reasonable defaults. Serving 4K to every user by default wastes data and energy. Often, starting with 720p and letting the viewer bump it up is more than enough.
- **Compress and transcode**: Just like with images, modern formats matter. Encoding in efficient codecs such as AV1 or VP9 can cut file sizes significantly while preserving quality.
- **Set thumbnails intentionally**: Many embeds ship with oversized preview images. Replacing those with optimized thumbnails can save hundreds of kilobytes.
- **Avoid background video loops**: A subtle video header might look stylish, but if it plays silently in the background for everyone, it wastes enormous amounts of bandwidth for almost no gain. Consider using a still image instead.

Handled this way, video remains a powerful medium for storytelling and teaching, without compromising performance or unnecessarily increasing emissions.

A Picture Says a Thousand Words, but Only If It Loads

Whether it is an image or a video, the most carefully crafted media is wasted if it never reaches the user. Heavy assets that take too long to appear, or that people abandon before they are fully loaded, consume energy without delivering value. From both a performance and sustainability perspective, this is the worst outcome: emissions rise, patience drops, and experience suffers.

This is why reducing asset weight matters so much. It ensures that media actually gets seen, rather than being stranded halfway across a slow connection. And it sets us up for the next piece of the puzzle: performance.

Less or Faster

Most of the time, optimizing websites to deliver and render as quickly as possible also makes them more sustainable. A smaller page weight, fewer requests, and efficient rendering mean less data traveling across the network and less processing on devices. The goals of performance and sustainability often move in the same direction.

But not always. Some performance techniques improve the perceived speed of a site while quietly driving up emissions in the background. They make things feel faster for users, but they achieve that by doing more work, not less. This is where we need to pause and look carefully at the trade-offs.

Figure 7-7 illustrates this relationship. In many cases, performance improvements and sustainability reinforce each other. In others, they pull in opposite directions, where techniques that make a site feel faster can increase overall resource use.

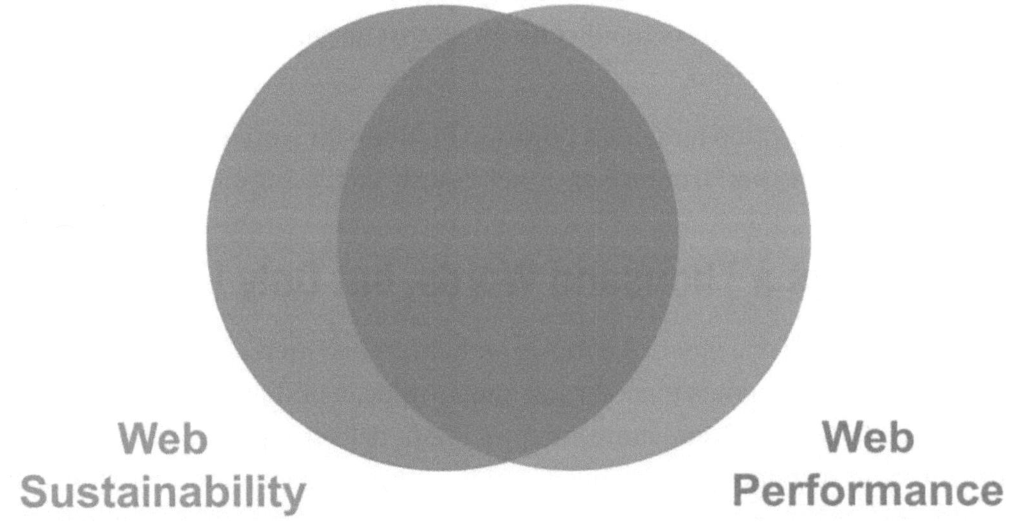

***Figure 7-7.** Relationship between web performance and web sustainability*

The most common examples are preload and prerender. These techniques allow us to fetch resources or even render entire pages before the user explicitly requests them. When a prediction is correct, the experience feels seamless. When it is wrong, we have burned bandwidth, CPU, and energy on something that never delivered value. The same applies to over-caching, preloading media "just in case," or configuring service workers to cache everything by default. On paper, the site may appear faster. In reality, we could be doing more work than necessary. This does not mean that preload or prerender are inherently wasteful. They are powerful tools when used narrowly and deliberately. Problems arise when they are applied broadly, without strong signals or validation, and treated as a default optimization rather than a targeted one.

Speculation rules are a newer browser feature that refines how prefetching and prerendering work. Instead of scattering <link> hints across the page, we can define structured rules in JSON that describe which navigations are worth preparing, and under what conditions. This makes speculative loading more predictable and measurable, and in supported browsers, reduces much of the guesswork and waste associated with traditional prerendering. Used carefully, speculation rules can preserve the feeling of instant navigation while staying more efficient with resources.

Here's how to stay fast without drifting into waste:

- **Preload deliberately**

  Preload is a hint that tells the browser, "You will definitely need this soon." It is perfect for the main CSS file, the hero image, or a critical font. But once we preload everything, nothing is prioritized. Preloading a script that turns out not to be used just shifts the waste earlier in the timeline.

- **Be cautious with prerendering**

  Prerendering goes further: it lets the browser fetch and render an entire page before the user navigates to it. This can make transitions feel instant, but if the prediction is wrong, we have downloaded and rendered a page no one ever saw. That is wasted data, wasted energy, and wasted CPU cycles.

- **Measure with care**

  Real-user monitoring tools can help validate whether these preloads and prerenders are actually paying off, but they also carry a cost. Every extra metric collected means more data transferred, processed, and stored. It is worth measuring, but also worth being deliberate about what is measured and how long it is kept.

- **Defer media until requested**

  Video and other large media files should not be preloaded "just in case." The import-on-interaction pattern ensures they only load when the user actually wants them, saving bandwidth for everyone else.

These techniques highlight the tension between speed and sustainability. Tools like real-user monitoring can help validate whether preloads or prerenders are actually worthwhile, but they also generate their own footprint. Every metric collected has to be transmitted, processed, and stored. Measuring is essential, but measuring everything "just in case" is like leaving every light on in the house "just in case" someone walks into the room. The principle is the same as with code and assets: be deliberate.

We have examined assets, code, and performance from the perspective of making them lighter, faster, and more efficient. The pattern is clear: less is almost always better, and speed often aligns with sustainability. But there are limits to what optimization alone can achieve. At some point, we need more than just tricks to shave off bytes and milliseconds. **We need a way of thinking that embraces constraints from the start, that ensures access for every user, and that works in harmony with the reality of limited resources.**

This is where progressive enhancement comes in. And when we add carbon awareness on top, the result is more than optimization. It becomes a framework for sustainable front-end development in the decade ahead.

Progressive Enhancement and Carbon-Awareness

Progressive enhancement is one of the oldest ideas in front-end development, but it might also be one of the most future-proof. The principle is simple: build the core experience in a way that works everywhere, then layer on enhancements that improve the experience when the browser, device, or network can support them. Instead of designing for the latest flagship device and then trying to degrade gracefully, we start from the most resilient baseline and move upward.

From a sustainability perspective, this principle becomes even more powerful. In Chapter 3, we explored how inclusive product choices can broaden access, and in Chapter 6, we looked at how design decisions can enable or block users. Progressive enhancement is the technical side of that same philosophy: a baseline built with clean HTML and CSS ensures that no one is left out, whether they are on an old phone, a patchy connection, or relying on assistive technology. Enhancements become optional, loaded only when they bring real value or when the user chooses to opt in, rather than being imposed by default. This approach shifts control back to the person using the site, allowing them to decide when richer, heavier features are worth the extra cost in data, energy, or attention.

A Foundation That Evolves

At the beginning of this chapter, we described front-end development as resting on three layers: structure, presentation, and interactivity. Progressive enhancement builds on this same foundation, but adds a decision-making mindset. It is not just a way to build, but a way to decide when and why to build.

At its core, progressive enhancement asks a simple question: **what is the minimum a user needs to succeed right now?** The answer defines the baseline. That baseline is clean, semantic HTML that works everywhere, regardless of device, browser, network conditions, or assistive technology. From there, we layer on CSS to improve clarity, readability, and visual expression. Only after that do we introduce JavaScript to add interactivity and advanced behavior where conditions allow.

Approached this way, front-end development becomes more resilient by default. Nothing is taken away from users who can support richer experiences, but no one is blocked from accessing the essentials. Enhancements are exactly that: optional improvements, not prerequisites. If JavaScript fails, loads slowly, or is never requested, the experience still holds together.

This approach aligns naturally with sustainability. A lean baseline reduces unnecessary data transfer and processing. Optional enhancements are loaded only when they provide clear value, rather than being shipped to everyone by default. Control shifts back to the user, who implicitly decides, through their device, connection, and choices, how much of the experience they want to load.

Progressive enhancement also resolves a tension we often feel in front-end work. It does not reject modern tools, frameworks, or dynamic interactions. Instead, it places them where they belong: as layers on top of a solid core. Designers retain freedom to create expressive interfaces. Developers still get to build rich, interactive systems. Users get reliable access, even in constrained environments. And because the foundation remains lightweight, we avoid wasting energy on features that never get used.

In this sense, progressive enhancement is not an old-fashioned best practice. It is a practical blueprint for building digital products that can scale across devices, contexts, and time. It allows the web to remain inclusive while still evolving.

And with the tools available today, this blueprint can go even further. By adding carbon awareness into our decision-making, front-end code can begin to respond not only to users and their devices, but also to environmental conditions. At that point, progressive enhancement becomes more than a technical strategy. It becomes a way to consciously balance experience, performance, and planetary limits from the very start.

Adding Carbon Awareness

Most front-end developers are already familiar with the idea of progressive enhancement through responsive design. We adapt to different screen sizes, respect dark mode or reduced motion preferences, and sometimes respond to slower networks. The browser gives us signals, and we adjust the experience accordingly. Carbon awareness builds on that same idea, but extends it beyond the device.

What if the web responded not only to users and their hardware but also to the conditions of the energy system powering it?

This is the core idea behind carbon awareness. The electricity that runs servers, networks, and devices is not equally clean at all times. Its carbon intensity, the amount of CO_2e emitted per kilowatt hour, changes constantly depending on how much renewable energy is available. When wind and solar generation are high, electricity is cleaner. When the grid relies more on fossil fuels, the same computation results in higher emissions.

A carbon-aware system can react to this signal in much the same way it reacts to bandwidth or motion preferences. When the grid is carbon-intensive, a site could delay non-essential background tasks, reduce visual effects, or load a simpler version of the interface. When cleaner energy is available, richer experiences can be enabled where they provide clear and meaningful value to the user.

The Green Web Foundation has been pioneering this idea through its Grid-aware Websites project. Using data from services such as Electricity Maps, WattTime, national grid operators, and projects like carbon-aware-computing.com, the initiative explores how real-time or forecast carbon intensity can inform design and development decisions. Experimental examples, showcased on Branch Magazine, include grid-aware indicators and subtle shifts in visual behavior depending on how clean or dirty the grid is at that moment.

However, it is important to be honest about the current limitations of this approach. Grid carbon-intensity data is highly dependent on how electricity markets and transmission networks are structured. In countries with many smaller grid zones, the signal can be relatively precise. In others, it is much less so. Germany, for example, operates largely as a single grid zone shared with Luxembourg, which means local conditions are often flattened into a single average value. Excess wind power in one region and fossil-fuel generation in another can cancel each other out in the data, even though the real-world situation is far more uneven.

There are also cases where grid-level data fails to reflect what is happening at the point of consumption. Recently my parents installed solar panels, and their household often produces more electricity than it consumes (it is a very sunny place). While visiting, I experimented with several carbon-intensity tools and quickly noticed a mismatch. Even when the house was powered almost entirely by on-site solar generation, grid-based tools still reported relatively high CO_2e values. This is because those tools reflect average conditions of the national electricity network, not what is happening behind the meter.

Due to these constraints, carbon awareness should be understood as an informed signal, not a hard truth. It works best when combined with the principles discussed throughout this chapter: progressive enhancement, user choice, and restraint by default. Heavy features should already be optional. Carbon signals simply add another input into deciding when those features are worth enabling.

Seen this way, carbon awareness is not a magic switch or a guarantee of lower emissions. It is an extension of responsible front-end thinking. It introduces a new condition into our decision-making, one that connects user experience with planetary impact. The signal may be imperfect today, but the direction is clear. As data improves and tooling matures, carbon-aware approaches have the potential to reduce emissions at scale by aligning when and how the web does its work.

Bringing the Concept to Life

The goal is not to create separate "green" versions of websites, like we once did with dedicated "mobile sites." We have already learned that maintaining parallel experiences is inefficient and exclusionary. Responsive design taught us to build adaptable interfaces that work everywhere. But in focusing on screen size, we often forget the other constraints that mobile experiences once forced us to consider: slower networks, limited power, and smaller data plans.

Progressive enhancement and carbon awareness bring those lessons back. They remind us that responsiveness should extend beyond layout to include performance, accessibility, and energy context.

We already have everything we need to build sites that adapt to people, devices, networks, and even the planet itself. Turning that potential into practice is where the real fun begins.

This section is aimed at developers comfortable with modern front-end workflows: SSR or edge rendering, service workers, and feature flags. The following techniques show how to make a site adaptive and efficient in real-world conditions.

Build a Resilient Baseline

Every sustainable experience starts with HTML that works on its own. Buttons should trigger their core action even if JavaScript fails. Forms should submit through native browser behavior. Links should always navigate, regardless of what framework or script sits on top.

Once the base is solid, layer on enhancements. Add features progressively, using feature detection instead of user-agent assumptions. This keeps the experience stable even when scripts break or networks fluctuate.

```
<button type="submit">Send</button>
<script>
  document.querySelector('button').addEventListener('click', sendForm);
</script>
```

If the script fails, the button still works. That is resilience in practice.

Respond to Context

Modern browsers expose a range of signals that describe a user's context: their preferences, their device constraints, and sometimes even environmental conditions. These signals allow us to adapt experiences intelligently, without shipping more code or assets than necessary. Instead of guessing, we can listen.

The table below summarizes some of the most useful signals available today, what they tell us, and how they can be applied in practice.

Signal	Context we get	How to use
prefers-reduced-motion	User wants fewer or no animations	Disable transitions, parallax, and non-essential motion
prefers-color-scheme	Preference for dark or light theme	Switch styles to match system setting
navigator.connection.saveData	Data-saving mode is enabled	Serve compressed media, skip autoplay, avoid prefetching
navigator.connection.downlink	Approximate connection speed	Limit speculative loading, serve lower-resolution assets

(*continued*)

Signal	Context we get	How to use
Battery API (where available)	The device is low on power	Pause background syncs and heavy effects
Carbon intensity (server or edge)	Current grid CO_2e intensity	Delay non-essential work, reduce visual complexity

These signals let us make small, respectful adjustments that improve usability and reduce unnecessary energy use, without fragmenting the experience or maintaining separate versions of a site.

Some practical examples:

- **Reduced motion** preferences can be handled entirely in CSS, with no JavaScript required. This improves accessibility and avoids unnecessary GPU work for users who explicitly opt out of motion.

```
@media (prefers-reduced-motion: reduce) {
  .animation { animation: none; transition: none; }
}
```

- **Data-saving mode** can be respected at runtime using the Network Information API. This ensures that users who are actively trying to conserve data are not forced to download large assets they did not ask for.

```
if (navigator.connection?.saveData) {
  loadLowResImages();
  skipVideoAutoplay();
}
```

The common thread across all of these examples is restraint. We are not adding features. We are deciding when not to use them. By responding to context instead of assuming ideal conditions, we build experiences that are lighter, more respectful, and more sustainable by default.

Make It Carbon-Aware

Carbon awareness can live alongside any other adaptive feature in front-end development. Just as we respond to user preferences or network speed, we can also react to the energy context our sites run in. The idea is simple: when the grid is cleaner, we can allow heavier features; when it is dirtier, we scale back and save energy.

The most efficient way to apply carbon awareness is at the server or edge, where one request can serve many users in the same area. An edge function can fetch regional carbon intensity, cache it for a few minutes, and decide which version of the page to serve:

```
const intensity = await getCarbonIntensity(region).catch(() => null);
const lowEnergy = intensity ? intensity > 400 : false;
renderPage({ lowEnergy });
}
```

For smaller, session-level adjustments, the browser can further refine the experience. The carbon-intensity value can be passed from the server or fetched asynchronously, triggering visual or behavioral changes without blocking rendering:

```
if (carbonIntensity > 400) {
  document.body.classList.add('low-energy-mode');
}
```

```
.low-energy-mode video,
.low-energy-mode .background-animation {
  display: none;
}
```

This pattern works well for pausing video, toning down visual effects, or delaying optional scripts. The goal is not to remove functionality but to reduce unnecessary work when energy is more carbon-intensive.

In practice, the most effective approach combines both layers. The edge makes coarse decisions about what to send, and the browser fine-tunes the experience during the session. This balance avoids waste while keeping interfaces responsive and personal.

A few good practices to keep in mind:

- **Cache by region and time**: Carbon-intensity data typically updates in fixed intervals, often every 15 minutes, similar to electricity price data. Caching decisions should align with this update frequency rather than attempting near-real-time updates.
- **Set thresholds carefully**: A typical value is around 400 g CO_2/kWh, but it varies by region.
- **Avoid blocking rendering**: Never wait for carbon-intensity APIs before showing content. Carbon awareness should enhance the experience, not delay it.
- **Respect privacy**: Derive the region from the IP at the edge without storing the address.
- **Keep it inclusive**: A low-energy version should remain fully functional, accessible, and pleasant to use.

If you want to experiment, the Green Web Foundation's open-source Grid-Aware Web repository is an excellent starting point. It demonstrates how to integrate carbon-intensity signals derived from grid data into both server- and client-side logic, while acknowledging the limits of what those signals can represent.

Let Users Stay in Control

Automatic adaptation should never remove choice. If a site loads a lighter version due to higher grid carbon intensity or limited bandwidth, it should clearly communicate why and give users control over the experience.

For example:

> *"You're viewing a low-impact version to save data and energy. You can switch to the full version at any time."*

Provide a visible toggle to move between versions, and make it reversible. If a user chooses the full experience, respect that choice and allow them to switch back later if their needs change.

Preferences can be stored locally, for example, in localStorage, and honored on subsequent visits. Transparency and reversibility turn adaptation into collaboration rather than restriction, and ensure that sustainability features empower users instead of surprising them.

Keep Data Close

Efficiency is not only about how much data we ship, but also how far it has to travel. Edge computing allows us to serve regional variants of a site and make carbon-aware decisions closer to the user, without repeated round trips to an origin server. Service workers and smart caching extend this idea into the browser, keeping assets and responses local so repeat visits cost almost nothing.

For example:

- Precomputing common pages at the edge to avoid regenerating the same content on every request
- Caching JSON responses and static assets with service workers so repeat interactions do not trigger new network requests
- Serving simplified templates or deferring non-essential features in regions with consistently carbon-intensive grid

Each of these actions reduces unnecessary data movement. Every byte that does not cross a network saves time, energy, and device resources.

Bringing progressive enhancement to life means treating context as a design input: user needs, device capabilities, network conditions, and now energy context. When we design and build with these signals in mind, the web becomes more resilient, more ethical, and better aligned with both people and the planet.

Conclusion

Front-end development has always been about connecting people and technology. But today, that connection reaches further. Every choice we make, every image, script, or animation, carries an environmental cost as well as a user impact. The front-end sits at the intersection of both. It is where design becomes real, where performance decisions meet user experience, and where sustainability can make a measurable difference.

This chapter explored how much influence front-end engineers truly have. Through clean structure, optimized assets, mindful performance, and adaptive patterns, we shape how energy flows across the web. Each decision, from how an image loads to when a script executes, determines whether our sites act as silent polluters or quiet advocates for efficiency.

Progressive enhancement and carbon awareness show a way forward. They remind us that we can build for everyone without compromise, that inclusivity, resilience, and sustainability are not competing goals but shared ones. A site that adapts to its users, respects their preferences, and responds to real-world conditions is not only more ethical, it is also more efficient, stable, and enjoyable to use.

The tools are already here: edge functions, browser APIs, carbon data, and, most importantly, the discipline of writing better code. What matters next is intention. Do we use these tools to chase artificial speed and complexity, or to craft a web that endures?

Those of us who build the front-end have the privilege of shaping what billions of people experience every day. With that comes the responsibility to make those experiences fast, fair, and future-ready. Because when we code with care for both people and the planet, the web becomes what it was always meant to be: a space that connects, empowers, and sustains.

Back at the beginning of my front-end journey, my biggest challenge was aligning a div (back in the pre-flexbox and CSS grid days). These days, the challenge feels a little bigger: aligning people, technology, and the planet all at once. Maybe that is what front-end development was preparing us for all along.

Summary

Front-end development sits at a critical intersection between user experience and environmental impact. Every line of HTML, CSS, and JavaScript we ship is executed on real devices, consuming energy, data, and attention. This chapter explores how front-end engineers can take responsibility for those costs while still building rich, modern experiences.

Starting with the foundational layers of the web, the chapter examines how growing complexity, heavy frameworks, third-party scripts, and media-rich assets have driven page weight and energy use steadily upward. It shows how principles such as interoperability, openness, accessibility, and security are not optional extras but essential building blocks of a sustainable front end.

Through practical examples, the chapter demonstrates how to reduce unnecessary JavaScript, question framework choices, control third-party dependencies, optimize fonts, cache assets effectively, and deliver images and video more responsibly. It also highlights the tension between performance techniques that improve perceived speed and those that quietly increase resource use.

The chapter then introduces progressive enhancement as a decision-making mindset, ensuring that core functionality works everywhere while optional features are layered on only when they provide real value. Building on this, it explores carbon awareness as an emerging signal, allowing front-end systems to adapt not only to users and devices, but also to energy conditions, while acknowledging the current limits of grid-level data.

Finally, the chapter brings these ideas together with practical patterns for building adaptive, resilient front ends that respect user choice, respond to context, and minimize unnecessary work. The takeaway is clear: sustainable front-end development is not about sacrificing quality or innovation, but about intention. By choosing what to ship, when to load it, and for whom, front-end engineers can create experiences that are faster, fairer, and better aligned with both people and the planet.

References

Standards, Specs, and Core Web Documentation

- **W3C Sustainable Web Guidelines, Web Development:**

  https://w3c.github.io/sustainableweb-wsg/#web-development

- **HTML (MDN):** https://developer.mozilla.org/en-US/docs/Web/HTML

- **JavaScript (MDN):** https://developer.mozilla.org/en-US/docs/Web/JavaScript

- **CSS Media Queries (MDN):**

  https://developer.mozilla.org/en-US/docs/Web/CSS/Media_Queries

- **prefers-reduced-motion (MDN):**

  https://developer.mozilla.org/en-US/docs/Web/CSS/@media/prefers-reduced-motion

- **prefers-color-scheme (MDN):**

  https://developer.mozilla.org/en-US/docs/Web/CSS/@media/prefers-color-scheme

- **HTML <picture> element (MDN):**

  https://developer.mozilla.org/en-US/docs/Web/HTML/Element/picture

- **Speculation Rules API (MDN):**

  https://developer.mozilla.org/en-US/docs/Web/API/Speculation_Rules_API

- **Network Information API (MDN):**

  https://developer.mozilla.org/en-US/docs/Web/API/NetworkInformation

- **Battery Status API (MDN):**

  https://developer.mozilla.org/en-US/docs/Web/API/Battery_Status_API

- **Service Worker API (MDN):**

  https://developer.mozilla.org/en-US/docs/Web/API/Service_Worker_API

- **Cache-Control header (MDN):**

  https://developer.mozilla.org/en-US/docs/Web/HTTP/Headers/Cache-Control

Industry Reports and Benchmarks

- **HTTP Archive Web Almanac 2024:** https://almanac.httparchive.org/en/2024/
- **Web Almanac 2024, Sustainability chapter:**

  https://almanac.httparchive.org/en/2024/sustainability

- **HTTP Archive:** https://httparchive.org/

Performance Tooling and Measurement

- **Firefox Power Profiler:** `https://profiler.firefox.com/`
- **Chrome DevTools (docs):** `https://developer.chrome.com/docs/devtools/`

Performance, Constraints, and "Cost of JavaScript"

- **Russell, Alex. "The Performance Inequality Gap"**

  `https://infrequently.org/series/performance-inequality/`
- **"Transitioning to Modern JavaScript" (YouTube):**

  `https://www.youtube.com/watch?v=cLxNdLK-yI`
- **"The Cost of JavaScript" (YouTube):**

  `https://www.youtube.com/watch?v=ZKH3DLT4BKw`

Patterns and Practical Implementation Guides

- **Import on interaction pattern (patterns.dev):**

  `https://www.patterns.dev/vanilla/import-on-interaction/`
- **Browser-level image lazy loading (web.dev):**

  `https://web.dev/browser-level-image-lazy-loading/`
- **Responsive images guide (web.dev):** `https://web.dev/serve-responsive-images/`
- **Video optimization (web.dev):** `https://web.dev/fast/#optimize-video`

Images, Formats, and Encoding

- **WebP (Google for Developers):** https://developers.google.com/speed/webp

Accessibility and User Safety

- **The A11Y Project: Never use autoplay:** https://www.a11yproject.com/posts/never-use-auto-play/

Progressive Enhancement

- **Progressive Enhancement (MDN glossary):** https://developer.mozilla.org/en-US/docs/Glossary/Progressive_Enhancement
- **ProgUX (Netcentric, GitHub):** https://github.com/Netcentric/progux

Carbon-Aware and Grid-Aware Web

- **The Green Web Foundation, Grid-Aware Websites (GitHub):**

  https://github.com/thegreenwebfoundation/grid-aware-websites
- **Green Web Foundation developer docs:**

  https://developers.thegreenwebfoundation.org/
- **Green Web Foundation, "Introducing the grid-aware web"**

  https://www.thegreenwebfoundation.org/news/introducing-the-grid-aware-web/
- **Designing a Grid-Aware Branch (Branch, Issue 9)**

  https://branch.climateaction.tech/issues/issue-9/designing-a-grid-aware-branch/

- **Electricity Maps API:** https://www.electricitymaps.com/platform/api
- **UK National Grid Carbon Intensity API:** https://carbonintensity.org.uk/
- **Sustainable Web Design:** https://sustainablewebdesign.org/

Energy Systems and Grid Zones

- **ENTSO-E (bidding zones/review material)**

  https://bid3.afry.com/publicpages/publications/client-studies-pages/2025-04-02-entso-e-bidding-zone-review-for-the-2025-target-year.html

Books

- **McGovern, Gerry. World Wide Waste:** https://gerrymcgovern.com/books/world-wide-waste/

Podcast

- **Environment Variables (Acast), "Root & Branch and SCI-Web" (Ep. 124):** https://shows.acast.com/environment-variables/episodes/root-and-branch-and-sci-web

CHAPTER 8

Content and Marketing

Ines Akrap[1]
[1]Munich, Germany; inesakrap.com

"Content is king." That was one of the first sentences I heard on my first day as a trainee front-end developer. I was sitting in the third row of desks in an open-plan office that had been arranged to look like a classroom. I was part of an Academy program, being trained to develop front ends for a specific, monolithic CMS. As someone who had just spent years studying mathematics, physics, circuitry, networks, and software programming, I wasn't particularly excited by the talk of content. Yeah, yeah, give me some code, please. By the time I "graduated" from our Academy, my perspective definitely changed.

Our Academy program was split into three weeks of learning and three weeks of project work. For the project phase, we were divided into small teams, each tasked with delivering a functioning website powered by the CMS. The brief was clear: focus on CMS and content creation functionality. We were instructed to choose something like a bank, an insurance portal, or a news site. I still remember my thoughts wandering off, trying to figure out if there was a bank that didn't already have a website. The "lightbulb" moment happened instantly: Gringotts, the wizarding bank from Harry Potter. My teammates loved the idea, and so we set out to build a CMS-powered Gringotts website (shown in Figure 8-1).

C. Chinchilla and I. Akrap, *Building the Sustainable Web*, https://doi.org/10.1007/979-8-8688-2521-7_8

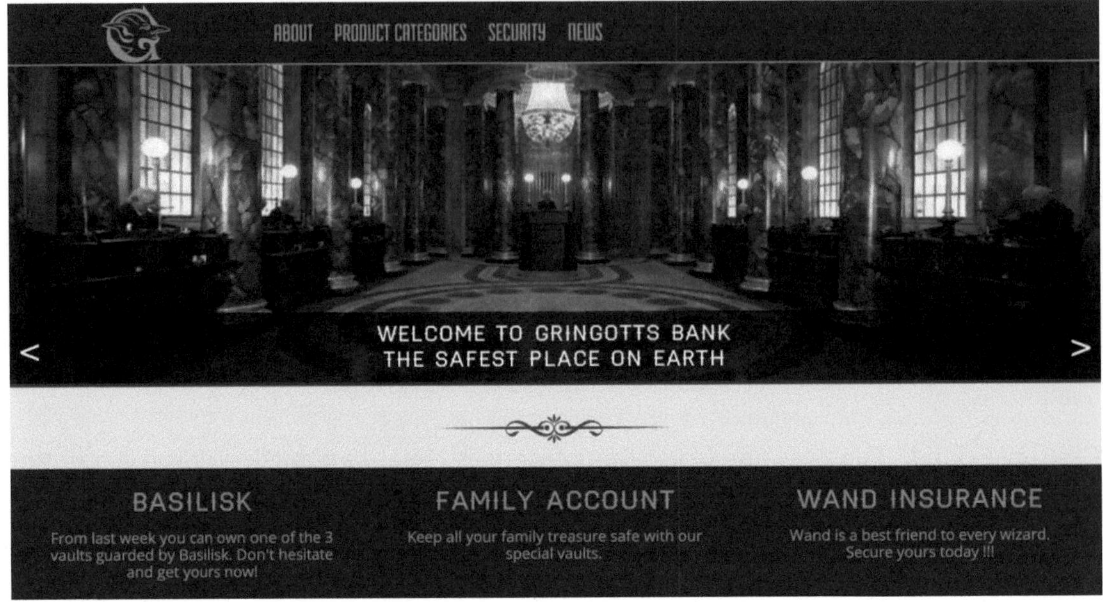

Figure 8-1. *Screenshot of Gringotts Bank website project home page*

Over the following weeks, we configured the system, built components, defined color schemes, and refined accessibility features. By the end of the sprint, everything was ready except one thing: the content.

I took that task on myself, pulling a late night to fill the site with copy, images, and mock stories to showcase what we had built. To my surprise, it was much more fun than I ever thought (probably something to do with my Harry Potter obsession). Every component we created was designed to organize and display content. Yet, until that point, we had focused almost entirely on the technical requirements of the components, rather than what they were meant to display.

That project remains one of my favorite things I've ever built. Not because it was the most advanced technically, but because it taught me that everything else we design and develop is actually in service of content and not the other way around.

The Core of the Web

"Content is king." The phrase is usually credited to Bill Gates, who wrote an essay under that title in 1996. He predicted that content would drive the Internet's value, just as programming had driven the software industry. Nearly 30 years later, the statement still holds, but it has evolved. Content remains the reason people visit a website or use a service, yet the scale and speed of its creation have grown far beyond what anyone imagined. That growth brought with it new layers of complexity, something we've encountered in every stage of digital creation.

In the previous chapters, we explored how strategy, design, and development create the foundation of good digital products. Yet it is the content that fills that structure and turns it into something meaningful for users. Words, images, video, data, and the small pieces of text that guide or reassure users, such as button labels, error messages, and short instructions, all come together to inform, guide, or inspire the user. All of these elements together form the language of digital communication. They shape how we experience products, how we understand information, and how we connect with organizations. Content remains the heart of every digital interaction.

People come online for a reason: to read the news, check a balance, buy a ticket, find a recipe, or learn something new. They do not come for the layout, animations, or code behind it, no matter how elegant those may be. The content is what ultimately matters to our end users, and everything else exists to support it.

However, in the life cycle of many websites, content is often treated as an afterthought, coming at a later stage after design and development are already complete. By the time content authors and marketing teams start their work, the site's technical and visual framework is already set, making it more challenging to adapt for sustainability, accessibility, or relevance. When content is seen as an afterthought, it becomes just another thing to fit in, rather than the foundation upon which everything else is built.

Yet, in practice, content is not only what users care about most but also where the real consequences of our digital choices appear. Every story told online consumes both energy and attention, shaping how people think, act, and connect. The way we plan, create, and maintain content determines whether those connections enrich people, respect the planet, and create lasting value, or quietly deplete them all.

The Weight of Words

The web carries more content than any one person could read in a lifetime. As we write this, there are over 1.12 billion websites worldwide, yet only about 17% of them are considered active. That contrast reveals a hard truth: more than 80% of the web sits unused, filled with pages, images, and domains that rarely see a visitor but still exist, still draw power, and still occupy storage. This imbalance shows how easily digital creation outpaces digital care.

Content is both the soul and the load of our digital world. Once created, it begins to accumulate in databases, backups, and caches, where it is rarely reviewed or retired. The more we publish, the heavier the web becomes.

In theory, digital content is easy to change or delete. In practice, it lingers. Old campaigns, outdated press releases, and product descriptions from long-forgotten launches often remain stored, indexed, and retrievable. Each item sits on a server somewhere, quietly using resources that few ever think about. This quiet permanence is one of the web's great contradictions. We celebrate speed, agility, and constant change, yet behind every update sits a growing archive that never sleeps. Storage seems limitless and inexpensive, but in reality, it depends on physical machines that consume electricity and water, which must eventually be replaced.

The result is an enormous amount of digital weight carried by content that no one reads, maintains, or removes. The cost is not only environmental but also social and economic. For users, it makes information harder to find and trust. For organizations, it creates clutter that slows teams and confuses strategy.

Reducing this weight starts with awareness. Every word, image, and data entry should have a lifespan. **Treating content as a living system, one that needs pruning as much as growth, is the first step toward making our digital ecosystems lighter, more transparent, and more sustainable.**

The People Behind the Words

Content does not create itself. Behind every page view and campaign lies a series of choices made by content and marketing teams. They decide what gets published, when it appears, and how it is delivered. These decisions shape what we read, watch, and interact with online, and by extension, how much energy and data the web consumes in the process.

The scope of this work is broad: creating, publishing, promoting, and measuring content. Each step leaves a trace. The words, images, and videos produced determine the amount of data users need to load. The platforms and tools chosen to distribute and track that content determine how many scripts, cookies, and network requests are triggered each time a page opens. Even well-intentioned actions, such as adding analytics to understand users better or embedding interactive widgets to boost engagement, can introduce hidden costs that multiply at scale.

This is not about limiting creativity or communication. It is about recognizing influence. Every decision, from tone of voice to tracking method, affects the speed, efficiency, and trustworthiness of a digital experience. The stories we tell, and the systems we use to tell them, directly shape the web's environmental and ethical footprint.

To see how these forces play out in practice, we can look at one of the most familiar content types online: the recipe post. It offers a clear example of how convenience, search optimization, and revenue models can quietly weigh down both user experience and sustainability.

When Algorithms Drive Experience

Recipe websites offer a familiar, everyday example of how marketing systems can quietly undermine both user experience and sustainability. The pattern is instantly recognizable: a long introduction filled with personal anecdotes, pop-ups layered over the text, videos that start playing automatically beside ads, and somewhere far below, the actual recipe (Figure 8-2).

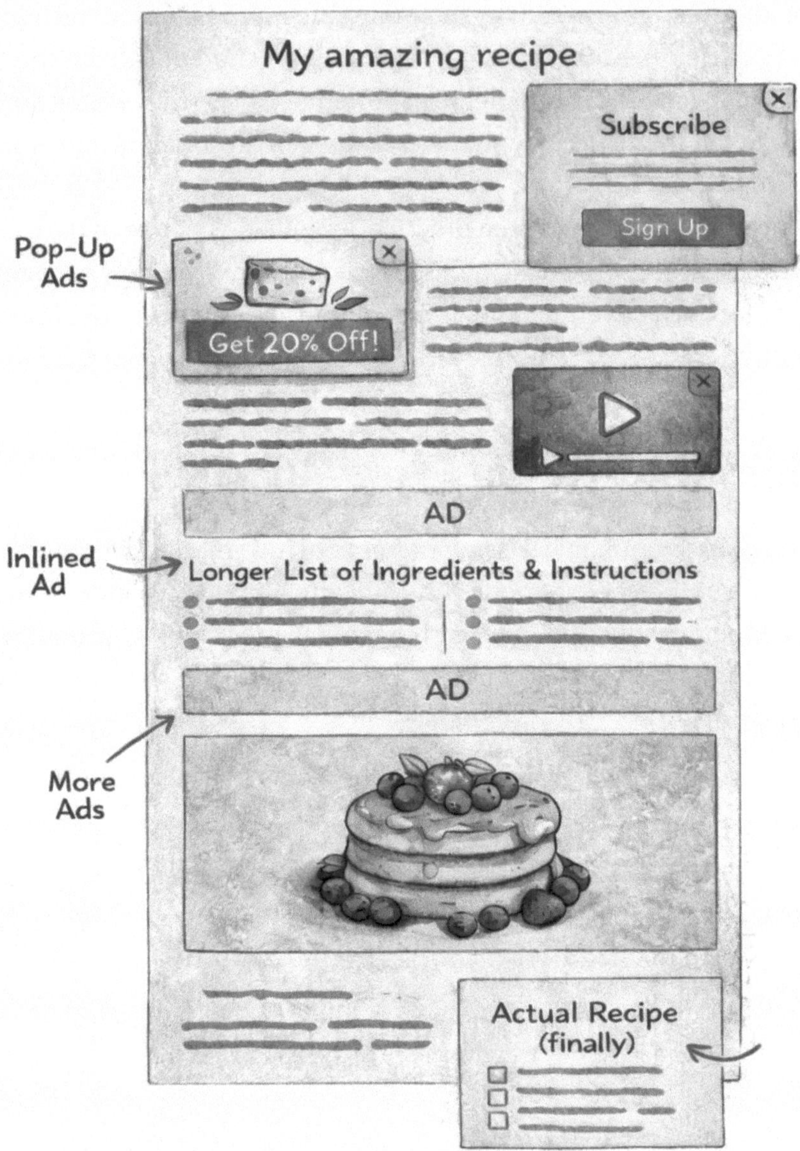

***Figure 8-2.** Anatomy of a typical recipe page, illustrating how advertising and engagement elements push the core content further down the page*

This did not happen by accident. It emerged from the intersection of search engine optimization and ad-based revenue models. For years, search algorithms rewarded length, keyword repetition, and time spent on a page. More words and more scrolling signaled valuable content. At the same time, advertising systems paid for impressions and engagement, turning every extra paragraph, image, or embedded video into another opportunity for monetization.

Together, these incentives created a feedback loop where success depended on volume and visibility rather than clarity or usefulness. Pages grew longer, heavier, and more complex, even when that complexity actively worked against the user's goal.

Alisa Bonsignore, author of *Sustainable Content* and a leading voice in sustainable content strategy, describes this dynamic as a systemic failure rather than an individual one. Content bloat, she argues, is rarely the result of bad intentions. It is the outcome of incentives that reward accumulation, discourage deletion, and treat digital storage and distribution as effectively free. In practice, this leads to what she calls "digital landfills": vast amounts of content, tracking data, and media that continue to consume energy long after their value has faded.

The recipe page is a perfect illustration of this phenomenon. What should be a straightforward exchange of information becomes an obstacle course designed to satisfy algorithms and ad platforms rather than people. The longer and heavier the page becomes, the better it performs for machines, even as it frustrates the humans it was meant to serve.

We have all experienced this shift. What began as a way to help people find information has slowly turned into a system that serves itself. The race for visibility rewards quantity over clarity and activity over usefulness. Each additional image, script, tracker, and video request adds a small, often invisible cost in energy, data transfer, and attention. Individually, these costs seem negligible. At scale, across billions of page views, they are anything but.

From a sustainability perspective, the imbalance is clear:

- Heavy pages transfer large amounts of data, increasing energy use for both hosting and delivery.
- Third-party scripts for ads and tracking trigger multiple requests across networks.
- Autoplay videos and oversized imagery consume bandwidth and battery power, especially on mobile devices.
- User frustration leads to repeated loading, refreshing, and abandonment, resulting in unnecessary data traffic.

The environmental cost mirrors the social one. A simple task, such as finding a recipe, can easily become an obstacle course of interruptions and delays. For users on slow connections or with assistive technologies, such pages are often completely unusable. What should be a straightforward exchange of information instead prioritizes metrics over meaning. And it usually ends up with me calling my mum for the recipe, which one may argue is not too bad an outcome. Most of these patterns were not designed with bad intentions. They grew out of an effort to reach audiences and measure success, but over time, they have created a web that is heavier, slower, and less human.

Sustainable content design takes a different approach. It values clarity, relevance, and respect for attention. A well-structured recipe page with a concise introduction, accessible layout, optimized images, and the option to jump straight to the recipe serves both people and the planet. It loads faster, wastes less energy, and builds genuine trust.

This example is a reminder that the web works best when it serves people, not algorithms. However, when visibility and data collection become the primary goals, experience and sustainability often suffer. Building a more balanced and responsible web begins with understanding how marketing systems influence what we create and how we share it.

If this is what happens on a single recipe page, imagine its impact at scale, where millions of campaigns and automated systems follow the same logic, each adding to the weight of the web.

Beneath the Campaigns

When we talk about marketing on the web, we often think of visibility, reach, engagement, and conversion. In principle, digital marketing was meant to make communication smarter. Collecting and analyzing data promised to help teams understand what people want and deliver it more efficiently.

In practice, the system has outgrown its purpose. Over the years, the accumulation of new tools, integrations, and performance metrics has made reaching people more complex than communicating with them. Every pixel, tag, and tracking script loads extra code. Every personalized ad triggers requests that travel across multiple servers. Every optimization adds another dependency. What began as a way to connect people has evolved into a web of overlapping systems: analytics dashboards, ad networks, social media integrations, customer relationship management platforms, automation flows, tracking pixels, pop-ups, and SEO tools. Each has its own reason to exist, but together they create weight, noise, and constant motion.

The irony is that many of these tools were designed to make marketing more efficient, yet their combined effect slows everything down. The more we optimize, the heavier and slower the web becomes.

The problem is rarely intentional. Marketing teams often work in isolation from developers and designers, following inherited practices or vendor recommendations. Even today, documentation for tracking tools still instructs teams to place scripts at the very top of the page to ensure every event is captured, a small choice that improves analytics precision but harms performance, accessibility, and sustainability.

These practices are not the result of negligence but of disconnection. Each team optimizes for its own metrics: visibility, reach, conversion. Few people stop to consider how those local gains impact the larger system. The outcome is a web that works harder than it needs to, and often, harder than anyone ever intended.

Toward a Sustainable Digital Strategy

The web has long celebrated growth. More content, more campaigns, more updates. Activity became a measure of success. For many teams, the question was "What should we post next?" rather than "Do we need to post at all?" The result is a digital world filled with noise, repetition, and weight that few ever pause to question.

A sustainable content strategy begins by slowing that rhythm. It shifts focus from constant production to meaningful communication, from chasing metrics to building trust and long-term relationships. It invites teams to ask not only what to create, but what not to create. Every new page, image, or campaign carries a cost in energy, time, attention, and credibility. **Recognizing that cost is the first step toward creating with intention.**

Restraint becomes a creative skill and a mark of maturity. Knowing when something is complete, when to update instead of duplicate, and when silence communicates more clearly than another campaign makes digital communication lighter and more respectful. It reduces waste, both technical and mental, and helps the work that truly matters stand out.

Earlier in the book, we drew inspiration from Marie Kondo's philosophy of keeping only what serves a purpose. The same idea applies to digital strategy. Content should earn its place. If it no longer informs, supports, or inspires, it is time to let it go. The goal is not to empty the web, but to make it intentional, filled with information that still holds meaning.

Every decision, from the first brief to the last published page, contributes to the weight or lightness of our shared digital world. By creating with care and publishing with purpose, we can make the web a place that informs, connects, and endures, not through endless growth but through thoughtful balance. We need to stop treating the web like it has no limits.

What Sustainable Looks Like

Sustainability starts with intention. It asks us to pause before creating, to understand why something exists, who it helps, and what impact it leaves behind. Making digital communication sustainable means focusing on what matters most and letting go of what does not.

Sustainable content and marketing prioritize quality over quantity, long-term trust over short-term reach, and collaboration over isolated goals. They recognize that every article, image, and campaign leaves a trace, and that each of those traces carries both social and environmental weight.

Practicing sustainability in this context means asking different questions: Does this content serve a clear purpose? Is it inclusive and accessible? Does it respect attention, privacy, and energy use? Each answer becomes a small design decision, shaping how the web communicates and how responsibly it grows.

This is what sustainable communication looks like in principle. The following sections will explore what it looks like in practice, from how we plan, write, and maintain content to how we track, promote, and measure impact in ways that support both people and the planet.

Content Creation: Quality Over Quantity

We usually create websites to tell stories, share knowledge, and promote ideas. Over time, though, the rhythm changes. Publishing becomes routine. We write because the calendar says it's time, not because there is something new to say. We publish because the web rewards activity. Algorithms favor what's fresh, even when it adds little value. So we post again: new campaigns, new headlines, new keywords. The result is a growing archive of content that often repeats itself, becomes outdated, or quietly loses relevance.

To build a more sustainable web, we need to shift focus from volume to value. **The real question is not what to create next, but what people truly need from us and what might be better to retire.** Choosing what stays and what goes helps reduce noise, storage, and confusion. It also helps people find what matters faster and with less effort.

When we create with intention, we guide users instead of overwhelming them. Every page, article, or campaign becomes part of a clearer story that respects their time, attention, and goals. This clarity strengthens our relationships with audiences, building trust, respect, and loyalty, the foundation of any lasting and profitable brand.

Quality, in this sense, is not polish or perfection. It is relevance. It is usefulness. It is empathy for the person on the other side of the screen, who came not to admire our work but to find an answer, learn something, or make a decision.

Sustainable content begins where noise ends. It is about slowing down, making space, and choosing meaning over motion.

Putting it into practice:

- **Audit regularly**: Review existing pages and assets before creating new ones. Identify what is outdated, duplicated, or unused.
- **Define purpose**: Every new piece of content should answer a clear "why": who it helps, and how.
- **Plan for endings**: Include expiry or review dates for campaigns, articles, and assets.
- **Write with clarity**: Use plain, concise language. The fewer words it takes to communicate an idea, the lighter and more inclusive it becomes. Consider your audience and make it inclusive. Maybe not everyone is a native speaker.
- **Favour maintenance over expansion**: Improve what exists before adding more. Minor, thoughtful updates often have a greater impact than new production.
- **Celebrate deletion**: Removing irrelevant content saves storage, reduces crawl load, and helps users find what matters.

Sustainable Marketing Practices

Marketing connects people to products, ideas, and causes. When done with care, it helps the right message reach the right audience at the right moment. Yet the same systems that enable this connection can also create waste when left to run unchecked. Automation, constant optimization, and endless tracking can turn good intentions into unnecessary complexity.

Sustainability in marketing begins with awareness of that impact. Every click, open, and impression travels through servers, scripts, and databases. When multiplied by millions, those actions shape both the energy use of the web and the quality of our shared experience.

Sustainable marketing is guided by purpose. It means focusing on what truly matters: messages that inform rather than interrupt, data that helps rather than harvests, and strategies that build trust rather than dependency. It asks teams to create with intent and to let go of what does not serve either people or the planet.

When practiced this way, marketing becomes more than a growth engine. It becomes part of a balanced digital ecosystem, one where success is measured not only in conversions but in clarity, trust, and long-term relationships.

Putting it into practice:

- **Question every script**: Before adding analytics or tracking, ask: Is this essential? Is there a lighter, privacy-friendly alternative?
- **Use ethical analytics**: Tools like Plausible, Fathom, and Matomo provide insights without relying on invasive tracking or cookies.
- **Optimize ad delivery**: Avoid using autoplay videos or large third-party ad networks when static or contextual placements are available.
- **Segment with care**: Send fewer, but more relevant, emails and campaigns. Quality outreach reduces carbon emissions and enhances engagement.
- **Limit retention**: Store marketing data only as long as needed. Delete outdated leads and reports that are no longer relevant or serve a purpose.

- **Collaborate early**: Work with developers and designers when implementing tags or tracking scripts to reduce performance and energy impacts.
- **Respect privacy**: Transparent communication and opt-in choices build user trust and reduce unnecessary data processing.

Ethics and Privacy

As marketing becomes more data-driven, the line between engagement and intrusion becomes increasingly blurred. Every decision about how we reach people, how much we track them, and how transparently we communicate those choices shapes the kind of web we build.

Digital marketing thrives on data. It helps creators understand what resonates and what converts. But that insight often comes with a hidden cost. Tracking scripts, audience pixels, and email analytics collect far more information than most users realize. Each interaction generates data that moves through multiple systems, stored, sold, and shared across networks that few ever see. This constant exchange consumes energy and erodes trust.

When marketing prioritizes collection over connection, the result is a web that feels intrusive instead of inviting. People become data points, and attention becomes a commodity. Ethical marketing works differently. It values clarity over capture, consent over convenience, and transparency over manipulation.

Sustainable privacy practice begins with restraint. Ask what you genuinely need to know, and why. If a campaign cannot function without invasive tracking, it may not be the right campaign. Building relationships through honesty and respect for people's time, attention, and autonomy is not only better for privacy but also for long-term trust and for the planet.

Putting it into practice:

- **Be honest about tracking**: Make it clear what data is collected and why. Avoid hidden pixels or silent retargeting.
- **Limit analytics**: Use privacy-focused tools that track trends rather than individuals.
- **Avoid manipulative design**: Do not use dark patterns or misleading consent prompts to gain clicks or sign-ups.

- **Respect inboxes**: Avoid unnecessary follow-up emails or remarketing loops that feel invasive and waste energy.
- **Store responsibly**: Delete campaign data, lead lists, and contact details once they are no longer relevant.
- **Lead with transparency**; Make privacy a visible part of your brand communication, not a footnote in your policy.

Trust built through ethical communication extends naturally to how we use one of marketing's oldest and most direct tools: email.

Email Marketing

Email remains one of the most effective and enduring forms of digital communication. It is personal, measurable, and one of the few channels organizations truly control. Unlike social platforms that depend on algorithms and paid reach, email allows a direct, permission-based connection between creators and their audiences.

However, with each campaign stored, processed, and transmitted through countless servers, one email may seem insignificant, but multiplied across millions of inboxes, the impact becomes tangible.

Automation and segmentation make it easy to stay in touch, and just as easy to overdo it. Newsletters are sent to inactive lists, while updates are directed to those who have already made a purchase. Additionally, campaigns persist even after they have lost relevance. The result is a steady stream of messages that use energy, storage, and attention without much value in return.

Industry data shows that the HTML portion of a typical marketing email averages around 45–55 KB. With images and other assets included, best-practice guidance suggests keeping the total under about 100 KB to avoid clipping, improve load times, and reduce wasted data. Sending a 100 KB email to 50,000 subscribers transfers roughly 5 GB of data in a single campaign, a reminder that even small things add up.

Sustainable email marketing is about quality, timing, and respect. It favors fewer, more meaningful messages over constant contact. It means maintaining clean lists, optimizing images and limiting tracking pixels. It also means making subscription choices clear and easy to manage.

A well-crafted message that provides genuine value will always outperform a dozen automated ones that do not. Less noise leads to stronger engagement, clearer insight and lighter impact. It also means applying the same design principles discussed earlier in the book: readable typography, balanced contrast, support for dark and light modes and lightweight layouts that work across devices.

Putting it into practice:

- **Audit mailing lists regularly**: Remove inactive subscribers and bounced addresses. It reduces data storage and ensures your emails reach only those who want them.
- **Optimize assets**: Compress images, use modern formats like WebP, and keep attachments to a minimum. Smaller emails load faster, reducing both emissions and user frustration.
- **Be transparent about tracking**: If you use pixels or open-rate tracking, disclose it clearly. People appreciate honesty; it builds trust and helps you comply with privacy standards.
- **Choose efficient formats**: Plain text or lightweight HTML templates render reliably across clients and use far less data than image-heavy layouts. They are also more accessible for screen readers.
- **Design with care**: Respect users' system preferences, including dark and light modes. Use clear typography and ensure good contrast for readability on all devices.
- **Empower your audience**: Make it easy to subscribe, adjust preferences, or unsubscribe entirely. Avoid manipulative designs or hidden links. A transparent exit is part of a trustworthy experience.
- **Focus on value, not volume**: Send fewer but more relevant messages. Measure engagement not by quantity but by genuine connection and usefulness.

Accessibility and Inclusion

Accessibility has become an essential part of creating and maintaining digital content. It is no longer something handled by specialists at the end of a project, but a shared responsibility for everyone involved in communicating online.

Since June 2025, the European Accessibility Act (EAA) has made accessibility a legal requirement across the European Union, building on the W3C Web Content Accessibility Guidelines (WCAG) that define how digital content should work for everyone: perceivable, operable, understandable, and robust.

For content and marketing teams, this shift is about more than compliance. It is a reminder that clear, inclusive communication is both good practice and good business. Accessibility makes messages easier to find, read, and trust. It invites more people in, strengthens credibility, and reduces waste by ensuring that our creations are both usable and understandable.

Accessible content is also sustainable content. The clearer and easier the information is to access, the less time, energy, and attention it takes to deliver and consume. Simplicity serves everyone: users, teams, and the planet.

Putting it into practice:

- **Write for clarity**: Use plain, inclusive language and keep sentences short. Avoid cultural references or metaphors that may not translate well.
- **Structure for navigation**: Use clear headings, descriptive subheadings, and logical order so both readers and search engines can follow easily.
- **Describe visuals meaningfully**: Provide alt text for images, captions for videos, and transcripts for audio. Marketing visuals should communicate even when images are turned off.
- **Respect reading modes and preferences**: Test how emails and landing pages display in dark mode, mobile view, or text-only readers.
- **Make links descriptive**: Replace “click here” with meaningful phrases that tell users where the link leads.

- **Ensure campaigns are accessible**: Avoid flashing animations, auto-playing videos, or motion-heavy visuals that can cause harm or distract.
- **Audit content regularly**: Include accessibility checks in content reviews and marketing workflows to ensure new updates don't break usability.
- **Include accessibility in brand guidelines**: Make it part of how tone, visuals, and interaction are defined across all communications.

Governance and Maintenance

Sustainability is not a project with an end date. It is a practice of care about what we create, how we maintain it, and when we let it go. Governance gives that care structure. Without it, even the best sustainability intentions fade once campaigns end or teams change.

In most organizations, content and marketing decisions are made across many roles and tools. Without clear ownership, updates accumulate and outdated assets remain online, leaving it unclear who is responsible for pruning or reviewing them. Over time, this leads to duplication, confusion, and waste. A sustainable content system relies on shared accountability, which involves knowing who decides what stays, what goes, and what gets updated.

Good governance does not mean bureaucracy. It means clarity. Establishing simple workflows and review cycles helps ensure that content remains accurate, relevant, and aligned with accessibility and sustainability goals. The same applies to marketing systems. Tags, tracking pixels, and automation scripts should be reviewed and cleaned regularly, just like the content they support.

Maintenance, meanwhile, is where sustainability truly lives. Every time we edit, archive, or delete outdated content, we prevent unnecessary storage, data transfer, and user confusion. Regular pruning lightens infrastructure, clarifies messaging, and builds trust. And it saves money.

In practice:

- **Assign ownership**: Every page, campaign, and asset should have a clear owner responsible for updates, accuracy, and removal.

- **Establish review cycles**: Schedule periodic content and tag audits to identify outdated or redundant content.
- **Document workflows**: Maintain a shared record of processes for creating, approving, and retiring content to ensure consistency as teams evolve.
- **Monitor sustainability metrics**: Track page weight, data transfer, and engagement quality alongside traditional analytics.
- **Archive or delete with purpose**: Not everything needs to stay live forever; removal can be an act of sustainability.
- **Educate teams**: Incorporate sustainability and accessibility into the onboarding and performance reviews for all communication team members.
- **Close the loop**: When a campaign ends, review its impact, retire assets, and apply learnings before starting the next.

Sustainable governance is an act of long-term care. It recognizes that the web is never finished but constantly evolving. By tending to what already exists before creating more, we keep our digital spaces lighter, more coherent, and more humane. What we maintain with care today becomes the foundation for a better web tomorrow.

A Note on Artificial Intelligence

Generative AI has made it easier than ever to produce content at scale, but ease and abundance are not the same as value. Automated writing, imagery, and recommendations can quickly fill the web with repetition and noise. When quantity becomes effortless, the discipline to create with intention becomes even more important.

For a long time, I kept my distance from AI, declaring it unsustainable and unnecessary. A few early reports cemented the idea in my mind that "one prompt uses as much energy as eighty search queries." It felt wasteful, detached, and at odds with the principles of sustainable design. Then two things happened that changed my perspective.

The first was reading Andy Masley's article A Cheat Sheet for Conversations About AI, where he shared data showing that generative AI's footprint, while real, is much smaller than early headlines suggested.

The second was the proper "I-am-in" moment. As I struggled to fill out pages of paperwork for my parental leave, I decided to give AI a chance. In 15 minutes, I had all the forms completed that had frustrated me for days. It is a German bureaucracy game-changer.

It was a reminder that, like any other technology, AI is not inherently good or bad, sustainable or unsustainable. Its impact depends on how, why, and where we use it. It's just that, a tool. Like any tool, it can help or harm depending on how we use it. Our task is not to resist it or embrace it unquestioningly, but to understand it, apply it for the right purposes, and stay responsible for what we create with it.

In the context of content creation, AI is not a replacement for human creativity or judgment; it is an amplifier. Used thoughtfully, it can help analyze performance, summarize insights and speed up routine work. Used carelessly, it generates a large amount of low-quality material that burdens both users and infrastructure.

Chapter 9 continues this conversation, exploring AI's role in creativity, the ethical questions it raises, and the shared responsibility we all have in shaping its impact. For now, what matters is not what the technology can do but what we choose to do with it.

Conclusion

Content and marketing shape what the web becomes. They decide what fills our screens, what messages reach us, and how much energy is spent along the way. When they are driven by curiosity, respect, and purpose, they can connect people, share knowledge, and build trust. When they chase visibility for its own sake, they fill the digital world with noise, clutter, and waste.

The goal of sustainable communication is not silence; it is intention. Every word, image, and campaign should serve a purpose, reach the right people and respect their time and attention. That requires collaboration across roles: marketers working with developers to minimize tracking, writers partnering with designers to create clarity, and teams agreeing on what truly needs to exist.

In a world where publishing is effortless, the challenge is not creating more but creating better. Lighter, clearer, more honest work benefits everyone: users find what they need faster, organizations build credibility, and the planet carries a little less digital weight.

Sustainability in content and marketing is a practice of care, not a checklist. It is about making space for what truly matters: people, stories, and trust. And while we keep working toward that, if you are lucky enough, you can call your mum to get that recipe. She will most likely not track your clicks.

Summary

This chapter explored the role of content and marketing in shaping the sustainability of the web. While design and development provide the structure of digital products, content determines what fills that structure, how often it changes, and how much data, attention, and energy it consumes. Content is not an add-on to digital systems; it is their core purpose and one of their largest sources of impact.

We examined how the pressure to publish, optimize for algorithms, and measure everything has led to an increasingly heavy and cluttered web. From overlong recipe pages to tracking-heavy campaigns, many common marketing practices prioritize visibility and metrics over clarity and usefulness, resulting in slower experiences, higher energy use, and growing user frustration.

The chapter highlighted how sustainable content strategies shift focus from quantity to quality. By treating content as a living system with a clear purpose and lifespan, teams can reduce digital weight, improve trust, and make information easier to find and maintain. Practices such as regular audits, clear ownership, intentional deletion, and inclusive writing all contribute to lighter, more resilient digital ecosystems.

We also looked at sustainable marketing through the lenses of privacy, ethics, and restraint. Ethical analytics, careful use of automation, respectful email practices, and transparent consent mechanisms help reduce unnecessary data processing while strengthening long-term relationships with users. Accessibility emerged as both a legal requirement and a sustainability principle, reinforcing the idea that clear, inclusive communication benefits people and the planet alike.

Finally, the chapter addressed emerging challenges such as generative AI, emphasizing that scale and ease of creation increase the responsibility to act with intention. Sustainable content and marketing are not about producing less by default, but about producing better. By creating with purpose, maintaining with care, and letting go when content no longer serves, teams can reduce waste, build trust, and help shape a web that informs, connects, and endures.

References

Web Statistics and Scale

- Amount of websites and active ratio (DemandSage):

  `https://www.demandsage.com/website-statistics/`

Sustainable Content Strategy and Governance

- GreenMellen Media, "Should you update, rewrite, or delete outdated content?":

  `https://www.greenmellenmedia.com/should-you-update-rewrite-or-delete-outdated-content/`

- Mightybytes, "Stop writing web copy that over-explains":

  `https://www.mightybytes.com/blog/stop-writing-web-copy-that-over-explains/`

- CarbonCrane (identify high-impact or redundant assets): `https://carboncrane.io`

Marketing Systems, Advertising, and Performance

- Schepp.dev, "Ad integration in 2020" (tracking and performance):

  `https://schepp.dev/posts/ad-integration-in-2020/`

- Web.dev, "Loading ads and page speed":

  `https://web.dev/articles/loading-ads-page-speed`

Privacy-Friendly Analytics Tools

- Plausible Analytics: `https://plausible.io`
- Matomo Analytics: `https://matomo.org`
- Fathom Analytics: `https://usefathom.com`

Research on Environmental Impact of Digital Content

- Nature Communications paper on sustainability of digital content consumption:

  `https://www.nature.com/articles/s41467-024-47621-w`

Books and Long-Form Sources

- Bonsignore, Alisa. *Sustainable Content*. Greenleaf Book Group, 2024: `https://greenleafbookgroup.com/titles/sustainable-content`
- McGovern, Gerry. "Crap Data Everywhere" (LinkedIn): `https://www.linkedin.com/pulse/crap-data-everywhere-gerry-mcgovern-zixqe/`

Accessibility Standards and EU Policy

- W3C, Web Content Accessibility Guidelines (WCAG):

  `https://www.w3.org/WAI/standards-guidelines/wcag/`
- European Accessibility Act overview (European Commission):

  `https://ec.europa.eu/social/main.jsp?catId=1202`

Email Marketing and Operational Metrics

- Email marketing statistics (DemandSage):

  `https://www.demandsage.com/email-marketing-statistics/`

AI and Content Creation Impact

- Andy Masley, "A Cheat Sheet for Conversations About AI":

  `https://andymasley.substack.com/p/a-cheat-sheet-for-conversations-about`

Practical Eco-Design Guidance

- Designers Éthiques, Guide d'écoconception:

  `https://beta.designersethiques.org/fr/thematique-ecoconception/guide-d-ecoconception`

CHAPTER 9

The Impact of AI

Chris Chinchilla[1]
[1]Berlin, Germany; `https://chrischinchilla.com/`

While it's important to point out that artificial intelligence (AI) is nothing new, it would be naive to say that the years since 2022 and 2023 haven't seen a massive uptick in the usage of AI-based tools and applications. Many words have been written about the broader impact of this increase. This chapter focuses on the environmental impact of increased AI usage from the following direct and indirect perspectives:

1. Using artificial intelligence as an end user and as part of an application
2. Using and implementing artificial intelligence in the development process
3. Training and maintaining artificial intelligence models

The Impacts of Artificial Intelligence Overall

Throughout these sections on artificial intelligence (AI), I believe it's essential to address an age-old technological adage: "Just because you can, doesn't mean you should." Attributed to *Practically Radical* by William C. Taylor, it has become a phrase of warning to idealistic engineers and overly enthusiastic business people for at least a decade.

I remember a concept called "abstraction" from my University studies of what was then called Human-Computer Interaction (HCI), now more commonly known as user experience (UX). Abstraction means making something very complex seem simple and easy to use. The current giant wave of generative AI is a classic example of this.

After a little thought, you can type a short snippet of text into a chat interface, and boom, back comes an image, a lengthy essay, answers to research, a piece of music, or more. It's almost too easy, and that is probably why generative AI tools have been (as far

C. Chinchilla and I. Akrap, *Building the Sustainable Web*, https://doi.org/10.1007/979-8-8688-2521-7_9

as we can tell) immensely popular. This abstraction belies the enormous complex web of technology and processes that respond to you at that moment, and the work that came before for that to make it even possible.

And before anyone gets ready to fire an email (there's a carbon impact there too), yes, I know that what a lot of companies and consumers now call "AI" we called machine learning (ML), natural language processing (NLP), and other terms in the past. But that was an eternity ago, back in 2022, and now times have changed. The motivation for this chapter is the current trend and its environmental impact, but it tries to use the correct terminology in the correct places and refer to the current wave of tools and older ones when relevant. This is also a technology area moving at breakneck speed, and books move slower, so it's highly likely that some of what is said in this chapter is outdated by the time you read it. Between starting to write this chapter and finishing, a LOT has happened in the AI space, and a lot has happened regarding monitoring and containing its environmental impact.

Generative AI large language model (LLM)-based tools are different and, in some ways, worse than more traditional applications in that they have an environmental impact when you use them and when the models they use to respond to you are trained. More on that shortly.

There is also an increasing trend for people to run models locally on their devices, which makes perfect sense. Doing so offers privacy and security benefits, as well as the ability to refine a model to suit your specific needs. Several tools are now available that make the process relatively easy, and I am increasingly doing it myself as well. However, reiterating a point made several times in the book, once application processing ends on local devices, you lose the ability to measure the carbon impact at scale. There's a certain irony here, as I am all for local-first, user-controlled distributed computing. In terms of environmental impact, unless people opt in to reporting, which is unlikely, there is no real way to determine the metrics. Is that spike in domestic power use people running local LLMs, or coffee machines? And once you factor in the transmission cost of these local devices, sending bits and bytes back and forth, the potential environmental impact is possibly even bigger. It would be fascinating to see a study on this, but it would be hard to implement. In reality, I like to think and I hope that, due to most people not running cooling systems, massively over-provisioning their local devices, or being able to afford to buy the kinds of servers that hyperscalers use, cloud data centers still have, by far, the greater impact.

In addition to this energy impact, AI is causing significant disruptions to jobs, politics, the creative industries, and other sectors. The impacts are difficult to measure and are not directly a topic for this book, but they are a classic example of the unintended consequences that naive engineers often witness when unleashing their technology on the world.

On a more practical level, hosting and running generative AI tools is quite expensive (giving a hint of the energy impact), meaning that the financial cost is often greater than the return. There are positive outcomes from many of the old and new wave of AI tools, such as medical research that can accomplish things far quicker than a group of humans ever could. But are the positive outcomes outweighed by the negative? It's hard to say right now, but it's worth considering.

In summary, just because you can use or create a chatbot that responds to a customer query with support data doesn't mean you should.

The Environmental Impact of Artificial Intelligence

Now, let's return to focusing purely on the energy impact. And as always, what's better? One 1kW GPT or ten 100W GPTs? As mentioned so many times in this book, as these new AI tools become more efficient and easier to run for the typical user, will we save any energy? Or will people use them more, with no actual net benefit to energy saving?

It's important to remember that any AI tool or service is fundamentally just another series of applications running on a server and the server's software. All the issues and impacts associated with those in other chapters also still apply. It's important to single out AI's impact as it's a growth technique and technology that is causing a dramatic shift in the usage and design of the technology industry. AI industry analysists, semi-analysis predict that AI usage of data centers will take over traditional usage (however you interpret that) by 2028.

One of the key differences between AI and "traditional" applications is that many AI applications need "training" before they are useful. Not only is this process unique to AI, it's also the singular most energy-intensive part.

Overview of LLM Energy Impacts

LLMs consume energy at various stages of their life cycle, and as every stage has different energy impacts, a quick primer is useful.

- **Training** is the first phase and may involve a process of trial and error, or showing the model examples of the desired inputs and outputs, or both.
- **Inference** uses the trained model to make predictions on new and previously unseen data as people use the model. Each prediction uses less energy than training, but the infrastructure used to deliver the predictions does consume energy.
- The energy impact of **tooling** using the tool is likely less but broader, depending on what the tool generates and how you use it.

A report written mid-2024 between Hugging Face and the Allen Institute for AI summarized the carbon emissions during inference for common AI tasks per 1000 queries and found that, unsurprisingly, image generation was by far the most intensive, with one image generating the same carbon emissions as charging an average smartphone to full.

This makes sense. After all, generating an image requires far more data than plain text, and I shudder to think of the carbon emissions required to generate audio or video. The report showed that "generation tasks" consume more than tasks such as summarizing or translating. Again, this makes sense. They do more work.

The same report states that most recent work has focused on the impact of training. There's less on inference, which typically uses less computing resources than training, but as it happens more frequently, it likely has a greater impact over time. Potentially, 60–90% of AI and ML computing demand over time, depending on the source.

While they are less well-known models, there are reports available for the Bloom and Noor models that provide a more detailed analysis of the energy impact of training particular models. There are only estimates for the impact of training closed-source proprietary models, and for training GPT-4, the current estimate is around 62 GWh. This is about enough to power a mid-sized city for several days. In contrast, the BLOOM model, albeit older and less sophisticated, used 433,196 kWh. However, bear in mind that tools and services used trained models for a reasonable period of time.

In research from Alex de Vrie, who created similar reports for the impact of Bitcoin, he provided some sober reading. He laid out (in 2023) what he considered a reasonable scenario for 2027, where new AI servers sold that year alone could use between 85 and 134 terawatt hours (TWh) annually. That's similar to the energy consumption of Argentina, the Netherlands, and Sweden in a year, and is about 0.5% of the world's current electricity use. As he could not obtain the numbers directly, he postulated these results based on the energy consumption of Nvidia A100 servers used by most AI providers. However, these numbers don't factor in any efficiencies the companies running them might be using, or the amount of capacity used during the day, they also don't factor in cooling and infrastructure. Even if the consumption in 2027 is equal to one-third of the estimations, that's still high, and is just one part of the server consumption picture.

There is also an indirect environmental impact of the training process that's easy to overlook, which is the impact on the content owner. There have been a handful of reports from open-source projects and communities, such as Wikipedia, but the most comprehensive is this piece from Libre News. It's not explicitly about environmental impact, but more the sheer amount of unblockable traffic that the infrastructure of projects now has to cope with due to AI scraping for training. Extrapolating this into exact numbers is hard, but it's certainly a significant increase, which equals higher strain on servers, and thus, a greater environmental impact.

Sating the Thirst of AI

As always, we should also talk about water. An appropriately titled paper from 2025, "Making AI less 'thirsty,'" makes for dry reading. It claims that Microsoft used over 700,000 liters of water to train its GPT-3 model and that global water demand in 2027 for AI purposes could be 4.2–6.6 billion cubic liters, which is half the water consumption of the UK in one year. However, the report itself states that many companies keep these numbers secret. While I don't want to dismiss the fact that any computing-intensive process uses a tremendous amount of water, most of the paper's numbers are highly informed estimates. However, with hotter summers, increased forest fires, and water supply and distribution issues, there's an increased movement on social media (ironically) to stop using tools such as ChatGPT due to the water and energy consumption. Still, it's not stopping the impact on water supply to the communities that house data centers. The US state of Nevada is experiencing an increase in data center construction, despite being the driest state. And while only indirectly connected to AI, Taiwan Semiconductor Manufacturing Company (TSMC) has its own water issues at home, as well as in Arizona, another of the driest US states.

Finally, compounding the three emissions scopes outlined in Chapter 4, most AI workloads perform best when run on custom hardware and with as many resources as possible allocated. We have all witnessed the seemingly constant unquenchable demand for graphical processing units (GPUs), especially those from certain vendors, such as NVIDIA.

All of this increased energy, water, and resource usage also has a financial cost. One factor many rushing to implement AI solutions don't stop to assess is whether it's actually *worth it*. Implementing an AI chatbot for customers to interact with your service or documentation can bring benefits and new options, but is the monthly cost worth it just because it's what everyone else is doing? And we are still in the midst of a potential AI bubble and yet to see if the financial costs to the companies behind AI infrastructure are worth it.

On a hyper scale, De Vries estimated in the same paper that it would cost Google $100 billion in up-front server costs to implement AI inference in web searches. Google makes a lot of money from search traffic, but is it worth that much? At the time of writing, it seems that it is worth it to companies like Google. But will enough people *want it* to warrant the cost?

A great resource, and almost an equivalent to this section, is The Green Web Foundation's AI report.

The Impact of Using and Implementing Artificial Intelligence in the Development Process

In much the same way as the front end of an application has an almost impossible-to-measure impact on energy usage, what developers use as part of their personal development process is the same. While the development servers, services, containers, etc. are counted as part of the general cost of cloud, their transience can make them harder to track and have a full picture of with regards to AI. This applies even more in the case of using assistive AI.

If you run models locally or remotely, while many of the other impacts and caveats in this chapter apply, you have a degree of visibility into their impact on your machines. Any models or tools you run locally are trackable, but as covered in Chapter 4, tools for tracking the power consumption of local machines aren't all made equally. Much like tracking remote instances, they involve a complex web of dependent systems and services. However, with enough determination and the tools mentioned in Chapter x4, it's possible.

Where things get grayer is tracking the impact of services you have no control over. Two of the most popular developer editors and IDEs now bundle AI tools, Copilot for VSCode, and AI Assistant for IntelliJ. There are also new stand-alone tools such as Cursor and Windsurf that are "AI-first," putting assistive tools front and foremost. In addition, it's now possible to add AI to almost every stage of the developer workflow, and companies are hungry to sell you a solution.

In short, it's all too easy to refer and defer to these assistants during the development process. But every "explain my code" or "write the documentation for me" query has an impact that is completely unclear to you beyond broad data center usage. I find myself doing it increasingly regularly, as when you use them effectively, AI assistants can work exceptionally well for some tasks, getting you better answers than time spent on web searches. While comparing one to the other is complex and begins to take into account the inherent carbon impact of a human being's time, too, at the moment, they still have a greater energy impact than multiple browser searches and site visits.

According to research from kanoppi in February 2025, the differences are the following:

Metric	Google Search	ChatGPT	Difference
Energy per query	0.0003 kWh	0.0029 kWh	~10x higher for AI
CO_2 emissions/query	0.2g	68g	~340x higher for AI
Daily energy use	~10.8 MWh	~621.4 MWh	~58x higher for AI
Annual home equivalent	~2,000 homes	~21,600 homes	~11x higher for AI

However, these numbers are at best estimates, and at worst, complete conjecture. These numbers also don't include the impact of training. Although remaining pragmatic and balanced, I don't think any reported numbers for search engine searches also include the impact of building and maintaining their search indexes. Now that many search engines include a degree of AI-powered results, the differences are narrowing, in the wrong direction.

Also, the ChatGPT website alone is now estimated to be the fifth-most visited website in the world. I don't think this includes any ChatGPT app usage, and is only one among hundreds of other AI tools. In short, the numbers in the table above really start to matter.

At the time of this writing, Microsoft was exploring the possibility of opening its own power station to fuel its and the public's growing interest in AI. Of course, it's hard to say how much of that has to do with something like Copilot, but it's an example of how much the interest in AI has increased the overall energy impact of computing.

As with many other technical solutions to problems, it's not that you shouldn't use it, but more that you should consider if you need to use it. Ask yourself if you need an AI assistant to solve a small problem, firing off a succession of Internet pings and hops and their subsequent carbon impact. Perhaps you can save that impact by not feeding the AI data machine with more inputs, and give your brain a little exercise by solving the issues yourself after a few minutes of thought.

However, there are times when AI assistants prove more useful than traditional searches, Q&A forums, or hours banging your head against a wall trying to figure out a solution. As a long-term writer and maintainer of documentation, I proposed a "docsbot" chat interface for interacting with and interrogating documentation several years ago, during the first, and underwhelming, wave of chatbots. At the time, people thought it was a crazy idea, as the chat technology available was a glorified decision tree and frequently led to frustrating conversations that led nowhere. However, finding an answer to a specific question in documentation has always been a challenge. AI chat interfaces to documentation genuinely provide a new way to find answers that didn't exist before. The proliferation of Q&A-style forums, despite all their pitfalls, showed that all people ever really wanted to do was ask a question and receive an answer, not trawl pages of documentation trying to find what they want to know from a sea of words that are often instead what the writer thinks you want to know.

I have used AI chat interfaces for documentation to find (correct) answers I couldn't find before, and I know of others with the same experience. Likewise, code assistant tools can help you find solutions you might have never found before by analyzing millions of other examples and drawing parallels a human brain would never have noticed.

While I feel the frequent selling point of AI is that it could help humanity solve the big problems we never have time for is overblown, it's not completely without merit. When used correctly and intentionally, it can achieve wonderful things. Save it for that and not the lazy patchwork of throwaway asset generation. This has many other negatives, besides its energy impact, that we are all aware of, such as job losses, cost cutting, reduced opportunities for juniors, devaluation of creativity, deepfakes, and much more.

On the positive side, well-implemented AI systems can process quantities of data at a scale impossible for humans, spot patterns, and create connections that would have taken human researchers years to find. This has led to advances in medical research, cybersecurity mitigation, and yes, even more creative pursuits, allowing you to assess multiple ideas and approaches as you work that you might have never seen or thought of.

I like to think of the current wave of AI tools as "assistive" rather than "generative." Ideally, they run alongside you, giving advice and suggestions and providing proactive insights as you work. This is the ideal anyway. While I can see the ideal implementation of this, I fear that we will actually end up with a plethora of new walled gardens. One company can provide actionable insights to one data set but not another, so have you gained much?

The rise of generative AI came when the broader tech industry was experiencing a downturn in revenue and funding, and it provided a potential new source for both. I still wonder what the level of interest might have been if the wider industry had been in a better state. What is the real level of user interest in the tools and services? If the amount of money and infrastructure companies pour in is anything to go by, it's wonderfully successful. However, the tech industry has always been motivated by stimulating growth at the cost of all else, hoping that user uptake will eventually reflect their investment. But at the moment, we don't know (and they don't tell us) if it's all been worth it financially. In addition, the unbridled rush for energy and resources makes it hard to justify whether it is or will be worth it in the long run.

Making AI More Efficient

Things are not without hope, though. Like many other technological shifts, sometimes, after an initial wave of unbridled enthusiasm, developers start to consider improvements and broader sustainability. Since starting to write this book, there have been positive and negative developments in AI energy efficiency.

During my time working with the sustainability movement in the early 2000s, I remember that while domestic personal solar panels were often seen as a great solution for generating renewable energy, especially where I was in Australia, they were too expensive for most people. Then came cheaper panels from China, which, combined with some government incentives, made them more affordable and widespread.

It might be a strange comparison, but I wonder if the sudden appearance of more efficient models such as DeepSeek and its apparent low cost and resource usage in comparison to other generative AI tools and models might be a similar moment. I am not alone in wondering about DeepSeek's impact on AI sustainability. Chris Adams of The Green Web Foundation also mused on the subject and reached a similar, "too early to say" conclusion. It doesn't matter if DeepSeek remains in use. It's enough that it was a paradigm shift to show that other methods are possible and that you don't always need a lot of money and resources to make something effective. If generative AI tools are here to stay, I hope the disruption caused by DeepSeek encourages a wider and more global approach to them.

All Other Advice Still Applies

Training and running models is still a task that runs on a computer, just like any other. Therefore, much of the advice presented in this book so far remains applicable.

- Use the most efficient hardware in the most efficient way possible, powering down when not in use, shifting loads to the most low-carbon data centers, etc.
- If possible, use operating systems and infrastructure as code software to automate and optimize resource and workload usage as efficiently as possible.
- Use the most efficient programming languages and techniques for the training and inference of models. For example, Python is a popular choice for ML training, but by default it is not the most energy-efficient programming language; but many of the common Python ML libraries, such as NumPy, use C code at their core, which is far more energy efficient

Reducing the Size of Models

Many tools the general public is most familiar with (ChatGPT, Claude, Gemini) are examples of general LLMs, or if you like, "large large language models." They possess broad knowledge of many subjects and, as a result, have a larger number of parameters. Without getting too deep into model training principles, the more parameters, in theory, the more the model "knows," the larger the model, and the more resources it uses.

Suppose you use an AI tool with a particular focus, such as coding, medical-related, or the works of Shakespeare. In that case, you could be using an example of what is called several different terms, including "small language model," "specific language model," "custom language model," and "domain language model." They are more efficient because, in theory, they require less training, inference, and prune the parameters deemed unnecessary for the specific topic. For simplicity's sake, the rest of this chapter sticks with the term "small language model" (SLM).

In addition to using smaller training datasets limited to the more relevant expertise domain, SLMs also use several other techniques to reduce their size and increase their efficiency, all of which fall under the general umbrella term of "compression."

Knowledge distillation is a process in which an LLM transfers its knowledge to an SLM. As there is still an LLM involved, albeit to a lesser extent, I wondered about the energy impact of the process. There has been research from Vrije Universiteit Amsterdam, but largely on the impact on the resulting SLM. The research showed more than a 40% reduction in energy consumption for a distilled version of the BERT model and nearly 30% for a distilled version of GPT-2. At the time of writing, widespread usage of SLMs is growing, as is the research on their effectiveness for usage and energy impact.

Quantizing the way the model represents the training data by using different types to store that metadata efficiently. For example, using integers instead of floating-point numbers.

Pruning removes unnecessary parameters, reducing model size and improving efficiency without significant accuracy loss.

Other approaches take some of these methods and propose different approaches.

For example, CompactifAI uses compression algorithms to increase efficiency without reducing the actual amount of data in a model. When testing with LlaMA 7B, they claim to reduce the memory size needed by 93%, with an accuracy drop of 2–3%.

Linearity in neural networks uses a familiar mathematical concept that offers predictable scalability to reduce the intensive attention mechanism used by many LLMs that use transformers (the "T" in ChatGPT, etc).

Another is FrugalAI, which is especially popular in the French industrial sector. While it is still in the theoretical and principles stage, the one main practical explanation of plans I could find (in English) was this paper, which discusses using existing models as a base for adding context-specific models. It's like cascading dependencies in software, which sounds like knowledge distillation in SLMs. To find out more, mostly in French, there is an in-progress Association Française de Normalisation (AFNOR) specification for FrugalAI.

I recommend this awesome list on efficient LLMs for even more ideas and examples of projects using those ideas.

Are RAG and MCP Solutions

Retrieval-Augmented Generation (RAG) and Model Context Protocol (MCP) are two emerging techniques for supplementing model reasoning with up-to-date data. They benefit model accuracy and could improve their sustainability impact if they don't need to pack everything in at training and inference time. There is not much research done on the sustainability angle of these techniques, but I wonder if the impact of fetching data through more traditional methods has less impact than constant retraining and inference. However, some models can use RAG and MCP techniques to bring energy impact statistics knowledge into applications. This isn't an encouragement to do so, but it is an interesting idea.

More Optimized Hardware

In terms of providers, all hyperscalers are opening new power plants to support the demands for AI. While researching for this chapter, I found more useful public research from Google. As a company, they have been involved in "traditional" AI, ML, and NLP for a long time, and before the recent explosion in usage, they were typically the go-to hosting provider for that kind of work. David Patterson, now a distinguished engineer at Google, who previously worked on reduced instruction set computing (RISC) and redundant arrays of inexpensive disks (RAID), has written a lot of Google's AI and sustainability content. While much of it was written before the recent boom and drive for AI revenues that pushed some sustainability efforts out of the way, a report from 2025 looks specifically at the life cycle emissions of specialized AI hardware. This builds upon some of what Chapter 4 covered to look at Google's custom Tensor Processing Units (TPUs). Google has also outlined other techniques it uses for more efficient AI, such as speculative decoding, sparse models, quantized training, and its "4Ms" (model, machine, mechanization [use the Cloud], and map [use cleaner energy]). However, despite a post in 2022 claiming Google uses these 4Ms, I couldn't find much other material referencing them, and several sustainable Cloud experts have debunked Cloud hosts' claims around their sustainable AI practices, especially when those practices involve using **their** cloud and **their** specialized components.

On the flip side, Salesforce published a post demonstrating how switching to more efficient TPUs resulted in a two-time energy efficiency increase over the previous generation of TPUs. Comparing the long-term energy efficiency to the impact of replacement and production is challenging.

Other, more vendor-neutral hardware options include other alternatives to using GPUs, such as SpiNNcloud's custom architecture that claims to be 78% more energy efficient than GPUs by using a technique called "dynamic sparsity." This is a relatively new idea, already employed by some models, including DeepSeek, that (in summary) adapts the structure during training to learn more effectively though a combination of compressing input and selecting the most relevant and up-to-date information from a model.

How to Evaluate Models

Hugging Face and EcoLogits

This book has touched upon energy rating systems across the board, and Hugging Face, one of the best-known and longest-established communities for machine learning and AI models, recently announced AI energy score ratings. It's standardized, measuring energy consumption during specific set tasks and contributes to a publicly available leaderboard across these tasks, meaning you can look for the models most efficient at the tasks you want to do. The leaderboard gives an overview of the range of energy use for each task and is useful for understanding what can affect that energy use.

Some factors are more obvious. A model with more parameters, such as the 11 billion version of Google's t5, uses three times the energy of the 3 billion parameter version of the same model. It also corroborates some of what this chapter has already covered. Even the image generation model currently labeled as the most efficient (mitsua-diffusion-one) uses 186Wh instead of the most efficient text generation model (distilgpt2), which uses 1.31Wh. None of this is unexpected, but it's much easier to decide what models to use when you can see it so clearly. Alongside this leaderboard and submission process, when you add a model to Hugging Face, you can submit it to the leaderboard that displays carbon footprint information.

It's an opt-in submission, but for open-source models, the process is automated, allowing anyone to submit any model for consideration. For proprietary models, you use a Docker image to run the tests and submit the outcome yourself. Hugging Face plans to update the leaderboard biannually, which feels a little infrequent, but it is a small organization. The project itself is an interesting overview of tools and methodologies for evaluating AI models, some of which this chapter touches upon.

Continuing with Hugging Face tools, they also have a calculator built on top of EcoLogits' framework that lets you select from various pre-trained models from different providers and see an estimate of different environmental impacts based on sample prompts. It's basic but a great, quick, and easy way to get a rough idea. For those who want to delve a little deeper, there's an expert mode where you can tweak the parameters, the electricity mix, and the location.

For Python programmers, things are more interesting. You can use EcoLogits as a library in your code and get estimates by using models and prompts.

For example, using the following code:

```
from ecologits import EcoLogits
from openai import OpenAI

# Initialize EcoLogits
EcoLogits.init()

client = OpenAI(api_key="<OPENAI_API_KEY>")

response = client.chat.completions.create(
    model="gpt-4o-mini",
    messages=[
        {"role": "user", "content": "Write a summary of the energy impact
        of using AI"}
    ]
)

# Get estimated environmental impacts of the inference
print(f"Energy consumption: {response.impacts.energy.value} kWh")
print(f"GHG emissions: {response.impacts.gwp.value} kgCO2eq")
```

Gives, when I ran it, the following output:

```
Energy consumption: 0.0007276084883333335 to 0.0023992267283333337 kWh
GHG emissions: 0.0004481344673662768 to 0.0014351882624849968 kgCO2eq
```

The wide range is due to the OpenAI models being closed source and multimodal, so the library uses estimates rather than accurate information. As with any of the options presented in this book, and especially in this chapter, open models give better results.

ML.energy

Another energy consumption leaderboard is from ML.energy. Again, it breaks down energy consumption rates by task and the GPU on which the tasks run, with measurements of the energy consumed per response (be that answer, image, etc.) in Joules. It includes different models, but much like the Hugging Face leaderboard, as you expect, the more parameters, the greater the energy usage, and image and video generation consume more energy. Behind the scenes, it uses the Zeus project from ML. energy to measure energy consumption, a library for measuring the energy impact of arbitrary lines of Python code. It's optimized for deep learning workloads (one of the methodologies behind training a model) as it focuses specifically on the energy usage of GPUs. In addition to measurement, it also offers three energy optimizers you can apply to learning processes.

CodeCarbon

Similar to Zeus, but more widely known, CodeCarbon is another Python library for measuring the CO_2 equivalents for training and deploying models by tracking blocks of code. It has a lot of configuration options for setting country, region, Clouds used, and more.

CodeCarbon adds some interesting extras, especially in visualizing the energy impact. You can run the library over blocks of code and get the energy consumption written out to the terminal for the run, or run CodeCarbon on a machine in the background and get the overall energy impact, plus labelled tasks. I initially hoped this meant you could also track any task running on the machine, but I am not completely sure if that's the case.

It also writes a CSV file with the energy consumption and powermetrics logs, which many tools, including most operating systems, use to report various data about CPU usage.

You can choose to output the collected metrics to CodeCarbon's central dashboard to visualize the energy impact of your projects and opt to make the project's data public. If not, you can also output to Prometheus, Logfire, an HTTP webhook, or a Python Logger.

If you want to try the library with a production-level experiment, the CodeCarbon team has a Jupyter notebook from the GreenIO event in 2024 that you can try.

Blocking AI Scrapers

Finally, this chapter mentioned the additional resource strain and environmental impact of AI scrapers. Traditional website scrapers such as those used by search engines generally respect the robots.txt file that defines what they can and cannot scrape. Technically, AI scrapers should also respect the robots.txt file, but many don't. It's a constant battle between site owners and AI projects as they try to determine which traffic is from scrapers and which is legitimate. That said, it might be worth setting up a more aggressive blocking strategy if you notice sudden spikes in traffic that are causing you issues.

Summary

More than any other chapter in this book, writing this chapter was a constant moving target. Almost daily, a company or community announces a new or significantly changed AI-powered tool or model.

Many predict that, like other emerging technologies of the past, the hype will slowly die down, or if not, the underlying technology will become more efficient. Some predict this is already happening, but as this chapter and book have repeated multiple times (once more!), more efficient doesn't mean less impact. It's also too early to tell if the efficiency of research, work, and environmental savings will be realized to offset the race for energy consumption currently prevalent in AI companies and projects.

CHAPTER 10

Looking Ahead

Chris Chinchilla[1], Ines Akrap[2]
[1]Berlin, Germany; `https://chrischinchilla.com/`
[2]Munich, Germany; `inesakrap.com`

If you have made it this far, you already know that building digital products responsibly is not about a single technique or framework. It is about patterns, trade-offs, and long-term thinking.

In this final chapter, we zoom out. We touch on a few areas that did not fit neatly elsewhere, reflect on the current state of computing sustainability, and focus on how individuals and teams can keep making progress in an uncertain and changing landscape.

The State of Computing Sustainability in 2026

During the writing process of this book, a lot has changed in computing and sustainability, and it would be amiss not to mention this.

When we started drafting and writing this book, sustainability was something that most large tech companies happily promoted as a positive aspect of their business. Some companies did this because it was something they genuinely believed in and thought was important. Others did so because regulations demanded and required it. While others did it because at the time, it was in the zeitgeist.

For data centers and companies in some parts of the world, such as the European Union, not much has changed (yet). But in other parts of the world, such as the United States, policy and attitudes have changed a lot since we began this book. In the mainstream zeitgeist, sustainability is less important, and many tech companies are now showing their true colors.

As much of this about-turn in computing sustainability coincides with the rapid growth in AI-based technologies and the rush of momentum to pursue them for the anticipated productivity and economic growth, many other concerns have been quickly

C. Chinchilla and I. Akrap, *Building the Sustainable Web*, https://doi.org/10.1007/979-8-8688-2521-7_10

cast aside. Instead of heeding some of the concerns voiced in much of this book and by many of those affected by rapid data center growth and needs, increasingly, tech companies are ignoring them.

While this book has many examples of concerning growth and expansion, it was always possible to find examples of tools, projects, and people wanting to improve the impact of the rapid growth, or at least acknowledging the problem and knowing that improvements would be needed in the near future. But from the second quarter of 2025 onward, this has changed. As the unfettered demand grew, the enthusiasm for computing sustainability went in the opposite direction. And if there's anything that well-meaning projects and people need more than anything else, it's enthusiasm and energy.

In short, when we started this book idea, it felt like the best time to talk about computing sustainability, but now, as we finish it, it feels like the worst time to be discussing the subject.

Or is it?

Any self-respecting person passionate about a topic you feel others should care about knows that often the best time to bring up and fight for a subject is when it seems like the worst time. And as many tech companies have revealed their true beliefs and motivations over the past year or so, there is also a general malaise with much of tech culture and what we have allowed them to do and get away with. There has never been a better time to seek out alternatives, and all over the physical and digital web, efforts to make a difference continue.

The bulk of the time writing this book was during the peak of the AI hype cycle. Even as builders are laying bricks for the data centers needed to sustain the AI boom, there are whispers that enthusiasm is already waning. This, plus more efficient models reducing the environmental impact, means that maybe things won't be as bad as we feared. To quote Vlad Coroam$_2$ of the Roegen Centre for Sustainability again, "this is not the first time." Computers used to be giant room-sized machines, and while I have no idea of their power consumption, I am certain it was significant. We found a way to reduce that over time, and we will do the same again. However, this time, the combination of Jevons' Paradox and the desperate clamber for economic growth and productivity right now is the differing and dangerous factor.

So where does this leave you? You can focus on what you can influence. Make sustainability practical within your own product work. That is where progress still happens, even when the bigger picture feels messy.

How to Bring This Back to Your Team

At this point, you might be wondering how to bring these ideas back to your team. You may even be the first person in your organization who sees how digital sustainability connects to your product, your users, and your responsibilities. That can feel exciting and a little overwhelming. The good news is that you do not need to transform your whole team at once. Change usually starts with one person making the topic visible and practical at the right moment. Small moves open the door for bigger ones, and momentum builds from there. The suggestions below offer concrete ways to help your team take those first steps.

Start with Shared Understanding

Teams move faster when they share the same mental model. Sustainability is no different. If each person has a different idea of what "sustainable digital products" means, the work stalls before it begins. The first step is simply making the topic visible.

Most people in tech still don't realize how much their everyday decisions affect energy use, hardware lifespans, or infrastructure demand. So share what you've learned. Share this book with teammates who might not even know this space exists. Give them the same context you now have. A common baseline is powerful.

You don't need a big workshop to get going. A short intro session, a link to the Web Sustainability Guidelines, or a quick walkthrough of where your current product creates waste is often enough. Designers start to see how accessibility and choice connect to sustainability. Developers connect performance to energy. Product managers begin to spot trade-offs that were invisible before.

Once everyone on the team shares the same vocabulary, conversations become easier, and decisions improve. Sustainability stops being abstract and becomes something your team can act on together.

Look for Small Wins

Small improvements often deliver results faster than people expect. You don't need to overhaul an entire architecture to make meaningful progress. Many teams start by scanning for a few obvious opportunities and fixing those. It builds confidence, creates momentum, and proves that sustainability and practicality can work together.

One of the easiest places to look is images. They are often the heaviest part of a page, and most websites ship files that are far larger than necessary. At one point, while helping a team investigate why a page felt unnecessarily slow, I started experimenting with responsive image techniques. A simple srcset adjustment, combined with serving more appropriate image sizes, dramatically reduced the total page weight. Nothing about the design changed, and the visual experience stayed exactly the same. The only difference was that the browser stopped downloading oversized assets it didn't need. Changes like this rarely feel groundbreaking when you make them. But the impact adds up quickly.

Plenty of other opportunities follow the same pattern. If you don't have time to audit all running services or containers, or right-size instances, then instead, switching to a green hosting provider is often a single configuration change. Removing old dependencies or unused JavaScript can cut load times without touching the user interface. Clearing out outdated assets or heavy libraries that no one relies on anymore reduces storage and processing for every request. None of these changes requires redesigns or big budgets, but each one moves the product in the right direction.

Small wins are how teams build momentum. They reveal what's possible, they make sustainability visible, and they create the buy-in you need for greater improvements later.

Make Progress Visible

Once a team starts making changes, it helps when the results are easy to see. People stay motivated when they can see the effect of their work, even if the improvements feel small at first. You don't need a sophisticated dashboard to get started. A shared spreadsheet, a lightweight internal page, or a quick report pulled from your existing analytics tools is often enough. What matters is that the team can track a few meaningful indicators over time, such as how heavy key pages are, how long they take to load on real devices, how many requests they trigger, or how energy estimates shift after improvements. These numbers do not need to be perfect. They just need to give the team a sense of direction.

Making progress visible also changes conversations with stakeholders. Talking about "making the product more sustainable" is usually too abstract to move anything forward. But saying that a refactor reduced page weight by 40%, or that a cleanup brought load time down by a full second, immediately lands differently. Throughout our work with large corporate teams, we've repeatedly seen that the moment sustainability improvements connect to prosperity metrics, the whole topic starts to gain traction. Faster pages, reduced infrastructure cost, fewer abandoned sessions, more conversions, etc. People understand the value because they can see it.

It is also important to remember that not every number is supposed to go down. Sometimes an increase is a good sign, too. Better accessibility might add a small amount of markup. A security improvement might introduce a slight delay. You and your team need to understand the trade-offs and make informed decisions.

And finally, celebrate the wins. Sustainability work can feel abstract and long-term, so marking progress keeps energy high. A quick before-and-after comparison in a team channel, a shoutout in a retro, or a short message highlighting a small improvement is enough. These moments remind everyone that their effort matters and help build a culture where good decisions are noticed and repeated.

Connect Sustainability to the Goals the Team Already Has

A common mistake is treating sustainability as something separate from the team's main work, a kind of bonus objective that only gets attention when everything else is finished. In reality, sustainability fits naturally into the goals your team is already measured on. The trick is making those connections visible.

Most product teams care about performance, accessibility, reliability, user experience, cost, and long-term maintainability. All of these overlap with sustainability. Faster pages generally consume less energy. Cleaner codebases are easier to maintain and often require fewer resources to run. Supporting older devices expands your user base and reduces frustration. Reducing unnecessary data transfer lowers infrastructure costs. Improving accessibility almost always improves efficiency as well. The alignment is already there. You just need to point to it.

When sustainability supports the goals teams already recognize as important, resistance drops quickly. It stops being “extra work” and becomes a way to reach targets the team is already chasing. For product managers, that means sustainability becomes part of delivering value. For designers, it becomes part of creating flexible, inclusive experiences. For developers, it becomes part of writing efficient, resilient systems. For leadership, it becomes a path to reducing cost and risk while improving user satisfaction.

This framing also helps with prioritization. Instead of asking for time to “make the product more sustainable,” tie your proposal to an existing KPI. If you want to reduce page weight, connect it to performance. If you want to clean up unused dependencies, connect them to stability and security. If you want to optimize images, connect them to conversion rates on mobile. The motivation becomes obvious.

You're not trying to convince your team to care about a completely new idea. You're showing them that sustainability strengthens all their existing goals. Once that link is clear, the conversation shifts from "Why should we do this?" to "Why wouldn't we?"

Bring Sustainability into Everyday Work

Teams change fastest when certain topics become part of everyday work, rather than being reserved for special meetings. Sustainability is no different. If it only comes up during a quarterly strategy session or at the end of a project, it never has the chance to shape decisions when it actually matters.

Start weaving it into the conversations you already have. When discussing new features, ask a simple question about impact alongside the usual questions about users, scope, timelines, and cost. When planning sprints, point out opportunities to combine performance or accessibility improvements with sustainability benefits. If something feels heavier than it needs to be, say so. You are not pushing a new agenda. You are making visible a dimension of quality that has always been there.

Normalizing the topic also means being clear about what sustainability actually adds. Most teams already care deeply about clarity, performance, accessibility, reliability, cost, and maintainability. The challenge is that these concerns often live side by side rather than together. Sustainability provides a shared lens that connects them, helping teams reason about how decisions interact, accumulate, and play out over time.

Instead of introducing a new set of values, it strengthens existing ones by grounding them in system reality. Design intent is discussed alongside how interactions behave on real devices. Performance work becomes about efficiency and longevity, not just speed in ideal conditions. Product decisions gain a clearer view of long-term cost, risk, and resilience. Sustainability gives teams a common language to explain and defend better choices, especially when trade-offs appear or deadlines apply pressure.

Seen this way, sustainability is not extra work layered on top of what teams already do. It makes good practice more explicit, more consistent, and easier to sustain. Over time, it stops feeling like an added concern and simply becomes part of how thoughtful product work gets done.

Progress Won't Be Linear

Even with the best intentions, this work rarely unfolds smoothly. You will meet resistance. Sometimes it will be explicit, sometimes it will be quiet. A proposal gets deprioritized. A new feature undoes a performance improvement. A stakeholder agrees in principle, then never quite finds the time. This is normal.

Digital sustainability often challenges habits that have been rewarded for years: shipping fast, adding features, and optimizing for growth above all else. When you question those defaults, it can feel uncomfortable for teams and organizations, even if the underlying ideas make sense. That discomfort does not mean you are wrong. It usually means you are touching something real.

There will also be moments where progress goes backward. A redesign adds weight. A new dependency sneaks in. A deadline forces compromises. That does not cancel out the work you have already done. Sustainability is not a straight line, and it is not about perfection. It is about direction. What matters is whether the overall trajectory is improving over time.

It can also be emotionally tiring to care about something that others do not yet prioritize. I've felt this many times in my own work, especially when advocating for topics like performance or accessibility. If you find yourself frustrated, discouraged, or doubting whether the effort is worth it, that is a sign to slow down rather than give up. Take breaks. Pick your battles. Focus on what you can influence right now.

The goal is not to win every argument or fix everything at once. The goal is to keep the topic alive long enough for it to take root. Over time, ideas that once felt inconvenient start to feel obvious. What feels like friction today often becomes tomorrow's baseline.

Keep an Eye on Standards and Regulations

You do not need to become a legal expert to work sustainably, but it helps to stay aware of how standards and regulations are evolving. In digital sustainability, this landscape is still uneven and often unpredictable. Some initiatives gain traction, others are weakened or delayed, and many remain voluntary for a long time.

The value of paying attention is not about trying to guess what will become law and when. It is about understanding direction. Accessibility showed this clearly. Long before deadlines were enforced, expectations were already shifting. Teams that understood the principles early felt far less pressure later, even as timelines, interpretations, and enforcement details changed.

Keeping an eye on standardization and regulation can be simple. Follow a small number of trusted guidelines, working groups, or organizations. Notice what topics keep resurfacing. Notice which practices are framed as "good practice" today. You are looking for signals that help you make better decisions now, rather than reacting under pressure later.

This awareness also helps when talking to stakeholders. Referencing emerging standards or shared frameworks often carries more weight than personal opinion. It shows that sustainability is not an isolated concern but part of a broader shift in how digital products are expected to behave.

Don't Do It Alone

If you are the first person at your company to think seriously about digital sustainability, it can feel like a lot to take on. But you are not supposed to do this alone. There is a whole global community working on the same questions, facing the same obstacles, and sharing what they learn as they go.

Joining that community gives you perspective, support, and practical tools. It also reminds you that even if your team is not fully on board yet, you are part of something bigger. You can learn from others, borrow their examples, use their language, and share your own experiments. When you bring these ideas back to your team, you arrive with confidence and evidence, not just enthusiasm.

Resources Worth Following

These organizations and tools can help you stay connected to the broader community and to the evolving conversations around sustainable computing. There are many more resources worth considering. Some are mentioned throughout this book and others we will keep up-to-date in the GitHub repository for the book.

Standards, Guidelines, and Frameworks

- **Web Sustainability Guidelines (WSG)**

  W3C guidelines that cover a wide range of recommendations to make web products and services more sustainable. Created and maintained by W3C Sustainable Web Interest Group.

https://www.w3.org/TR/web-sustainability-guidelines/

- **Sustainable Web Manifesto**

  A simple set of principles for guiding sustainable design.

  https://www.sustainablewebmanifesto.com

- **Ecodesign of digital services (RGESN)**

  France's official ecodesign standard for digital services. Good reference even outside France.

  https://ecoresponsable.numerique.gouv.fr/publications/referentiel-general-ecoconception/

Organizations Shaping the Space

- **The Green Web Foundation**

  An independent non-profit that tracks how much of the Internet runs on green energy and that advocates for a more sustainable and just Internet.

  https://www.thegreenwebfoundation.org

- **Green Software Foundation**

  A non-profit under the Linux Foundation that promotes software that is responsible for emitting fewer greenhouse gases. Their focus is reduction, not neutralization.

  https://greensoftware.foundation

- **Sustainable Digital Infrastructure Alliance (SDIA)**

  A global industry group focused on reducing the environmental impact of digital infrastructure, with research and tools for procurement, architecture, and hardware life cycles.

  https://sdialliance.org

- **Bundesverband Green Software**

  A non-profit association advancing green software practices across Germany and Europe. Its work spans policy, education, and practical implementation, including stewardship of the Blue Angel for Software, the world's first ecolabel for software. The organization also maintains an interactive landscape of software sustainability measurement tools, runs introductory education programs, and collaborates with academia to integrate sustainability into IT curricula.

  `https://www.bundesverband-green-software.de/`

  `https://landscape.bundesverband-green-software.de/`

- **Boavizta**

  An open-source initiative providing data, tools, and methodologies to assess the environmental impact of digital services and hardware, with a strong focus on life cycle analysis and embodied carbon. Boavizta's models are widely used to estimate the footprint of devices, infrastructure, and cloud services, supporting more informed design and procurement decisions.

  `https://boavizta.org/`

Communities and Networks

- **ClimateAction.tech**

  A global community of people in tech who want to work on climate issues. Provides events, working groups, a lively Slack community, and a huge library of shared resources.

  `https://climateaction.tech`

- **Sustainable UX (SUX)**

  An active Slack community and movement focused on sustainable design. Great for learning, sharing, and connecting with practitioners applying sustainability in UX and product work.

`https://sustainableuxnetwork.com`

- **Green I/O**

  A podcast and event series highlighting practitioners, researchers, and organizations advancing sustainable digital practices around the world.

  `https://greenio.tech`

People and Publications

- **Branch Magazine**

  A creative, critical, and hopeful publication about the climate impact of the tech industry. Produced by ClimateAction.tech and the Green Web Foundation.

  `https://branch.climateaction.tech`

- **Chris Adams**

  Technologist, writer, and organizer whose work bridges engineering, climate action, and policy. Shares practical insights on sustainable computing.

  `https://rtl.chrisadams.me.uk`

- **Fershad Irani**

  Writer and researcher exploring sustainable software, ethical tech, and the human implications of digital systems. Insightful essays and analysis.

  `https://fershad.com`

- **Tim Frick**

  Author of *Designing for Sustainability* and long-standing advocate for ethical, inclusive, and sustainable digital design. His articles provide clear guidance for teams starting their journey.

  `https://www.mightybytes.com/insights/`

Showcases and Directories

- **Lowwwcarbon**

  A curated collection of websites built with low energy use and sustainable design principles. Great for inspiration or benchmarking when teams need concrete examples.

  `https://lowwwcarbon.com`

Book Authors

- **Chris Chinchilla**

  Senior technical writer and developer working across documentation, podcasts, and video. With experience in sustainability organizations, he supports non-profits and communities building more sustainable digital technologies.

  `https://chrischinchilla.com/`

- **Ines Akrap**

  Front-end software engineer advocating for fast, sustainable, and accessible web products. Contributes to W3C web sustainability work and shares practical knowledge through teaching and public speaking.

  `https://inesakrap.com`

How to Use This List

These are just starting points. The ecosystem is growing, and you'll see new ideas and initiatives develop over time. You can pick one or two organizations, join a community, and follow a person whose work resonates with you. Digital sustainability is a broad field, and staying connected to others doing similar work makes the journey more practical, grounded, and far less overwhelming.

Conclusion

We wrote this book to be shared. Passed between team members. Referenced in planning meetings. Used as a companion when updating a design system or reviewing an architecture diagram.

Sustainability is a long journey, and long journeys require people who know how to keep momentum alive. Many sustainable decisions take more time at first and pay off later. The early work is visible. The benefits often appear quietly, through happier users, lower costs, fewer outages, simpler systems, and teams that feel proud of what they build.

Your influence as an individual is more powerful than it might feel. You do not need to change everything at once. You only need to begin. A conversation. A metric. A small clean-up. A question asked at the right moment. One choice creates space for the next.

And, as always, progress happens the same way we described earlier in this book.

Page by page.

Line by line.

Byte by byte.

Where you go from here is up to you.

But we hope you go forward with intention, curiosity, and confidence.

The work is worth it.

Index

C. Chinchilla and I. Akrap, *Building the Sustainable Web*, https://doi.org/10.1007/979-8-8688-2521-7

F

I

J

K

L

M

N

O

P, Q

R

S

T

U

X

Y, Z

MIX
Papier aus verantwortungsvollen Quellen
Paper from responsible sources
FSC® C105338

If you have any concerns about our products,
you can contact us on
ProductSafety@springernature.com

In case Publisher is established outside the EU,
the EU authorized representative is:
Springer Nature Customer Service Center GmbH
Europaplatz 3, 69115 Heidelberg, Germany

Printed by Libri Plureos GmbH
in Hamburg, Germany